MOTHERS AND DAUGHTERS

WOMEN OF THE INTELLIGENTSIA IN NINETEENTH-CENTURY RUSSIA

MOTHERS AND DAUGHTERS

WOMEN OF THE INTELLIGENTSIA IN NINETEENTH-CENTURY RUSSIA

BARBARA ALPERN ENGEL

University of Colorado

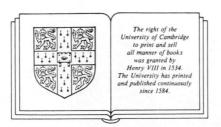

The right of the
University of Cambridge
to print and sell
all manner of books
was granted by
Henry VIII in 1534.
The University has printed
and published continuously
since 1584.

CAMBRIDGE UNIVERSITY PRESS

Cambridge

New York   New Rochelle   Melbourne   Sydney

Published by the Press Syndicate of the University of Cambridge
The Pitt Building, Trumpington Street, Cambridge CB2 1RP
32 East 57th Street, New York, NY 10022, USA
10 Stamford Road, Oakleigh, Melbourne 3166, Australia

First published 1983
First paperback edition 1985
Reprinted 1986, 1987

Printed in the United States of America

Library of Congress Cataloging in Publication Data
Engel, Barbara Alpern.
Mothers and daughters.
Bibliography: p.
Includes index.
1. Women in politics – Soviet Union – History – 19th century.
2. Mothers – Soviet Union – History – 19th century.
3. Daughters – Soviet Union – History – 19th century.
4. Intellectuals – Soviet Union – History – 19th century.
5. Radicalism – Soviet Union – History – 19th century. 6. Soviet
Union – Social conditions–
1801 – 1917. I. Title.
HQ1663.E53   1983   305.4′2′0947   82-14611
ISBN 0 521 25125 7 hard cover
ISBN 0 521 31301 5 paperback

CONTENTS

PREFACE

This book presents a brief history of some of the women who participated in the Russian radical movement. It also examines the evolution of women's consciousness in a specific setting, and the relationship between the social forces that prompted women to rebel and the nature of women's thought and activism.

Inspired by the recent reemergence of feminism and by my own discovery of the female heroes of the Russian radical movement, I began to research the subject in 1972, while a graduate student at Columbia University. Initially, a study of the history of women radicals seemed worthwhile in itself. One reason was that there were hundreds of them, actively participating in movements for social change, on virtually an equal basis with men. Another was that these women had been truly awe-inspiring: courageous, utterly dedicated, and remarkably free from the concerns about material comfort, family, and personal relationships that absorb the energies of most of the people I know. I wanted to tell their story.

I found a narrative approach increasingly unsatisfactory as I became more familiar with European and American women's history and acquired a comparative perspective. The extraordinary histories of the women I was studying raised broader questions: Why had there been so many radical women in Russia, as compared with Western Europe or America? How does one account for the unusual level of altruism that made these Russian women so much more self-sacrificing than their activist sisters in the West? Why was feminism, or indeed any concern with women's issues, so noticeably absent from their thought and action? Given their lack of personal ambition and the absence of interest in women's issues, how did women radicals come to play such prominent roles, sometimes leading roles, in the movements they joined? To answer these questions, I found that I needed to look at private experience as well as public activity – most particularly, at what being female meant to Russian women in rebellion against conventional roles. In this way, this book has become a kind of case study of how the personal became political in a time and place very different from our own.

Looking at Russian radical women this way made me aware of their weaknesses as well as their strengths, made them seem more human and more fallible; it also deepened my appreciation of their strength, courage, and absolute integrity. I have never met the like of the women who appear in this book. I feel privileged to have lived with them for ten years and to have been able to learn so much from them. I am immensely sad, as well as enormously relieved, to finish this book and to let them go.

During the years I devoted to this project, many more individuals and institutions than can be acknowledged here contributed to my work. I would particularly like to thank Columbia University for the grant of a Faculty Fellowship that enabled me to begin the research. Grants from the American Council of Learned Societies and the Council on Research and Creative Work of the University of Colorado allowed me to pursue postdoctoral research in Helsinki and the Soviet Union. A grant from the American Philosophical Society and a grant-in-aid from the Council on Research and Creative Work funded research at the Hoover Institute. I am grateful to Boris Sapir for assisting my research at the Institute for Social History in Amsterdam and to Anna Bourgina for graciously granting me access to the Nikolaevskii Archive at the Hoover Institute.

I am grateful to Clifford Rosenthal for the idea that eventually gave rise to this book. Lewis Engel first pointed out to me the enormous influence exercised by mothers over daughters, and Jay Rosenblatt helped me to understand the effects that influence might have on the experience of being female. In the early stages of the project, Marc Raeff and Leopold Haimson provided invaluable guidance, criticism, and advice. Richard Stites generously shared with me his knowledge of sources and has continued to give unstintingly of his advice and editorial assistance. The book has benefited immensely from his scrutiny. Richard Wortman's critical reading of the manuscript helped me to refine it and to focus my argument. Discussions with Nancy Frieden stimulated my thinking, and her careful and critical reading contributed vitally to improving an earlier draft of this book.

The women's movement and the community of women scholars influenced this book in many, many ways. Joan Kelly Gadol, Gerda Lerner, Renate Bridenthal, and Alice Kessler Harris showed me the possibilities of women's history at a time when I most needed encouragement. Rosalind Petchesky and Sarah Eisenstein helped me to comprehend the connections between the personal and the political, and Ellen Ross helped me to refine those insights and make them more explicit. Conversations with Rochelle Ruthchild stimulated and challenged my thinking about Russian women. Lee Chambers Schiller provided a valuable critique of an earlier draft of the manuscript, and our ongoing discussions have deepened my understanding of the ways in which Russian women resembled and differed from women elsewhere.

For their reading and comments on earlier drafts of this book, I would also like to thank Robert Pois, Robert Schulzinger, Joan Lord Hall, Katherine Edwards, Susan Armitage, Heather Hogan, Barbara Clements, Martha Gimenez, Marcia Westcott, and the members of the Seminar Series on Feminist Theory and Research Practice. Ruth Major cheerfully typed and retyped the manuscript. Finally, I am deeply indebted to William and Minette Alpern, my parents, for their unflagging faith and support over the years.

These people, and many more, contributed to this study. All errors, whether of fact or interpretation, are, of course, exclusively my own.

B.A.E.

NOTE ON DATES
AND TRANSLITERATION

All dates are given according to the old (Julian) calendar, which in the nineteenth century was behind the Western (Gregorian) calendar by 12 days, and by 13 days in the twentieth century. Russian titles have been transliterated according to the modified Library of Congress system, with я and ю rendered as ia and iu. Names of well-known individuals already familiar to the Western reader have been left in their anglicized form.

PART I

TRANSFORMING THE FEMALE TRADITION

INTRODUCTION TO PART I

During the 1860s and 1870s, Russian women seemed to be everywhere: on the barricades of the Paris Commune; at universities in Paris, Berne, and Zurich; with medical cadres at the front lines in the Russo-Turkish War. In Russia, they pursued social justice with pistols and propaganda leaflets in hand. European and American newspapers carried news of them and printed their pictures.

These women brought moral fervor to everything they did. Hundreds devoted their lives to educating or providing medical care for the Russian masses; hundreds more participated in movements for social and political change. All were dedicated to the cause of the Russian people, and some were self-sacrificing almost to the point of martyrdom. This made them different from their activist sisters to the West, who displayed neither their dedication nor their willingness to give up everything, including family ties, personal connections, and even children, in order to serve a cause. The moral fervor of Russian female activists inspired in their male comrades a respect bordering on adulation, and partly as a result, Russian women became far more likely than their European counterparts to occupy important positions in radical organizations. In the second half of the nineteenth century, women constituted a substantial and influential minority in the Russian radical intelligentsia.

Students of Russian history have paid the intelligentsia considerable attention. Its members left a rich legacy of documents, making their lives and ideas highly accessible to historians. Equally important, the intelligentsia themselves constituted a significant historical force. Nineteenth-century Russia remained an economically backward, rigidly stratified, and overwhelmingly agrarian society in which capitalist relations of production were only starting to develop. As a result, Russia lacked a bourgeoisie of the sort that provided impetus for the attack on hereditary privilege in the West, as well as a working class that might challenge bourgeois domination. Until late in the nineteenth century, a tiny group of alienated, socially conscious intellectuals provided the most trenchant critiques of the social order and were the most active participants in movements for social change. In the 1830s and 1840s, the intelligentsia was composed mainly of nobles, but eventually it drew its membership from all strata of society, including the peasantry. This increased its democratic quality and strengthened its claim to represent the nation as a whole.

Despite the high level of female participation, most historians have treated the intelligentsia as if it had been exclusively male, if not by excluding any mention of women then by ascribing to them the same motivations and experiences as men.[1] At the same time, historians have tended to approach both the men and the women of the intelligentsia as public beings, as social theorists and activists.[2] Rarely have historians analyzed in depth the private experiences that helped to shape a social conscience, and writers who have usually have been biographers who have treated such matters as if their subjects' experiences were individual and unique.[3]

Two recent works by Richard Stites and Vera Broido have given women of the intelligentsia the separate treatment they deserve.[4] In his monumental pioneering work, Stites provided a comprehensive account of the development of female activism between 1855 and 1930. Neither he nor Broido, however, probed deeply or systematically into the underlying social forces that prompted women to step outside the family-centered role, nor did they examine the value system that enabled women to challenge that role successfully.

In Russia, as elsewhere in Europe, law, custom, and tradition defined women primarily as daughters, wives, and mothers. Virtually every woman married, and those who did not either remained with their parents or lived in the families of others as domestics, companions, or governesses, or as the rather pathetic female relatives one encounters so often in Russian novels. Even when other options became available to women, as they did in the second half of the nineteenth century, traditional expectations remained for a long time unaltered, so that it required considerable courage and determination for a woman to undertake a life outside the family sphere.

Of enormous importance to the quality of female rebellion in Russia was the fact that in many instances it was religious values that provided women with a rationale for rebellion against the family-centered role. Mid-nineteenth-century Russia remained a traditional society, and religious values continued to be a powerful force in the culture. But whereas religious values still commanded respect at all levels, as a result of the formalization and secularization of official, public life, it was primarily the powerless and humble who tried to live according to religious principles.

This was especially the case with women, for whom religion provided not only a consolation but also a source of strength. Among the qualities that Russian Orthodoxy endowed with special meaning were humility and the capacity for suffering and self-sacrifice, and people who manifested such qualities could exercise considerable moral authority. This made a religiously based feminine ideal perfectly suited to women's position in the family, for while leaving the exercise of genuine authority to the male head of the household, it granted the wife a distinct, honorable, and in many respects gratifying sphere of her own. Women derived real satisfaction from living according to the loftiest precepts of their culture, especially because in Russia individual interests remained subordinated to the family or state, and individual self-expression was valued only by a tiny minority of people. Therefore, while religion helped to reinforce women's subordination to men and to the family, it also elevated and sanctified women's endurance and allowed women to feel a certain moral superiority.

In the nineteenth century, the belief in women's moral superiority served to justify demands for greater rights for them in public life as well as private life. As educational opportunities expanded, fostering an individualism that challenged their traditional submission to family authority, women claimed the right to defy "family despotism" for the sake of their own self-development and to fulfill an ethical vision by devoting themselves to society as a whole. Reference to a higher purpose legitimized – indeed, ennobled – women's rebellion in the eyes of many contemporaries. But by acting according to a perception of themselves as moral beings so as to exercise some options, many women ended up having to turn their backs on others. Political and social circumstances influenced that choice. So did the motivations of the women, for when women pursued a religiously based ideal outside the family, they left behind the socially prescribed roles that had traditionally contained and channeled their idealism. In order to right "the injustice reigning everywhere," some renounced not only their families of origin and the educational goals that had prompted their rebellion in the first place, but also sexuality and personal life. Their ethical vision and willingness to dispense with other attachments prompted women to an absolutism and intensity of dedication that most male radicals lacked. This led to a sexual division of labor within the movement, even though women enjoyed equal status with men, and it left an enduring mark on the quality of female radicalism in Russia.

CHAPTER 1

MOTHERS AND DAUGHTERS

Russian women of the nineteenth century differed from their sisters in the industrializing West, as anyone familiar with the Russian classics has sensed. The heroines of Turgenev, Dostoevsky, and Tolstoy impress the reader as intense and strong-willed, more active, more emotional, more multifaceted than, say, the rather one-sided heroines of Dickens, Flaubert's Emma Bovary, or Thackeray's Becky Sharpe. Indeed, Russian heroines often are more fully human and more positive than the heroes, as several critics have observed.[1]

The Russian heroine's special strength of character appears so consistently that it cannot be attributed to literary imagination alone. And although it is highly significant that nineteenth-century Russian heroines almost invariably derived from the nobility, whereas European heroines came from the middle class, class differences do not entirely explain the differences in character. Equally as important as these differences was their context. Economically, socially, and culturally, Russia remained at an earlier stage of development than the industrializing West, where bourgeois ideas about the domestic role of women were already determining society's expectations not only of upper- and middle-class women who could fit the image but also of increasing numbers of lower-class women who could not. Bourgeois conceptions of domesticity simultaneously strengthened the position of the woman in the family by elevating her role as wife and mother and weakened it by relegating the woman exclusively to the private sphere and denying her any legitimate function outside it.[2]

Owing to the peculiarities of her economic and social development, Russia lacked such a bourgeoisie, and as a result she never developed a comparable ideology of domesticity. To be sure, in nineteenth-century Russia, as elsewhere in Europe, to be female meant to be daughter, wife, and almost inevitably mother, and to be subordinate to males in all but the last of these positions. But the content of family roles and the quality of female subordination differed considerably from Western European patterns. In some ways the position of Russian women was more independent, because they retained their rights to property even after marriage and, depending on social position, fulfilled a variety of responsibilities that were vital to maintaining the family's economic and social status. Yet, from another perspective, women were more helpless: Because the authoritarianism that characterized Russia's autocratic political system also shaped family relations, the law and custom subordinated Russian women to men more absolutely than was the case for their European sisters. Family law required "unconditional obedience" of wife to husband and children to parents, and custom reinforced the legislation by granting men the right to use force to chastise recalcitrant wives and children.[3] In this way, the family hierarchy both reflected and reproduced the social hierarchy by teaching children to submit to patriarchal authority, but it allowed young males to anticipate a time when they, in turn, would exercise authority. The comparative strengths and weaknesses of Russian women provide one key to understanding not only the unique qualities of Russian literary heroines but also the psychology of those real-life heroines who tried to transcend and transform the world of the Russian woman.

The ways in which the position of Russian women shaped the relationships between mothers and daughters provide another key. Recently, several feminist scholars have argued convincingly that the mother-daughter relationship is the ultimate determinant of female personality.[4] Although this approach ignores both historical and cultural variables, it can nevertheless add significantly to our understanding of women's history, because patterns of mothering do vary considerably according to time and place, and there is good reason to believe that as a result the mother-daughter relationship varies, too. Variations occur not only in form, as a result of different social and cultural expectations of motherhood, but also in content, depending on what mothers actually convey to daughters about how it feels to be a woman.

It is relatively easy to trace developments in form. For example, there is considerable evidence to indicate that in premodern Europe, mothering represented only one of a number of roles a married woman performed and that it became the dominant focus of her life only after capitalism had removed production from the home, and only among those sectors of the population in which the ideology of domesticity had firmly taken hold.[5] In terms of form, Russia resembled premodern Europe at virtually every level of the social hierarchy, because peasant women – the vast majority – were expected to devote much of their time and attention to labor, whereas noblewomen managed complex households in the countryside or fulfilled a variety of social obligations in the city. Not until the middle of the nineteenth century did Western ideas about women's maternal role begin to be widely disseminated in Russia, and even then, few women adopted them as fully as their European sisters did.[6]

It is far more difficult to determine how the form of mothering affected either the emotional content of the mother-daughter relationship or the perception of womanhood that a daughter acquired. Only women speaking for themselves can tell us that, and only a tiny minority of Russian women were sufficiently educated to provide records of their feelings. About the rest, the illiterates, we know only the form, because that we can learn from the testimony of others.

Such testimony paints an almost overwhelmingly negative picture. Until 1861, most women, like most men in Russia, were peasant serfs. Peasants furnished most of the nation's wealth. To their landlords they owed rent in dues, labor, or kind, and to the state they paid a variety of direct and indirect taxes. Roughly half of the serfs belonged to noble landlords who held almost absolute power over them. Serf women, not counted among the "souls" that constituted the tax base of Russia, were in many ways worse off than the men, because the women spent most of their adult lives subservient not only to the nobility but also to their husbands and their in-laws. Because marriage was an economic arrangement, parents selected the spouses for both sons and daughters. It was the woman, however, who went to live with her husband's family and became subject to the authority of her in-laws, and if her in-laws proved despotic, she had nowhere to appeal. Sons, like daughters, were enjoined to submit to their parents. In addition, in the extended peasant household, where parents, their sons, and their daughters-in-law usually occupied one room, emotional intimacy between couples was difficult if not impossible, and loyalty between spouses was neither encouraged nor expected. Wives were valued according to their capacity to labor, to bear children, and to endure. Although the women worked at least as hard as the men, peasants regarded women's work, even fieldwork, as "unproductive." So they did not recognize a woman's contribution to the household economy, and they gave women no say in the disposition of household resources. This may help to explain the antifeminism of folk proverbs: "I thought I saw two people, but it was only a man and his wife." "A chicken is not a bird, and a woman is not a human being." Their lack of rights also made peasant women sexually vulnerable: to landlords, who sometimes kept serf harems, and to fathers-in-law, who took advantage of daughters-in-law when sons were absent or were underage.[7]

Despite their powerless position, peasant mothers looked out for their daughters by helping them to avoid the heaviest and most unpleasant labor, and a mother contributed what little income she had to her daughter's dowry. Great affection between parents and children was rare in peasant families, but mothers and daughters were closer than other family members, and they remained so even after daughters had left home.[8]

We know less about the village priests, who stood above the peasantry in social status but shared much of the peasant way of life. The parish clergy married, and they constituted a closed caste, priesthood passing from father to son whether or not the son felt a particular calling to serve

God. The majority of priests were poor and barely literate, reduced to tilling the land like their peasant flocks in order to feed themselves and their families. Among the priesthood, as among other social groups, marriage was based on calculation rather than inclination. Sons of priests married daughters of priests, and if it appeared that the aspiring cleric would not soon be taking over his father's parish, he might choose a bride with an eye to his future father-in-law's parish. For such a match, the personality of the wife, the compatibility of the couple, and even the consent of the bride were irrelevant. What mattered to the suitor was the position involved, whereas the parents of the girl sought guarantees for their old age, because after he succeeded his father-in-law, the son-in-law was expected to support his in-laws for the remainder of their days. Thus, either the bride left her parents for a home of her own or the husband went to live with his wife's family, and in such cases the daughter remained in the same household as her mother even after marriage.[9]

On the next rung of the social ladder we might expect to find a middle class, with the middle-class values and way of life that in Western Europe and America were so crucial in defining woman's place as being in the home, but there was no middle class in Russia. The nearest thing to a middle class was the merchantry, which was divided into a number of subcategories according to wealth and trading privileges. But even merchants belonging to the highest strata often were uncultured and illiterate, as well as crude in their personal and business practices. Dependent on the state and fiercely loyal to the tsar, they failed to generate the liberal economic and political theories of their Western European counterparts. Their family patterns also differed considerably from those found among the European middle class during a comparable stage of economic development. Trading usually took place at bazaar or market, instead of home or shop, so that a wife rarely participated in her husband's business, although a fortunate few might inherit businesses, trade on their own, or set up their own workshops, most often as dressmakers or laundresses. Because marriage in Russia did not automatically establish community property, a Russian businesswoman could manage her own funds and retain her own profits.[10]

Still, the urban household was rarely a unit of family production, and so the marriages of Russian merchants and craftsmen lacked the element of partnership that seems to have characterized the unions of their counterparts during the early stages of capitalism. For evidence of this, we need look no further than the *Domostroi*, or *Household Guide*, a sixteenth-century document attributed to the monk Sylvester that, according to some, was still very influential in nineteenth-century Russia.[11] Aimed at the upper strata of urban society, the *Domostroi* confined women entirely to the home and enjoined them to submit to their husbands in everything. Should a wife disobey, it was her husband's duty to punish her, physically if necessary; if the offense was grave enough, he was to use a lash: "privately, politely and without anger." Most accounts agree that merchant husbands treated both their wives and their children as chattels and that mothers, in reaction to the tyranny they themselves experienced, often tried to tyrannize over children in their turn.[12]

Even among the nobility at the summit of the social ladder, women's lot was far from easy. Most Russian nobles were not as proud, as wealthy, or as cultivated as their Western European counterparts, and the aristocratic way of life so faithfully depicted in the novels of Tolstoy was enjoyed by less than 1 percent of them. Another 10 percent of the nobility lived quite comfortably, received education, and enjoyed the fruits of Western culture. The remaining 90 percent were poor, in some cases so desperately poor that they lived on the same level as the peasantry.[13]

But even the lives of well-to-do noblewomen in many respects resembled the lives of their lower-class sisters. For one thing, biology shaped much of a noblewoman's existence. Society expected women to marry, and most women did, and marriage meant almost continual childbearing. On the average, married women bore close to five children in the early part of the nineteenth century, according to figures that unfortunately allow for no class distinctions.[14] It is likely that noblewomen became pregnant even more frequently than this, because they ate better and probably were in better health, and unlike women of the lower classes they rarely nursed their children themselves, and so they lacked even that unreliable means of birth control. For example, Varvara Bakunin, mother of the anarchist Mikhail Bakunin, bore eleven children in the first fourteen years of her marriage; Ekaterina Tsevlovskaia, mother of the memoirist Elizaveta Vodovozova, had sixteen children within twenty years; Ekaterina Figner, mother of the revolutionary, Vera Figner, delivered eight babies within twelve years. Biographical evidence in the following chapters also suggests that, on the average, upper-class women produced children every sixteen to twenty-four months during the early years of marriage.

Like other women, too, noblewomen were subject to the patriarchal authority of the male head of the family. In marriage, a woman vowed to obey her husband as head of the household, "to abide with him in love, respect and limitless obedience, and to render him every service and affection as keeper of the house."[15] Religious precepts reinforced the submission of women on every rung of the social ladder. Traditional Russian Orthodoxy taught that chastity was the most sublime state; it associated women with sexual attractiveness and therefore with sin. Orthodoxy might acknowledge sexuality within marriage as a necessary evil, but it forbade even legitimate sexuality on feast days, on fast days, and on the eve of a holiday. When a man intended to have sexual relations with his wife, he first removed his cross and turned the icons toward the wall. Early religious writings were stridently antifeminist:

"No wild beast can equal a malicious and bitter-tongued woman." "It is better to suffer from fever than to be mastered by a bad wife." "Rare is the wife who would not tell your secret to others." The cardinal virtues of the good wife, Orthodoxy taught, were obedience and silence.[16]

Yet while enjoining women to submission, Orthodoxy also provided models of strength and endurance in the *Lives of the Saints*, perhaps the most commonly read book in pious households. In addition, the *Lives of the Saints* (almost exclusively male, it should be noted) offered a kenotic ideal, extolling the poor and the humble, and elevating them above the mighty. Long after the requirements of state service had formalized and secularized the official, male domain, a traditional and religiously based system of values continued to shape the world view of noblewomen as it shaped the views of other less privileged women.

For all the similarities, noblewomen differed from other women in significant ways. Most important, unlike most married women in the West, noblewomen could own property – property that usually included peasant "souls." Thus, like noblemen, they enjoyed the dubious benefits of serfdom and sometimes tyrannized mercilessly over the people in their power. Some noblewomen managed their own property. Many more acted for their husbands who were away in service or were involved in other pursuits; others assisted their husbands by supervising the household, servants, and dairy. No one bothered very much about cleanliness in overcrowded noble households, where a dozen or more people might occupy four or five small rooms, with perhaps a wing added on to absorb the overflow, but noblewomen maintained a certain quality of life by making sure that clothing was manufactured and mended, that food was prepared and served, and that the household functioned smoothly. Although they rarely did heavy labor, noblewomen tended serfs and children who became ill; they fed and sometimes housed the beggars and religious wanderers who roamed the Russian countryside. If the family could afford it, they entertained a steady stream of visitors and patronized the impoverished female relatives for whom the expansive Russian household seemed always to have an extra place at the table and a corner in which to sleep.[17]

Despite the noblewoman's subordination to her husband, memoirs suggest that her responsibilities made the mother a positive role model for her daughters, even as they kept her from being as intimately involved with infants and small children as were middle-class mothers in the West. Motherhood was an important social role in Russia, but it meant something different from motherhood as the European and American middle classes were beginning to construe it. Childrearing was not the central focus of the noblewoman's life, as it was for the Western middle-class woman who had ceased to participate in her husband's business and was expected to embellish the domestic sphere and devote herself to her offspring. In fact, among the various duties a Russian noblewoman performed, childcare occupied a relatively insignificant place. Noblewomen bore their children, then turned their attention elsewhere, leaving them for others to raise. Because of the existence of serfdom, this did not necessarily mean that children were neglected. Serf women often were attentive, loving substitutes for the biological mother. If the family was sufficiently wealthy, the child passed from nurse to governess to tutor and then to school. One of the prerogatives of wealth seems to have been freedom from the daily responsibilities of childcare. The more conscientious mother might assume a supervisory role, but most seemed satisfied to inspect their children in the morning and evening and receive reports from nurse, governess, or tutor. "Relations between parents and children were defined quite precisely," recalled the daughter of a noble family of relatively modest means. "Children kissed their parents' hand in the morning, thanked them for dinner and supper, and took leave of them before going to bed. Every governess spent most of her time trying to keep the children as much as possible from bothering the parents."[18]

The distance between mother and daughter during a girl's early years meant that mothers, like fathers, were identified with the world of adulthood, rather than that of childhood, and that a girl entered her mother's world when she matured, just as a boy entered his father's world. To be sure, the mother remained central at every stage of a child's development, but her relationship with her daughter was mediated by other female figures. She left the care of her daughter to the wet nurse and then to the nurse during the formative first five years; when the time came to impose society's rules on an unwilling youngster, governess, tutor, or school usually served as the disciplining agent. These intervening figures attenuated both the primary attachment of infancy and the subsequent sense of loss in the daughter's feelings toward her mother. Equally important, a mother had nothing to gain from prolonging the infantile dependency of her daughter, since a woman's role had so little to do with childcare.[19]

Indeed, a mother's active role in relation to her daughter usually began just when a girl left childhood. It then became the mother's responsibility to make sure the daughter married. At about the age of sixteen, a girl entered her mother's world, the world of women. At that point, mothers in well-to-do families taught their daughters the requisite social skills and sometimes arranged marriages. In provincial families too poor to travel to the cities, a mother probably had more trouble finding a husband for her daughter, but the girl still remained her responsibility. For daughters whose families had access to society, a woman's world could appear compelling. "The doors to the parlor are open, and I can hear happy talk and laughter. Someone is playing a new polka in the hall. I sigh deeply and watch for a while. For me, this is heaven, the place I yearn for and for which they prepare me. But only at the age of sixteen can I be a full citizen there."[20] Not least among the pleasures of growing up was the possibility of unprecedented intimacy with the mother. "Mother drew me closer to her and talked with me. Our paths seemed to merge," wrote Ekaterina Iunge, the daughter of a successful society woman. "Mother's life was no longer separate from mine: we were always together. It seemed to me that before I had not understood her. I rejoiced in the change in our relations, and my love for her became a kind of idolatry."[21] Because it developed only as the girl grew older, such love, while intense, retained few traces of infantile dependency, and so represented little threat to a young woman's emotional autonomy. A Russian noblewoman could admire, emulate, and remain close to her mother without remaining a child.

For the most part, close mother-daughter ties operated conservatively, because they facilitated a girl's adaptation to her appropriate social role and ensured that she successfully passed from her father's authority into her husband's – the mother acting as a kind of unwitting agent for a male-dominated society. If a girl tried to choose a different path, the mother's duty was to keep her on the conventional one. Iunge, the young woman who so rejoiced in her new relations with her mother, also quickly acquiesced when the mother insisted on approving newly opened public lectures before allowing the daughter to attend them. Kazina, the young woman who yearned for the parlor, found that when she grew bored with the parlor, her relations with her mother became severely strained. Her need to stay close to her mother could lead a young woman to abandon unconventional aspirations; far less often a mother's desire to maintain intimate ties with her daughter might prompt the mother to revise her opinions.[22]

Under certain circumstances, however, the unusual mother-daughter relationship could actually sow the seeds of revolt. If the mother herself felt discontented with her lot, or if the values she transmitted were strongly at odds with official ones, this might inspire in a daughter a desire for a different sort of life, and provide an acceptable standard by which to judge the existing order. The lessons a woman learned from her parents about masculinity and femininity would shape not only her self-perception but also her political perceptions.

As judged on the basis of memoirs, most mothers, whether they acted as conservative or radicalizing agents, were perceived as loving and admirable figures, and daughters wanted to grow up to be like them. By contrast, fathers appeared cold as well as distant, less human beings than representatives of a rigidly hierarchical, authoritarian social order. Some, like the tyrant portrayed by Avdotia Panaeva in her semi-autobiographical *Tal'nykov Family*, actually beat their daughters.[23] Others did not need to resort to violence. "We feared him worse than fire," wrote Vera Figner of her father. "One glance, cold and penetrating, was enough to set us trembling."[24] From custom, law, possession of serfs, and even from their own socialization, men gained a sense of mastery –

if not in the political sphere, where noblemen served the autocratic state in either a civil or military capacity, then at least in the domestic one. Noblemen who had received military-style education often treated their children as if they were commanding an army, their only model for dealing with subordinates. Society, moreover, expected men to behave as they did.

Education reinforced the differences between the sexes, and as a result the men and women of the nobility were likely to subscribe to different value systems, to become discontented for different reasons, and to adopt different modes of rebellion. Boys went to school, where they acquired Western European values and an ideal of service to the state.[25] Girls remained traditional. Until well into the nineteenth century, only a minority could even read and write; fewer still attended school, and those who did were instilled with religious precepts and the necessity of subordinating themselves to husband and family.[26]

This meant that a woman's first source of discontent was likely to be marriage and family life, although traditional values prevented most discontented women from trying to change things. The earliest record of such discontent is to be found in the memoirs of Aleksandra Labzina, a woman from the lesser nobility. Labzina was born in 1759, the first child to survive in a deeply religious, relatively well-to-do noble family. Her father died when she was five, leaving her mother and her nurse to raise her. On his deathbed, the father offered traditional advice on the proper training of his offspring: "Teach them to love and share half of their goods with the poor and unfortunate," he told his wife. "For the love of God, do not accustom them to luxury or delicate food, but to harsh food and weather, and to simple dress."[27]

The widow ignored this advice for the first two years after his death. Instead, almost insanely bereaved, she went into total seclusion, refusing even to see her children, who might keep her from communing with what she imagined to be the spirit of her deceased husband. Only the determined efforts of her family restored her to a normal state, and then she assumed responsibility for her daughter. The seven-year-old Aleksandra actively assisted her chastened mother as she went about visiting prisons with money and supplies (including clothing the two had made), helping the poor, and treating the sick. If a person were seriously ill, the mother would sit by the bedside for days on end; even if the person were dying, Aleksandra would be present, helping her mother to ease the patient's sufferings. To prepare her daughter to earn a living, the mother taught the child to sew. To prepare her for life, she strengthened the child's body with exercise, made her work in the garden during summers, fed her coarse foods, and exposed her in a minimum of clothing to all kinds of weather. Religious observance was woven into the routine of Aleksandra's life. Mornings, she would kneel to say her prayers. Later, after dining on hot milk and black bread, the child would read the holy scriptures before taking up her work. Her mother constantly indicated to her the religious significance of events.

When Aleksandra was thirteen, her mother grew deathly ill. So as not to leave the child an unprotected orphan, the mother married her off to the son of a close friend. Aleksandra, who felt no attraction to her future husband, was advised by her mother immediately before the wedding: "Love your husband purely and passionately, and obey him in everything. It is not him you will obey, but God – God has given him to you and made him your master. Even if he treats you badly, endure everything patiently, try to please him, and complain to no one."[28]

The marriage was a disaster. The husband, who had received a secular education and had become a freethinker, mocked his wife's religiosity and entertained lovers in their home, even in their bed. He estranged the young bride from her family, gambled away her money or spent it on other women, and seemed to delight in inventing fresh torments for her. To all his cruelty she responded with patience, docility, frequent tears, and a self-righteousness that seems sometimes to have infuriated him. Several times Aleksandra considered leaving him, but each time, people she respected firmly advised her to remain. She must "endure everything," they maintained. To oppose her husband was to oppose God, whereas to suffer would strengthen and improve her, and ultimately she would be grateful for this test of her faith.[29] Labzina's mother-in-law tried repeatedly to intervene on the young woman's behalf, but she proved virtually powerless to influence her son. The marriage lasted close to twenty years, although husband and wife never reconciled their differences.

At the root of their problems were essentially opposite world views. Aleksandra, submissive, long-suffering, and docile, had been instilled with traditional values that legitimized and gave religious significance to the authority of the husband. To rebel against matrimony, a holy union, or to raise her voice in opposition to her husband's meant to rebel against God. By contrast, the husband had adopted secularized Western values that set him sharply at odds with his long-suffering wife. He conceived the aim of life as pleasure, not salvation (even his wife's pleasure, should she want it; he was forever urging her to take a lover). He did not hesitate to enjoy the traditional prerogatives of masculinity, but as a freethinker he had only contempt for the religious values that guided his wife. Because his society offered no system of morality that could serve to check his impulses, and because the state seemed as unwilling to restrain a husband as it was to restrain a serf owner, nothing remained to control his self-indulgent behavior.[30]

The Westernization of women only partially redressed the imbalance in the relations between the sexes. If we can trust complaints about the "immoral" behavior of noblewomen, at the upper levels of the nobility women as well as men had started to adopt Western ways by the end of the eighteenth century.[31] The autocracy had had a hand in this, as, indeed, it had a hand in just about everything. In his zeal to transform Russian society along the lines of Western Europe, Peter the Great had even tampered with people's personal lives. In 1714 he ruled that both parties to a marriage had to consent (a rule that was often ignored, as in the case of Labzina). He also required noblewomen to leave their customary seclusion, and he insisted that the sexes mingle in social gatherings, as he had seen them do in Europe. The belief that cultivated society required the participation of women encouraged men who shared his ideas to bestow on their daughters the fruits of Western culture, and eventually it led Catherine the Great to become involved in educating noblewomen.

The question was: For what purpose were they to be educated? Culture, ideas, and skills derived from the West prepared men for service to the state. With the exception of ladies-in-waiting and a few other positions at court, however, women had no place in state service. This did not matter much at the time that Catherine the Great was still in power: At the end of her reign, fewer than 900 girls, from a population of about 40 million people, had been educated in the Smolny Institute for Girls of Noble Birth (founded 1764), and several thousand more had been enrolled in public schools where students acquired basic literacy as well as religious and moral training. Catherine's aim was to improve life in Russia by educating better wives and mothers, and she was prepared to encourage women to participate as fully as possible in the intellectual life of the nation. Catherine even appointed her friend, Princess Dashkova, to be president of the Academy of Sciences (1783–96). Well-educated men sought such women as wives. So long as Westernized secular education remained the prerogative of the upper crust of the nobility, the women who bene-fited from it moved in a world in which everyone else was educated, too, and where a veneer of culture enhanced a woman's marriageability.[32]

However, education could create problems when it became available to women further down on the social scale – women who lived in the provinces, women who had access to neither court nor aristocratic circles. Western ideas threatened to create contradictions in such women's lives by leading them to expect more for themselves without providing them the wherewithal to obtain it. So women had far less incentive than men to abandon a religiously based system of values that gave life meaning and dignity, even as it enjoined them to submit and endure. Consider what would have happened had it been Aleksandra Labzina who received a secular education, and her husband the traditional one. Among other things, her religion had helped Labzina endure her husband's treatment by teaching that a person should expect nothing from this life. What would happen to a woman just as subject to male authority who allowed reading to erode her religious faith and to raise her expectations?

Praskovia Ivanovna Tatlina was such a woman. Born in 1808, the oldest child of a relatively modest noble family, Praskovia was raised in the time-honored fashion. Her father managed the estates of the wealthy Count Sheremetev; her mother, an old-fashioned and religious woman, attempted to prepare her daughters for their lot in life. But at the home of a wealthy and Westernized uncle, Praskovia learned to read, and she developed a passion for books that soon superseded all other interests. She began to question many of her parents' most cherished beliefs, and her reading of Enlightenment philosophers, Voltaire in particular, shook her religious faith so profoundly that it terrified her. Eventually she grew estranged from her family, especially from her mother, for Praskovia now had little patience with her mother's long-suffering religiosity, and still less with the God-fearing old women who filled her parents' home. Reading had cost Praskovia not only her religion but also her taste for any "feminine" pursuit. She wanted nothing to do with the kitchen or the nursery.

Nevertheless, when she turned eighteen, Praskovia's parents married her off to a virtual stranger, a widower seventeen years her senior, a military man who lacked her intellectual interests and who held thoroughly conventional ideas about woman's place: "For him a woman was an object," Tatlina wrote. He proved unable to acknowledge, let alone respect, her intellect and her interests. Drawing on her reading, Praskovia tried to explain this. "Men," she wrote, "do not recognize their own individuality," because they "slavishly drag out their existence in official circles." By contrast, women, while expected to behave like slaves, are better able to appreciate their own humanity because they are free to feel.[33] Failing to find happiness in her marriage, and without access to the aristocratic circles where she might have found companionship, Tatlina channeled her considerable energy and intelligence toward the outlet that remained: her children, and especially her daughters. "A person should be happy in this world," she reasoned. Her own experience had convinced her that marriage brings misery and that therefore people should avoid it. But in order to do this, a girl had to be able to make her own way. Over the vehement opposition of husband, family, and friends, Tatlina provided her oldest daughter with musical training, in the hope that through teaching, the only suitable calling for a noblewoman, the girl might remain independent.[34]

In the first half of the nineteenth century, Russian society provided almost no options for a woman who thought critically about her family role and rejected the values that would have enabled her to endure it. Those, like Tatlina, who sought to expand women's prerogatives on an individual level acted in isolation, finding reinforcement for their unconventional aspirations in literature rather than in other people. Far more likely to win support and admiration were those women who accepted their family roles and adhered to their mothers' values, even when they used such values to challenge the official order. Such women were the Decembrist wives, whose story illustrates this alternative source of women's consciousness.

The history of the Russian revolutionary movement begins with the Decembrists. Deeply imbued with Western European values, and frustrated in their efforts to bring about reform through legitimate channels, the Decembrists attempted to liberalize Russia's political, economic, and social systems by staging an abortive coup on December 14, 1825. The attempt failed, and the participants were arrested and tried. Five of the leaders were hanged, and most of the rest were sentenced to hard labor in Siberia.

No women participated in the Decembrist conspiracy, and as far as we know, none had been privy to the plot. Decembrist documents mention women only rarely, and when they do, the aim is usually to bar women from public life and to channel their energies into "philanthropic and *private* societies" (emphasis in the original) and "the education of children in accordance with the principles of virtue and faith." The Northern Society, which carried out the abortive coup of December 14, not only would have prevented women from voting but also would have kept them from attending legislative sessions. And although four women had ruled Russia during the eighteenth century, in the constitutional monarchy these men envisioned they carefully specified that "women are excluded from the throne and do not transmit any rights to it." Instead, power would be passed through women, from father to son and from father-in-law to son-in-law.[35]

Their exclusion from political activity made the Decembrist wives rebel in a very different sense than their husbands. While the men sought a share of political power, the women challenged the values that upheld the political order by defying social strictures and following their men to Siberia.[36] Their stories varied. Maria Volkonskaia, whose father initially disowned her on account of her decision, had only recently been married. She went to Siberia, she explained to her father, out of a sense of duty to her husband: How could she enjoy her comforts while he suffered? Better to follow him, and through her own suffering to ease his. Camille Ledantu, daughter of the French governess of the Ivashev family, had long loved Vasilii Ivashev in secret. The change in his position after 1825 permitted Camille to confide her love to her mother. When Vasilii learned of her willingness to come to Siberia and marry him, he gratefully proposed, and she as happily accepted.

The dozen or so women who followed their men to Siberia were all of noble birth and gently raised, and it was an act of immense self-sacrifice to give up their privileged positions to live in primitive quarters in frozen desolation. Those with children had to leave them behind. Because a woman had the right to divorce a political criminal (one of the very few instances in which divorce was possible), their sacrifice was freely chosen. Many of the Decembrist wives appear to have acted in a spirit of quasi-religious exaltation. The best known is Maria Volkonskaia, who "won immortality by throwing herself at the feet of her husband and kissing his fetters."[37]

It was this selfless devotion and readiness to act on their feelings in defiance of the cold, official male world that earned the Decembrist wives a revered place in the pantheon of Russian revolutionary martyrology. Aleksandr Herzen, a member of the first generation of the intelligentsia, wrote the following:

Nobody (except women) dared utter a word about relations or friends, whose hands they had shaken only the day before they had been carried off at night by the police.... Women alone did not take part in this shameful abandonment of those who were near and dear.... The wives of men exiled to hard labor lost their civil rights, abandoned wealth and social position, and went to a lifetime of bondage in the terrible climate of Eastern Siberia, under the still more terrible oppression of the police there. Sisters, who had not the right to go with their brothers, withdrew from court, and many left Russia; almost all of them kept a feeling of love for the victims alive in their hearts; but there was no such love in the men: terror consumed it in their hearts, and not one of them dared mention the unfortunates.[38]

Vera Figner (1852–1943), a revolutionary woman of a later generation, recognized the "heroism of Russian women" in the Decembrist wives. Noting the continuity between these women of an earlier generation and the radical women of her own, Figner inquired: "Should we not acknowledge them as our precursors, as lamps illuminating the past of our revolutionary movement?"[39]

By virtue of their willingness to relinquish their comforts and their privileges and to defy officialdom for the sake of a higher morality, the Decembrist wives became the first in a series of martyr heroines who inspired subsequent generations to challenge the existing order. Even as they did so, however, the Decembrist wives also perpetuated certain aspects of a traditional feminine ideal. Although the women who followed might later politicize the content of that higher morality, in their readiness to set aside personal well-being and to sacrifice themselves absolutely, the spiritual daughters of the Decembrist wives at the same time remained faithful to tradition.

CHAPTER 2

RISING EXPECTATIONS AND
SHATTERED DREAMS

The intelligentsia emerged during the harsh reign of Nicholas I, when public life became regimented as never before. Nicholas I ascended the throne under the cloud of the Decembrist uprising, which intensified his native suspiciousness and made him wary of the upper strata of society, to which the Decembrists belonged. Fearing the spread of dangerous ideas, Nicholas imposed stringent censorship on all publications, established the Third Section, a political police force, and tried to impose military discipline on every branch of state service and every sector of society.

Nicholas's efforts to control his people served only to intensify social conflict and to make an awakening Russian society more volatile. Economic development was already disrupting the traditional way of life. The productive forces of the nation were increasing, and although serfdom continued to act as a brake on those forces, it could not stop the growth of economic interdependence with the rest of Europe, which was by then well into the capitalist phase of development. Unaccustomed to viewing their properties with a businessman's eye, the majority of landowners had trouble keeping pace. Despite Nicholas's efforts to bolster the nobility, that class continued to decline. Nobles mortgaged, even sold, their estates, while the serfs grew more restless, and the number of uprisings increased alarmingly.

At the same time, the needs of a modernizing state set in motion forces the state could not always channel. The burgeoning bureaucracy required educated servitors, whose newly acquired expertise led many of them to assume greater responsibility and to expect more autonomy than the bureaucratic paper pushers of former times. The state needed its universities, which despite careful controls on curricula generated independent thought and planted the seeds of opposition.

The expansion of educational opportunities proved to be vital to the emergence of the intelligentsia. By providing access to Western European literature and to ideas about a more humane and just way of life, education promoted critical thought and inspired a minority of men and women to oppose the existing order. The men ran enormous risks; their

20

opposition cost many their freedom and some their lives. Nevertheless, in adopting a critical stance, in some respects these men were only traveling farther along a route the state itself had marked out. Already imbued with the secular ideal of service, they transferred their sense of obligation from the state to "society," then dedicated themselves to transforming the latter according to their vision of a better life.[1]

By contrast, contact with Western ideas created a profound conflict for women. Secular values challenged their religious world view, and notions about the individual's right to self-development and self-fulfillment directly contradicted their traditional role without suggesting a new one. The first generation of women of the intelligentsia sought to escape their dilemma by grafting their new ideas onto a traditional one. In women's higher morality they found justification for their dissatisfactions and for their efforts to redefine their traditional sphere, to raise its social value, and to make it more personally gratifying.

Rarely were these women's efforts successful, and their ideas failed to take root in the inhospitable soil of Nicholas's Russia. Nevertheless, these women's abortive rebellion demonstrated how a nascent individualism, just starting to challenge the authoritarian social order, might challenge the authoritarian family as well.

The intelligentsia, which would become the leading source of political opposition for the duration of the nineteenth century, arose during the 1830s in the shelter of the University of Moscow, an oasis of relative freedom where men could enjoy fellowship and understanding available nowhere else. At first, however, the aspirations of these men were political only in the broadest sense of that word. They were enamored of German romanticism, and although they knew that Russian reality was at odds with their sensibilities, instead of acting to change the world around them they consoled themselves by attending to their own feelings and perceptions. They sought freedom, to be sure, but in self-development and self-perfection, not in civil liberties or the right to cast a vote. Such a course was the safest in Nicholas's Russia, where for the slightest misstep a man might be condemned to years of prison or exile. It also left private life as the one realm in which men could act directly on their ideas.[2]

This led men to attribute special significance to the relationships they had with women. Romanticism, after all, stressed the primacy of feeling and subjective experience, and what feeling was more powerful and therefore more "true" than love? Love provided a means to merge with the Absolute; it elevated lovers and put them in touch with the forces of the universe. Their romanticism prompted some men of the intelligentsia to renounce the traditional patriarchal and sometimes brutal pattern of male-female relationships that many had experienced firsthand between their parents and instead to use women in their quest for self-perfection. This does not mean that women benefited from the new attitudes or that men learned to treat them as equals. Because these men regarded woman as a means to attain a higher state of existence, they elevated her on a pedestal so high they could barely touch her skirts. These men fell in love with their own ideal, not an earthly, flawed female being. So they eventually grew disillusioned, fell out of love, and fled, leaving the poor woman to cope as best she could. Nikolai Stankevich, Aleksandr Herzen, and Mikhail Bakunin all trifled with women's affections in this way.[3] It was difficult even for men with the best of intentions to give up the old habits of self-indulgence and domination. The old habits simply took different forms: Projection of woman as an ideal destroyed the individual woman as a person with her own personality and feelings.

There is every indication that this behavior did not make men particularly happy, either. Instead of attaining self-perfection, or a higher state of existence, they found themselves doing things that made them feel slightly guilty. Unwilling to return to the traditional male-female relationships, they were psychologically unprepared to create new ones. Some simply avoided intimate relationships with women altogether, as did Mikhail Bakunin (who may have been homosexual, bisexual, or impotent) and Nikolai Stankevich.

During the 1840s, Vissarion Belinskii, Aleksandr Herzen, and a handful of others set aside romanticism and turned to the writings of the French utopian socialists and George Sand. Descending from tne heights of romantic ecstasy to confront and try to change the world in which they lived, they came to reconsider their attitudes toward love, marriage, and the role of women. The writings of George Sand played an important part in this reevaluation. Immensely popular among both men and women during the 1840s, Sand's works were published in the rapidly proliferating "thick journals" that brought culture into even the remote provinces. Sand preached "freedom of the heart" and the need to obey its dictates, whether within marriage or outside of it. She did not advocate cold promiscuity (although certain of her Russian critics condemned her for doing so).[4] For Sand, love was the most elevated human emotion, and although it should not be limited by social conventions, neither should it be trifled with. In her own way, Sand argued for women's rights – not political rights, to be sure, but emotional rights, the right to be more fully human and to live according to one's feelings. Utopian socialists were more explicitly feminist, especially Charles Fourier, who wrote that "the extension of the privileges of women is the fundamental cause of all social progress."[5]

As a consequence of their own experiences, and under the influence of the utopians and Sand, a few men of the intelligentsia learned to approach women with greater sympathy and respect, and even to consider a woman's significance not merely in relation to themselves as men but also to society as a whole. Aleksandr Herzen and Vissarion Belinskii were the only ones to address themselves in writing to women's social role – Herzen in his diary and Belinskii in several critical essays. In 1849 Herzen wrote that in the communal society of the future, "woman will be more involved in general interests. She will be strengthened morally by education, and she will not be so one-sidedly attached to the family." Belinskii declared that it was unfair to confine women to home and family.[6] Both men assumed that participation by women would help to improve public life, but neither developed any comprehensive critique of women's position or the relationship between the sexes.

As a result of social position, women of the first generation of the intelligentsia reversed the men's priorities completely. Affected, although less directly than men, by the regimentation of public life, and suffering from similar conflicts between their sensibilities and the society in which they lived, these women experienced inequities in personal relationships that men did not. Moreover, because women's lives were confined to home and family because of the tradition of marriage and motherhood, as well as the absence of opportunities in the public domain, women did not enjoy even the circumscribed freedoms that men did, and certainly not the intellectual companionship. As a result, when women did begin to think independently and to strive for their own sort of freedom, they acted as individuals and addressed themselves almost exclusively to personal relationships, the sphere they knew best.

By affecting that sphere, the policies of Nicholas I unintentionally stimulated women's discontent, as they had stimulated men's. Anxious to control all social relations, the tsar turned his attention to family life as well as public life. In Nicholas's opinion, the family provided one of the cornerstones of social stability. The family was, after all, the basic unit of this patriarchal society, the place where loyal, God-fearing citizens received their initial training. It was logical, therefore, that Nicholas would have something to say about it. "Let parents turn their entire attention to the moral education of their children," declared Nicholas a year after ascending his throne. Education at home must prepare the character, and it must be in accord with the purposes of government. Religion was to provide the guidelines. One of Nicholas's leading ideologists wrote that "it is necessary to introduce into the family complete Christian teachings. . . . The most frequent possible contacts between the family and the Church are necessary."[7]

One way to ensure the stability of the family was to educate women in a manner that would reinforce their domestic role, and this changed the emphasis of state-sponsored schools for noblewomen. When Catherine the Great founded Smolny Institute, she aimed not only to prepare capable wives and mothers but also to provide the students with an education of high quality and to instill in them a taste for reading and intellectual work. When Catherine died in 1796, guardianship over Smolny passed into the hands of Empress Maria Feodorovna, the wife of Paul I

(1796–1801), who took a far more limited view of Smolny's goals. Raised according to the ideas of Jean Jacques Rousseau in a large, closely knit German family, the Empress Maria believed that the sole purpose of education was to train girls for domesticity. In the messages she sent to students and school officials, Maria constantly reiterated that a woman's place was in the home. In 1804, for instance, she advised graduates of Smolny "as daughters, to be obedient and respectful; as wives, to be faithful, virtuous, tender, modest, diligent and useful, and to promote the honor of the person with whom you have linked your fate... to be conscientious about the order, comfort and well-being of your household, and as mothers to try to combine warmth towards your children with sensible concern about their future well-being."[8] They were to seek comfort and pleasure only within themselves and their families. Maria had students read *Fatherly Advice to My Daughter*, translated from the German. Among other things, the book attacked women of the upper class for refusing to adjust to their vocation, which it described glowingly as middle-class domesticity.

During the reign of her son, Nicholas I, several new institutes were established, but Maria's guardianship continued, and so did the emphasis on domesticity. "Since woman is a delicate creature who is naturally dependent on others, her destiny is the family," asserted instructions issued to administrators of girls' schools in 1852. "She should learn that her fate is to submit to her husband, and not to command. She can only ensure her happiness and acquire the love and respect of others... by strictly fulfilling her family duties." Religion and morality remained at the very heart of such training.[9]

Despite this concern to adapt education to the woman's family role, school could nevertheless sow the seeds of discontent. This was not because school taught women to think for themselves, as universities sometimes taught men, but because what women learned had so little to do with the lives they would someday lead. The Empress Maria's notions of domesticity proved ill-suited to the lives of most serf-owning noblewomen. Why should such women devote themselves to domesticity when most had at least a few serfs to cook, clean, and sew for them? Why should they be solicitous mothers when they could leave the care of infants in the hands of a peasant nurse who knew how to do such things and would devote herself completely to her charge? Surely no one really expected a noblewoman to take on the work of servants.

Moreover, the very nature of institute education served to counteract the sort of training Maria had envisioned. Institutes removed girls from their families at the age of eight or nine and cloistered them until graduation. In such isolation, girls could hardly learn to mother. Indeed, the girls soon lost all family feeling, developing instead intense schoolgirl crushes, which they called "adoration," and which seem a kind of parody of adult courtship. Nor could girls acquire housekeeping skills when their mothers relied on serfs, and the lessons at school were useless. Nor could they learn any practical skills, for that matter, when institute education functioned to keep them thoroughly ignorant of the outside world (even the windows were greased so that they could not observe the world).[10] At the same time, girls acquired aristocratic pretentions. Maria had hoped to adjust institute education to the background of the student: "The majority of the girls are poor: we must prepare them for solitude. Some may have poorly educated parents: let them learn that they can live with anyone who is honorable."[11] Nevertheless, when institutes stressed learning at all, the subject matter was invariably decorative rather than practical in nature: languages, especially French, and manners.

This was not accidental. Marriage provided a woman's only avenue for social mobility, and a noblewoman's fate ultimately depended on the man she married. Because accomplishments presumably enhanced a girl's value on the marriage market, they might ensure her fortune. If she married well, then a noblewoman would indeed be able to consign household labor to others while she engaged in the social life for which her schooling had prepared her. Raised in isolation and ignorance of real life, and filled with romantic notions about their future, there was little incentive for pupils to interest themselves in the humdrum aspects of domesticity. It was far more pleasant to dream of the "good match" and the glamorous social life that would follow graduation: "parties, dances, toilettes and the courtship of brilliant cavaliers."[12]

How could they not be disappointed? Only a fortunate few would marry well and enjoy the social life of the capital. Some would not marry at all, but would become the female dependents we encounter so often in Russian novels, or, if their families could not afford to maintain them, governesses and teachers' assistants. Women viewed both positions as utterly unappealing. One student at Smolny, who learned that her sister would start work as a teacher's assistant (*klassnaia dama*), confided to her diary: "My God, who would have believed it! It seemed she would have such a brilliant future, full of love, wealth and fame – and now it has come to the position of *klassnaia dama* in the Smolny Monastery. . . . My poor Annette! . . . I feel so sad and melancholy, as if I were about to bury her."[13]

But even marriage ordinarily proved different from the romantic fantasies gained through reading or generated behind institute walls. Knowing nothing of real life, institute graduates were ill-prepared to choose husbands, and in many cases their parents arranged their marriages for them. Most women settled in the provinces with ordinary servitors, who had neither the time nor the taste for romantic flights of fancy. Such men expected their wives to know how to supervise a household and serfs, how to stretch a ruble if they were poor; so these women had to ignore what they had learned in school and set about acquiring practical skills. They were often lonely, too, for their neighbors in the provinces regarded institute graduates as eccentric "scholarly women." If they wanted to fit in, they had to hide their accomplishments.

Some women made the adjustment more readily than others. One was Aleksandra Stepanovna Gonetskaia, the daughter of a middling provincial nobleman. In 1828, sixteen years old and just out of school, she agreed to marry a man twenty years her senior when he promised to throw an enormous party for her. She was delighted by the prospect of a party and by the fact that she would be the first of her institute friends to marry, although they had rated her only ninth in looks. Aleksandra Stepanovna was relatively fortunate in her choice, if such a decision can be called a choice. Her husband, a retired military man, had acquired progressive ideas during campaigns abroad. He proved kind and gentle and was concerned for their children in a way that was still uncommon among the nobility of either sex. When they argued over childrearing, it was the wife who accused the husband of being too easygoing. Aleksandra Stepanovna grew accustomed to life in provincial isolation and stoically endured twenty pregnancies and eventual widowhood. After her husband died, she managed competently all the work connected with her estate.[14]

Elizaveta Shubert, born in 1821 to a geodesist and topographer, a member of the Academy of Sciences, found adjustment more difficult. Elizaveta did not attend school, but her father took pains to educate her, so that she was far better read than most institute graduates. When she married at twenty-two, she knew four European languages, was familiar with classical and modern literature, sketched, danced, sang, and displayed considerable musical talent. Soon after her marriage to forty-two-year-old General Vasilii Korvin-Krukovskii, she began to keep a diary. "So, I'm married," she wrote. "My future is full of hope. I have an excellent house...and a charming husband. I'll have to fulfill the most pleasant social obligations, and create the happiness of the man I adore." Such unclouded joy proved short-lived; within a few months she began to complain: "I cried all last night, while my husband lay beside me, senseless and snoring....In the evening we went to a meeting. When I was dressing, my gown stretched tight and my husband began to laugh because I was filling out with motherhood. I was glad at the thought, but then he began to make accusations, spoke contemptuously and demanded that our future child be named as he wished." Soon the husband took to visiting his club almost every evening, leaving her at home, and the diary entries assumed a depressing similarity: He was out, and she was at home with guests or by herself. After a while she simply ceased to write at all.[15]

In the first third of the nineteenth century, only a limited number of women were likely to acquire unrealistic expectations or to aspire to a life that was different from that of their mothers. For the most part, only families in St. Petersburg and the surrounding provinces took advantage of opportunities to educate their daughters at the expense of the state; even fewer bothered to educate girls at home. In 1802, some 2,007 girls attended school; in 1820 there were 5,791. By 1834, 4,864 girls (not all from the nobility) were enrolled in schools administered by the empress.[16]

How many young women left their parents' homes or their schools expecting more from life than it would offer them we cannot know for certain, but the proliferation of literary works attempting to redefine women's traditional role suggests that a substantial proportion of them continued to experience a sense of disappointment, a sense that human relationships should be more satisfying, a sense that their talents and capacities should be used more fully. In an effort to improve their lives, some of these women would develop a Russian version of the cult of domesticity that was flourishing to the West; they would try to elevate their sphere and, on that basis, to demand more scope for their own self-realization and more gratification from their relationships with men. From their midst emerged the first generation of women of the intelligentsia. Their intellectual inspiration, like that for their male counterparts, came from the romantics. Some expressed themselves in fiction and poetry that enjoyed considerable popularity during the 1830s and 1840s. Others tried to realize their ideas in practice. In both instances, women's rebellion began at home, and almost invariably in isolation.

One such rebel was Tatiana Passek (*née* Kuchina) (1810–89), who as a child played and studied with her cousin, Aleksandr Herzen, and then stayed home when he went off to the university. "I went into his room," she remembered, "and sat on the divan at the very table where we had read and studied together for several years. I took up a book and tried to read, but instead of reading, I fell into thought."[17] Tatiana's rebelliousness emerged in her choice of a husband, one of the few choices a woman had. Rejecting a more advantageous match, she accepted Vadim Passek, the child of a Polish rebel who had been deprived of his nobility for political reasons. Vadim Passek belonged to the circle that had formed around Aleksandr Herzen, and Herzen tried to prevent the marriage. "Vadim should not marry," he warned his cousin. "Family life is disruptive: it concentrates the attention on the self, on trifles, and takes one away from the common cause." To some extent, this warning proved justified. Although Tatiana Passek shared her husband's intellectual interests and did some translating of her own, her energies were primarily concentrated on raising her children and on creating the cozy domestic atmosphere that did, indeed, keep her husband at home and away from his friends and their social concerns.[18]

Other rebels included the following: the writer Avdotia Panaeva (1819–83), wife of the critic I. Panaev, whom she left for the poet Nikolai Nekrasov in the 1840s; the poet, novelist, and saloniere Karolina Pavlova (*née* Jaenish) (1807–93); the Bakunin sisters; the first wife of the poet and intellectual Nikolai Ogarev, Maria Ogareva (*née* Roslavleva) (1817–53), who refused to conform to anyone's expectations of her, enjoying a number of extramarital affairs before she and Ogarev separated for good. "I have never conceded anything to society," she confided to her diary, "not a single desire, not a single conviction, not a single impulse to love, not one of my caprices."[19] The fact that these women were related to men of the intelligentsia, or else moved in educated circles in which people were likely to sympathize with their aspirations, undoubtedly facilitated the efforts of these women to expand the limits of their sphere and may have eased their isolation.

Two of the foremost women of the intelligentsia, the writers Elena Gan and Maria Zhukova, enjoyed no such advantages. Raised in the provinces, married to the most ordinary of men, these women shared the experiences of many other women. It was not their feelings of alienation, nor their solitary striving to transcend their circumstances, but the fact that they took up the pen that most distinguished Gan and Zhukova from countless other restless and discontented wives of small landowners and petty civil servants. In the stories of these two women we can see the first stirrings of "women's consciousness."

As a general rule, fiction provides an unreliable means of ascertaining an author's ideas. If a literary work is of high quality, it is usually complex, subtle and rich, and it is not always easy to identify the author's message or to judge which of the characters, if any, speaks with the author's voice. Hence the well-plowed field of literary criticism. As a result, the historian who uses literature as historical evidence stands on shaky ground. Fortunately, the works of Elena Gan present few such problems. Gan's stories are openly polemical. They are fervent criticisms of women's lot. Her characters are poorly developed, and so are her plots, and the overall literary quality of her work is low. Contemporary critics recognized this, but some were willing to overlook it, because they recognized that the author spoke with an authentic woman's voice and that the medium, so to speak, should not drown out the message.[20] Her readers evidently agreed.

Elena Andreevna Gan was a woman who was educated too well for her station in life. Her mother, Elena Pavlovna, was born in 1788 or 1790 and was raised by her grandparents, members of the aristocratic Dolgorukov family, who gave her an excellent education. Under the influence of a woman friend of her grandmother's, she acquired a lifelong interest in botany, history, and archaeology. She corresponded with foreign scientists, collected birds and minerals, and filled dozens of volumes with her sketches of local flora. In 1813 she married a poor servitor, Andrei Fadeev, against the wishes of her grandparents.[21] They settled first in Astrakhan, then in the southern province of Ekaterinoslav. The daughter Elena, born in 1814, was educated by her mother, who shared with her children her knowledge of French, history, and botany.

This was more education than most women of her class received, but Elena found it insufficient. Later in life she would teach herself English, German, and Italian, and she read widely in European and Russian literature.[22]

When she turned sixteen, Elena married a cavalry officer, a man of thirty-two. We do not know who chose her husband, but because the Fadeevs were not wealthy and so could not dower their daughter lavishly, they probably regarded Gan as a good match. Petr Gan had obtained his education in the Corps of Pages, an aristocratic and military institution. He was intelligent and essentially good-natured, but practical, with a cold and rational approach to emotional life. For Elena, a romantic who had married in hope of "eternal love," the marriage proved a bitter disappointment. His cold practicality quickly dampened her romantic fantasies. In addition, their tastes were utterly incompatible: hers for books, for rapturous observations of nature, for conversations on elevated themes, for passionate expressions of feeling; his for cards, coarse jokes, and long, smoke-filled evenings drinking and roistering with his officer friends, who "expressed not a single thought."[23]

While her husband was serving in Poland, Elena's first child was born and died, leaving her severely depressed. Visits with her family provided some consolation in those early years of the marriage, but around 1833 the couple began to live a nomadic life, following the husband's assignments from one province to another. Everywhere, they stayed in the sort of makeshift quarters that Gan described in her first story, "Ideal": "A low room, with carpets covering the furniture; saddles and pistols hang on the walls...three similar rooms make up the entire dwelling."[24]

Elena Gan enjoyed none of the comradeship her husband did, and she found it difficult to make friends when they came to a new place. It was, as she put it, like stepping onto melting ice: "You keep feeling around to figure out where it's safe to put your foot." For men it was easy – a few hands of cards and they were on a familiar footing. Military wives faced all the problems. "The women judge all newcomers carefully and harshly on the basis of their dress, their features, and their character. They form two alien and hostile nations, and they don't merge quickly or easily."[25] Gan found the social life coarse and vulgar, and she sought relief from it in her children. After her two daughters were born, she threw herself into nursing and caring for them, going out as rarely as possible.

Then, for a brief but exhilarating period in 1836, Petr Gan was assigned to St. Petersburg. It was hardly safe for a woman to go about alone, but in the company of her husband's brother Elena wandered the streets, admired the sunsets, and attended the theatre. In literary circles she met for the first time people who thought as she did. She also made her first known literary effort, a translation from French published in the *Library for Readers* (*Biblioteka dlia Chteniia*).

Gan must have gained confidence from the realization that there existed other people who appreciated her and shared her values, but her experience in St. Petersburg also served to exacerbate the differences with her husband. There is one story, probably typical, about Elena and her brother-in-law rapturously admiring a sunset from the balcony of a restaurant, as Petr Gan sat impatiently waiting for them to come in to dinner. Elena grew increasingly intolerant of such "coldness." Even so, when Petr Gan received orders to leave St. Petersburg, Elena had to follow. After stopping for a while with her family in Astrakhan, where she wrote her first story, "Ideal," she went on to rejoin her husband and to resume their nomadic life. Without a room of her own to work in, she created the rest of her stories in a corner behind a curtain that shut her off from the children's nursery. Writing only at night, she published a new work almost every year under the pseudonym Zeneida R-va, even though from 1840 on she was almost constantly ailing (with what disease her biographers do not tell us). On June 24, 1842, shortly after a severe bloodletting that undoubtedly hastened her end, Elena Gan died at the age of twenty-eight, leaving three children to be raised by her mother.

Each of her stories touches on the central predicament of Gan's short life: the loneliness of the passionate, sensitive, and cultivated individual who has no outlet for her talents, who must live in a milieu in which no one can understand her, not even a lover, and certainly not her husband. Gan described her own fate in "Ideal," the story that reflects her life most faithfully: "Marriage! In that lottery, the odds are one thousand to one that an unusual woman will join her fate to the most ordinary and vulgar member of the opposite sex."[26] The heroine of the story, delicate and sensitive, is married to a military officer, who is cold, crude, and unresponsive to her emotional needs; he found the heart of a woman "an impenetrable secret." The provincial society in which the heroine must make her way is equally uncomprehending and equally unable to recognize, let alone appreciate, her superiority. "The position of a man of unusual intellect is unbearable in the provinces, but the position of a woman whom nature herself has placed above the crowd is truly horrible," wrote Gan. Other women envy and resent the heroine as a creature whose "intellect and feeling are superior to their frivolous and petty intrigues," while men, "among whom hardly one has an elevated soul," behave still worse. "They are frightened by her [the elevated woman] and use their crude strength to mock and degrade her." According to Gan, society lies in wait for a woman to make just one misstep, in order to throw her from her pedestal. "If we lose our balance even the slightest bit, society will trample us underfoot."[27]

In subsequent stories, Gan's message remained more or less the same. "Medalion" (1839) depicts a young woman who is seduced into loving a worldly and cold man and then loses her sight when he abandons her.

The central character is her older sister, who devotes her life to avenging this injustice. In "Teofania Abbadzhio" (1841), a poor but altruistic young woman sacrifices the man she loves, who does not appreciate her, so that he can marry a wealthy but frivolous society woman. In "Society's Judgement" (1840), society condemns a decent woman as immoral because she reveals her intelligence. And "The Futile Gift" (1842), one of the most tragic of Gan's stories, portrays a poor girl, the daughter of a steward, who possesses poetic talents that she is forbidden to express. Forced to deny her most precious gift, she becomes insane and dies at the age of eighteen. Only in "Liubon'ka" (1842), Gan's final story, does a lonely and misunderstood orphan heroine at last find happiness in marriage.[28]

The alienation of Gan's talented heroines reflects her own self-image. In St. Petersburg she might find sympathy, but elsewhere no one seemed to like her, hard as she might try to conform to provincial ways. "What do people want from me anyhow?" she inquired of a friend. "I receive them with the greatest possible courtesy, even with excessive attention, wasting my time trying to entertain them and to be interested in their conversation. And instead of being grateful, they regard me as a scarecrow at a fair (*iarmochnoe pugalo*), as a snake in flannel."[29] As Gan complained in another letter, society, "that three-headed monster," calls the talented woman immoral and with filthy comments defiles her most noble feelings and elevated ideas.[30] The one compensation for being a woman writer was that it gave her some freedom: Anything strange she might do was immediately attributed to "author's originality." "For example, in the Caucasus I attended five balls in a black dress and everyone considered it author's originality, and it occurred to no one that I simply owned no ball dresses,"[31] Gan wrote. While she might occasionally make light of being different from everyone else, Gan found it hard to endure. In 1839 she wrote her editor that she would either work or go mad, probably the latter, as a result of her total isolation "and the impossibility of sharing a single thought, of expressing the slightest feeling."[32]

The absence of any acceptable outlets occasionally led Gan to protest against the fate that had assigned such different spheres to men and women. In "Ideal," her heroine declares that "sometimes it seems to me that the world is created just for men. Men have access to the universe with all its secrets; they enjoy fame, art and knowledge; they have freedom and all the joys of life. But from the cradle, a woman is fettered by the chains of respectability; enmeshed by the terrible 'what will society think?'; and if her hopes for family happiness are not realized, what does she have left outside of the family? Her pitifully narrow education prevents her from devoting herself to meaningful work."[33] By contrast with the talented man, the gifted woman is doomed to "vegetate in the desert, in anonymity, away from the world, from all the great models, from all opportunities to satisfy her soul's thirst for knowledge, and only because she is a woman!"[34]

Logically, this reasoning should have led Gan to demand equality between the sexes – a demand being made elsewhere in Europe, as she knew. But Gan did not follow her own logic. Although she might concede that circumstances could force a woman to assume a masculine role, never did she contend that women, as women, had a right to the same prerogatives as men. One reason was that she believed in women's inferiority to men. "Although I am a woman who has suffered greatly from the conditions that fetter our sex," she wrote to a friend in 1839, "I'd never accept the idea that nature has created men and women equal. Our souls and bodies are weaker, our intellects more trivial, and nature has made our lot in life all too clear." "Our insignificance in all areas," Gan demonstrated by arguing that "there have been no great women artists or thinkers." Even without educational opportunities, she contended, "true genius should somehow have found its way."[35] Another reason was that Gan's romanticism confirmed what she could observe for herself: The male world was cold and formal, geared to the austere demands of service and allowing no scope for the cultivation and expression of feeling. Why would a woman want an equal place in such a world? Rather, a woman was better off making the most of the position she already had. According to Gan, a woman was first of all a loving wife and mother. "God gave women an excellent vocation, although not as glorious or as celebrated as He gave men. . . . The vocation of being the spirit of the household [domashnii penat], the comfort of her chosen friend, the mother of her children." This special vocation made women morally superior to men, although it left them inferior in other respects, and on the basis of women's moral superiority Gan argued for recognition of a woman's personality and needs, for more respectful treatment of women, and for a lessening of their subordination to men.

However, Gan's version of the cult of domesticity proved as ill-suited as the Empress Maria's to her circumstances and character, and never did Gan quite succeed in living up to her own ideals. For example, Gan believed that motherhood was a central feature of the woman's role. She herself wrote fiction, she insisted, for the sake of her children. This was true in that she used her earnings to hire teachers and governesses in order to provide her children with a better education and a better life than hers. "I would labor night and day, if only to preserve my children from what I had to endure," she wrote. In a letter of March 1840 she asserted that she hated to write, that it was like penal servitude, but nevertheless necessary for the sake of the children.[36] Yet by her own standards she was not an attentive mother, at least not after she started to write. Then she handed her children to nurses, governesses, and tutors, in the traditional manner of noblewomen. One of her daughters, the writer V. P. Zhelikhovskaia, remembered with a touch of resentment that her mother was almost always ailing and, when well, was forever hidden by the screen that secluded her "study" from the nursery.[37] Gan's letters also reveal her ambivalence toward her children. In 1838 she replied to her editor, who had asked if she intended to have more children, "Oh no! such a ludicrous notion has never even entered my head. May God preserve the two I have."[38] (She was nonetheless to have a third, the boy Leonid, in 1840.) Gan knew that her performance fell short of her own ideal of motherhood, and she often criticized herself for failing her children. "My illness has left me so irritable and nervous that I can't work with them. For children you need a tranquil temperament, unlike mine."[39] For all her disclaimers, she apparently felt more comfortable with her literary children, and more at home in her "study" than in the nursery a few feet away.[40] But never would she acknowledge this. If she derived pleasure from writing or from her literary success, she kept it to herself.[41]

An incurable romantic, Gan believed with Rousseau that a woman's vocation was to love, that her place was in the home, and she struggled to force her considerable talent, passion, and energy into that procrustean bed. It is no wonder that she was frustrated and that people found her difficult. Gan's demands on people were excessive and unrealistic, nourished by feelings she could not acknowledge, and legitimized by the very romanticism that led her to suppress her ambition and her desire to participate in the world of men. But given her perception of the male world, what choice had she? Capable of moral fervor and ready for self-sacrifice, a woman like Gan could find an outlet only in the family.

Much the same contrast between male and female spheres emerges in the works of Maria Zhukova. She was born in 1805 in the province of Nizhnii Novgorod, where her father served as a lawyer. Later they moved to Saratov. Like Gan, Zhukova spent her formative years in the provinces, where she acquired a love of nature and a critical yet affectionate appreciation of provincial ways. Her knowledge of languages and of foreign and Russian literature was exceptional for a girl born to such a provincial family. Because of her father's small salary, it is likely, as she hints in her stories, that she obtained this education neither at school nor from tutors but in the home of a wealthy noble family, who presumably raised her to be the companion of their daughter. In this family, too, Zhukova undoubtedly acquired the distaste for worldly and aristocratic society that characterizes almost all of her writings.[42] Like Gan, Zhukova was married early, at seventeen or eighteen, to a local landowner who served as a district judge in his region. The marriage proved unhappy. The husband loved to play cards and go on sprees, and although he was originally well-to-do, he soon lost all his money and ended up in debt. Eventually the two separated, but only after Zhukova had given birth to a son, her only child. Around 1830 she moved to St. Petersburg, and several years later she began to write to support herself and her child and to pay off some of her husband's debts. Her first story appeared in 1837, and she published regularly thereafter until her death in 1855.

Zhukova's works present a world even drearier than Gan's; society constricts her heroines still more tightly. Few of her women find personal happiness, although some aspire to it, and their marriages are rarely successful. When relationships fail, it is men who are at fault. "Men usually arrive in villages and towns to rest after a stormy youth spent in the capital. In district towns men are occupied with service, the latest decrees, the arrival of the governor, reports, responses to inquiries and so forth. Men who do not serve play cards, hunt and enjoy themselves, or spend all their time managing their accounts, and so can't be bothered with feeling. The world of emotion is not their department; it is a special article, which doesn't enter their desk register, nor their laws of bankruptcy."[43]

Zhukova's stories reflect her own disillusionment, and as a result her works have a more explicitly "feminist" tone. They call for other options for women besides marriage, and they depict women like herself who try to make their own way. These heroines are "ordinary" women, if also deeply feeling ones, who for one reason or another lack a husband to protect and support them. The heroine of "Self-sacrifice," for example, having given up her lover for the sake of her benefactress, ends her days in poverty, teaching in a provincial girl's school and supporting her aged mother. "The sense of my independence strengthens and comforts me in moments of sadness," she tells the narrator.[44] In "My Friends from Kursk," Zhukova mounts a virtual polemic on behalf of the unmarried woman and against the society that judges and ostracizes her. "As if an old maid has to be some sort of superfluous link in creation. Doesn't a woman have other duties, other goals in life than to bend herself to the fate of some man who saw fit to elevate her to the dignified status of his wife, to live for his happiness and then to pass away, leaving behind her several new beings?" Women should enjoy the same rights as men, Zhukova argues, and because men are never told that they have been born solely to reproduce themselves, why should women be? She assures her readers that this is not because women aspire to the public prerogatives of males – far from it. Rather, women must be granted the same "moral rights" as men, by which Zhukova presumably means that women should be valued, even if they do not marry. "So there won't be any misunderstandings, I declare that we have no pretensions to epaulettes, to judges seats no . . . nor even to author's spectacles: just allow us to have other goals than marriage and its consequences; allow us to believe that a plant that bears no fruit is not useless."

With the possible exception of her independent schoolteacher, however, the alternatives Zhukova suggests for the single woman are modest indeed: catering to the whims of parents, devoting herself to siblings, nephews, nieces, and the children of others, boiling soup for the poor, planting flowers. Her spinster anticipates no worldly success, aspires to no career. But then again, given the regimentation of public life and its domination by men, how could she? As Zhukova herself observes, "a female writer, a female petitioner, a female clerk, even in her own business, will hardly be forgiven by society."[45]

The stories of Zhukova and Gan invite comparison with those of their contemporary, George Sand, who influenced them both and addressed many of the same themes: the moral superiority of the genuinely loving woman; the unfairness of the social conventions that forbid her to act on her feelings; the injustice of men's domination over her. Nevertheless, Sand and the Russians also differ in significant ways. In Sand's work, eroticism, whether expressed within marriage or outside it, is inseparable from love. Sand's heroines fight to preserve their emotional integrity, and many manage to triumph over their circumstances in order to live according to their principles. By contrast, although the heroines of Zhukova and Gan do love passionately, their passion is seemingly devoid of eroticism; it is a passion of the soul that ennobles because of the women's readiness to sacrifice themselves for it, and it leads almost inevitably to suffering. Circumstances crush the Russian heroines, and in the rare instances when they triumph, they achieve moral victories, not personal happiness.[46]

In that sense, Gan and Zhukova were far less rebellious than Sand and far more in tune with their time and place. They accepted without question the idea of separate spheres for men and women and willingly relinquished any claim to male prerogatives in the public domain. Both firmly believed that a woman's highest calling was love and that marriage was the preferable place, if not the only place, to exercise it. Religiosity such as Labzina's rarely survived extensive reading of Western secular writings, but these women found romantic love a viable emotional substitute, and they gave it comparable moral value. (Elena, Gan's oldest daughter, seems to have taken the reverse route, becoming Elena Blavatskaia, one of Europe's more celebrated mystics.) So long as romantic ideals prompted women to work harder at being self-sacrificing wives and mothers, they threatened neither family nor social stability.

Yet an element of rebelliousness remained, and it became evident when women made use of this elevated domestic sphere to require more from their relationships with men. According to both Zhukova and Gan, a satisfactory relationship would require greater respect, more tenderness, and more sensitivity from men. Both writers agreed, however, that under existing circumstances, men were unlikely to provide this. The women thus offered a fundamental criticism of the way that men were socialized, as some of their more astute readers recognized. The critic Belinskii, for one, observed that Gan's most crucial perception was that "women know how to love, and men do not," and he acknowledged that she was right.[47]

The women's critique was also radical in its way, because by asserting women's rights as individuals to self-realization and self-expression on however modest a scale, they implicitly rejected women's customary subordination to the larger interests of family and state. To attain the sort of personal happiness both women wanted would have necessitated more than a change in the relations between the sexes. It would have required society to value people according to merit rather than social position. It would also have meant changing the way that noblemen were raised and educated and abolishing the customary and legal basis for their domination over others. To accomplish this, all social relations would have had to be transformed – from the hierarchical and authoritarian patterns characteristic of a state-dominated, traditional society to the more egalitarian relations of a bourgeois society in which an individual's accomplishments would determine his status and self-realization would become an accepted cultural value. Russia was still a long way from this stage of development. Serfdom retarded it; so did the estate system and the pervasive influence of the state.

To be sure, men of the intelligentsia had begun to challenge official standards of public and personal life, but such men remained few in number, and in the realm of personal life their attempts to be less domineering and to use their relationships with women as a source of gratification were proving only partially successful, at best. The majority of noblemen did not even try. Prepared in state institutions to command and obey, and dependent on service for their livelihood, they could scarcely afford to question their role. Even when such men aspired to personal happiness, they rarely attained it, as Richard Wortman made clear in his study of the legal profession. Bred to view morality as selflessness, men had difficulty embracing an ideal of personal happiness. Then, too, a servitor's fundamental loyalty was to the state, and when the demands of public life and private life came into conflict, the public inevitably triumphed. The requirements of service could squelch even the most ardent romantic.[48]

When women who had learned to expect emotional gratification failed to gain it in marriage, they were tempted to look for it elsewhere. This may be why George Sand's novels gained such popularity among Russian readers during Nicholas's reign, for they suggested ways that women might obtain satisfaction without having to change the social order. Although Sand's mystical socialism appealed to some men of the intelligentsia, it was the women of the 1830s and 1840s who found her a defender and a guide. In Sand's works, love is elevated, whether expressed in a socially sanctified union or elsewhere, so that if marriage has failed to satisfy, or if the love between husband and wife has grown cold, then for a woman to accept the love she is offered elsewhere becomes not only legitimate but indeed her highest obligation. As a result, women who were restless and dissatisfied with their domestic routine could find in Sand's works a rationalization for indulgence of their sexuality. Praskovia Tatlina, whose two daughters came under Sand's influence, found her books distasteful precisely because, in Tatlina's opinion, they awakened the impulse to "sensual love."[49] Other observers commented critically on the *Zhorzhzandovshchina* (George-Sandism), the phenomenon of noblewomen using the pretext of "elevated love" in order to deceive their husbands.[50]

No one took a poll to see whether upper-class women really became more adulterous during this period or whether people simply grew more upset about adultery. But given the superficial education of most noblewomen and the fragile restraints on self-indulgence, it would not be surprising if some women did seize the opportunity to enjoy male prerogatives. As Maria Tsebrikova, a feminist who wrote during the second half of the century, observed, "all the scandals of our daily life, all of women's licentiousness, created by women's ignorance and men's depravity, were ascribed to George Sand, as if George Sand, by elevating the ideal of love so high, was responsible for all the misunderstood women who emerged at the time, women who read her works for the love scenes."[51]

We know very little about the outcomes of such liaisons. Still, it is probably safe to assume that although they may have provided sensual pleasure, it is most improbable that they led to lasting happiness. Adultery is no more likely than marriage to change male behavior. An ardent suitor's vows of constancy and devotion often are forgotten after love is consummated, whether that love be marital or adulterous. The woman who sought a sustained, intense emotional experience was not likely to find it in adultery.

The tragic experience of Natalie Herzen, our third woman of the intelligentsia, provides an excellent case in point. Her story has been told several times, but it merits retelling because she took Sand's precepts so seriously and because her experience so richly illustrates the dilemma of women who found love the only route to self-realization.[52]

Natalie Herzen was born in 1817, the illegitimate child of the wealthy Aleksandr Iakovlev, who indulged the privileges of serf ownership to establish for himself a harem of women entirely subject to his whims. He sired many children with them, and almost all these children were sent to remote villages to live as serfs after his death in 1824. Her looks and her demeanor saved the seven-year-old Natalie from a similar fate. She was shy, with a delicate complexion and dark blue eyes. She caught the attention of a companion to her aunt, the Princess Maria Khovanskaia, and the companion selected her and another child from the group of illegitimate children and brought them to her mistress for inspection. The childless princess acted on a whim and decided to raise Natalie in her household.

Whatever maternal feelings the attractive child had stirred soon faded. The princess was no longer young and had no patience with children; so Natalie, already separated from her mother, was left with no one to nurture her. Instead, she was raised by tutors and ordered about by the companion. Later, she kept a diary in which she painted her unhappy childhood in the dreariest of colors:

My childhood was the gloomiest and bitterest imaginable. How often did I shed tears that were seen by none! How often, not yet understanding what prayer meant, did I get up in the night secretly (not daring even to pray except at the appointed time) and ask God to send someone to love and fondle me! I had no toy or plaything to divert or console me; for if they gave me anything it was with words of reproach and with the inevitable comment: "it is more than you deserve." Every trifle they gave me was bathed in my tears.[53]

Religion provided consolation by furnishing a world of escape, another and brighter "home," and it gave the fantasies of her childhood and youth a mystical and somewhat morbid tone. Her cousin, Tatiana Passek, relieved her isolation to some extent, bringing Natalie books and teaching her to read, but it was another cousin, Aleksandr Herzen, five years older than Natalie and also illegitimate, to whom the child really attached herself, first as a sister and subsequently as a lover and wife.

Aleksandr was a university student when they first got to know each other, and it is unlikely that he took this intensely religious, shy, self-absorbed child too seriously. His attitude changed in 1834, however, when he was faced with exile, bereft of his usual self-confidence and high spirits. Then, his seventeen-year-old cousin offered Herzen "a few words of sympathy" and brought him "to life again."[54] They began a correspondence that heightened in intensity as his exile progressed, culminating two years later in a mutual declaration of love in this world and the next. The correspondence, which runs to hundreds of pages, plainly reveals Natalie's exaltation, her eagerness to cover even the most earthly of passions with a cloak of divinity, and the resulting deification of the object of her affections, her beloved Aleksandr. She wrote, in one rather typical letter, "I felt like your sister, and thanked God for it. . . . But God wanted to show me another heaven, wanted to show that my soul could withstand still greater happiness, that there is no limit to the bliss of those who love Him, that love is higher than friendship. Oh Aleksandr – you know that paradise of souls, you've heard its song, you yourself have sung it, while its light illumines my soul for the first time – I revere, I pray, I love." His portrait became a sort of icon, and she knelt before it.[55]

Aleksandr, made of sterner, more earthly, more ironical stuff than his lonely and religious cousin, struggled briefly against such disembodied passion before he succumbed to it. Ambitious, by inclination both sociable and socially concerned, he had desires that family life alone could not satisfy – desires he found unthinkable in his future bride. As he wrote her in 1836, "your life has found its goal, its limits. . . . Your separate existence from me will disappear in my embraces; all needs, all thoughts, will drown in my love. . . . But my life is still not complete. Beyond private life I have an obligation to a diverse activity for the benefit of mankind, and feeling alone would be too little for me."[56] Nevertheless, his loneliness and his feeling of moral inferiority to his saintly Natalie led Aleksandr to submit to Natalie's vision.

Natalie was not only religious; she was also demanding in her own gentle and unobtrusive fashion. She wanted from Aleksandr the love she had never enjoyed as a child, and she wanted that love to belong exclusively to her. Never did she articulate this desire directly, of course, but she managed nevertheless to get what she wanted. Shortly before their marriage, Aleksandr wrote her: "My literary mission is nonsense . . . you are my mission. . . . I am writing to everyone: Friends, I do not wish to deceive you, I am not yours, I do not need you . . . my life is to live for Natalie, her life is life enough for us two."[57]

Both sets of relatives opposed the marriage, and the Princess Khovanskaia continued to press unwanted suitors on Natalie. So with the help of his friends and an accommodating priest (as first cousins, Aleksandr and Natalie were forbidden to marry), the two eloped on May 10, 1838, then settled in Vladimir, where Herzen completed his final year of exile. During this time Natalie had her husband all to herself, and it was probably the happiest year of her life.[58] The transition from heavenly love to earthly love apparently proceeded smoothly, as Natalie bore a son, Aleksandr, on June 13, 1839. She had read books on childcare before the birth, and afterward she became a devoted mother, laughing at her husband's clumsy efforts to tend the child and so establishing that as her own exclusive domain. She threw herself wholeheartedly into caring for "big and little Sasha," as she put it. The world of the family was more than enough for her.[59]

It was not, however, enough for her husband. When they returned to Moscow after a year, Aleksandr resumed his former interests: his friends, his writing, visits to the theatre, evenings out. Natalie preferred to stay at home. "I haven't been anywhere and don't want to be," she wrote, "but Aleksandr insists on taking me to the theatre." Aleksandr, for his part, felt guilty: "I've seen a lot here, and I've been doing many things, while poor Natasha has so devoted herself to Sasha that she does absolutely nothing else."[60] Their different personalities – his, outgoing, self-assured, ambitious; hers, shy, insecure, and intense – and their differing needs began to pull them in different directions. The gap between them grew greater when their next three children died shortly after birth. Both parents were grief-stricken, but Aleksandr could forget his sorrow in other interests, whereas Natalie was left alone with her grief, her feelings of inadequacy, her physical exhaustion, and an almost insatiable need for reassurance that Aleksandr was increasingly less inclined to provide. She resented the concerns that removed him from the family and from her. "I never see Aleksandr," she complained.[61] She resented the friends who appeared to threaten her monopoly of his affections. Her demands became burdensome to him, and he sought consolation elsewhere, first in the arms of a serving-maid (1842) and later in other liaisons, although none a real threat to the marriage. His first betrayal created a crisis not easily resolved, especially given Natalie's propensity toward feelings of abandonment, as well as her quite justifiable fear that they were growing apart.

In short, within a relatively brief period of time, the exalted "uniqueness" of their first love had degenerated into a not atypical relationship. Natalie, absorbed in domestic cares, felt neglected; she felt as if something had been lost. Aleksandr, wanting a wife to care for him and to raise his children, and devoted in his fashion, was absorbed in matters that took him far from his wife and was unwilling to resume the exclusive intensity of that first year. His personality proved the stronger of the two, and for a while Natalie appeared to accept his conception of their relationship. In 1846 she wrote to him: "Yes, Aleksandr, romanticism has left us, and we are no longer children but grown up people: we see more clearly and more deeply, feel more clearly. It is not the exalted enthusiasm of old, youth intoxicated with life and worshipping its idols – all that is far away, behind."[62] Not only had she abandoned her exalted love for him; in the face of his skepticism she had relinquished her religious faith as well.

However, neither "realism in love," in Martin Malia's phrase, nor skepticism suited Natalie's personality and needs. She continued to live through her feelings, and although she was unaware of it herself, she awaited only an excuse to express her passion. George Sand provided that justification, offering still another cult of love, if a more corporeal one than her first. In a letter of November 13, 1846, Natalie wrote of Sand: "Oh great Sand! Penetrating human nature so deeply, leading the living soul through degradation and debauchery so boldly, and bringing it unharmed through that all-consuming flame."[63]

In 1847 the Herzens left Russia for the West, and by March they had arrived in Paris. Aleksandr immediately made contact with the Russian émigré colony and resumed his old habits. The Herzens had left Russia just in time to observe at first hand the revolutionary wave that swept Europe in 1848. Herzen was elated when the workers rose in Paris; he was deeply disillusioned when the bourgeoisie defeated them the following June. Presumably, Natalie attempted to share both his enthusiasm and his disappointment, but it was difficult for her to stay interested in public events. "All Republics, revolutions and everything of that sort seem to me in the final analysis to be like knitting stockings, and they make the same impression on me," she wrote in December 1848.[64]

Natalie's restlessness could not be assuaged by defeated or even victorious revolutions. She sought emotional release, not political change. But where was she to find it? A devoted mother, she could not help but know that caring for children was as burdensome as it was gratifying. As she wrote that same December, "all morning, from the moment I open my eyes, I care for Sasha and Natasha [their second child to survive] and all day this is my responsibility. I cannot concentrate for a moment and I've grown so absentminded that sometimes it becomes painful." Or, writing of her children: "They have such different interests that it's terribly hard for me to satisfy them both at the same time, and even with all my desire to do so, and all my love and firmness, I do not always succeed, which exhausts me terribly." Her husband's friends, frequent visitors to their house, were more of a drain than a pleasure: "The evening passes, the children are put to bed, now perhaps I will rest. . . no, good people have come and it's even worse because they are good people. I could have been alone and now I'm not and I am insensitive to their presence, as if there were smoke before my eyes, and I have difficulty breathing. . . the following day it's the same, the next the same, again."[65]

A friend of her own, however, was an entirely different matter. In the spring of 1848, Natalie developed an intense, indeed a passionate, friendship with eighteen-year-old Natalie Tuchkova, the daughter of a landowner from Penza, who was then visiting Paris. During the seven months that this relationship endured, Natalie sent ardent letters proclaiming her devotion almost daily. Natalie Tuchkova she nicknamed Consuelo, after one of George Sand's characters. One such letter reads: "Consuelo di mi alma, dear child, my beloved, my Natalie. I say it from the depths of my soul, with all my strength, all my fullness, all my passion. Yes, I love you terribly! Your letters illuminate my love for you. It makes me happy, and it would make me happy even if you did not love me too." And another: "I have a picture that reminds me of you and sometimes I look at it for a long time. I love you, am in love with you. Whether or not I'll always feel that way, or it will pass, I do not know – but why should it? Now I love you, now I want you and that's that."[66]

She did not, as things transpired, continue to feel that way. Within the year her feelings for Natalie Tuchkova had ebbed, to be replaced by a no less passionate, but far less ethereal, relationship with Georg Herwegh, a German poet, a romantic, sentimental, and rather weak individual, and the closest European friend of the Herzen family. In the winter of 1848–9 the friendship à trois among Aleksandr, Natalie, and Georg, in the spirit of George Sand, ripened into a passionate affair between Natalie and Georg, with Herzen playing the unenviable role of deceived husband. Natalie threw herself into the relationship with all her pent-up passion and need. Georg was her lover, her child, her darling, the only man to whom she had ever truly given herself: "I have never given myself to anyone *as I have to you*, I was virgin before I knew you, I still am when you are away."[67] The affair was certainly no base adultery, but nevertheless it was to be kept from Aleksandr until the "appropriate time" came to reveal it. Surely, as a follower of Sand himself, he would understand.

When Aleksandr accidentally discovered the relationship, however, he proved far from understanding. Profoundly wounded in his self-esteem, and even perhaps in his feelings, he behaved remarkably like those bourgeois husbands they all despised, husbands who regarded their wives as property. Aleksandr managed to accomplish this without violating his own principles by insisting that Natalie had never actually loved Herwegh and that she had been, in effect, his innocent victim (which was manifestly untrue). Aleksandr's accusations led to a vicious epistolary duel between the two men, a battle they conducted over Natalie's ever more prostrate body. The husband effectively won this battle for Natalie. She agreed to renounce Herwegh, but only after he revealed himself as a thoroughgoing cad, clearly her husband's moral inferior, and most unworthy of her affection.

The experience left Natalie utterly crushed. To add to her grief, she had lost a son, a deaf-mute, when a boat on which he was traveling sank off the coast of France. So many losses in such a short span of time, compounded by two more pregnancies, doomed her attempt to return to her former existence. The victim of her own frustrated impulses, of the romanticism that encouraged them, and of the society that failed to provide an outlet, Natalie Herzen quietly passed away on May 2, 1852, after giving birth to a child who died shortly after.

By and large, these first female rebels were an unhappy lot. Relegated by their society to family life, and encouraged by romanticism to attend to their feelings, they found themselves at odds with their milieu, and often with their men. If they sometimes exaggerated their feelings and demanded too much of their loved ones, we should not judge them too harshly. They were, after all, passionate women whose talents and energies could find no acceptable outlet aside from personal relationships. They dealt with their situation the only way they could: by trying to elevate their relationships in order to gain greater latitude for themselves. But an attempt to find in emotional life the satisfaction of every need is bound to fail, especially in a society like the Russian, where Western ideas about domesticity had not taken root, and where men and women were defined so differently, with the one sex being given so much power over the other. The dilemma of the *intelligentka* would remain insoluble until the barriers to women's activity outside the domestic sphere had been lifted and changes in public life had provided reason for women to revise their critique of the male world, as well as their critique of men.

REJECTING THE AUTHORITARIAN FAMILY

INTRODUCTION TO PART II

When Nicholas died on February 18, 1855, educated Russians breathed a sigh of relief. His policies had grown even more repressive toward the end of his life; the revolutions of 1848 had caused him to restrict travel abroad still further, to impose more severe censorship on publications, and to make even greater inroads on university autonomy. It seemed as if Nicholas was trying to avert revolution through a supreme effort of his autocratic will. That effort severely retarded Russia's economic development and lost Nicholas the support of many of his most talented subjects. The cost of Nicholas's policies became evident in the Crimean War. Economic backwardness led to poor communications and difficulties in transporting troops and supplies. The army, Nicholas's pride and joy, proved unable to defeat Britain and France. The old regime, put to the test, had failed. Even the new tsar, Alexander II (1818–81), no reformer by inclination, perceived the need for change. If domestic order was to be maintained, serfdom clearly would have to go. On March 30, 1856, less than two weeks after the Crimean War had ended, Alexander II declared to an assembly of nobles: "It is better to abolish serfdom from above than to await the day when it will begin to abolish itself from below." The following year censorship was eased, and the press at last became free to discuss serfdom and the forthcoming emancipation.

As controls were lifted, social forces so long held in check burst forth in luxuriant profusion. Public opinion of a recognizable sort began to emerge, nourished by the proliferation of journals; at informal gatherings in private homes heated discussions of contemporary issues could last far into the night. People of diverse views and backgrounds debated, and some eventually joined forces to work for the betterment of society during those early, optimistic years. Convinced of the need for thoroughgoing change, socially conscious Russians subjected every traditional institution, including the patriarchal family, to reevaluation. They recognized that the family hierarchy reproduced and reinforced the social hierarchy and that the authoritarian relations between parents and children and husbands and wives perpetuated the despotism of the old order; so they advocated the transformation of family life as well as

45

political life. To produce the autonomous and independent-minded individuals that a more democratic society would require, family relations would have to be democratized, too.

Critics of the old society hoped that women would play a vital role in building a new one. In their view, women possessed qualities that made their participation essential. Preserved from the worst excesses of Nicholas's reign by their exclusion from public life, women retained a capacity for moral action that seemed so lacking in public life and so crucial to social regeneration. This led social critics to expect many things of women. Women should contribute their energies to movements for social reform, and at the same time take their domestic responsibilities more seriously in order to improve family life. A substantial minority of educated women proved responsive to these appeals. During the course of Nicholas's reign, their numbers had increased steadily, while their situation had remained fundamentally unchanged. The ferment that followed Nicholas's death not only opened the gates of public life to women but also made participation in public life seem worthwhile. Critiques of the authoritarian family helped to legitimize women's dissatisfaction with their family-centered role, and assumptions about the need for their special moral qualities suggested new avenues of activity for older women and encouraged younger ones, who had not yet settled into marriage and motherhood, to consider other options.

The discussions about family life and the role of women came under the heading of the "woman question." Women's responses contributed to making it one of the burning issues of the day. There emerged three approaches to the woman question. One sought to liberalize the family and the relations between the sexes and to expand women's prerogatives in the public sphere within politically acceptable limits. Another, which contemporaries called "nihilism," advocated more radical measures, contending that women should liberate themselves from "family despotism" and that the patriarchal family should be radically altered, even, in the opinion of some, abolished altogether. The third also involved a radical stance, but concentrated on social and political change rather than personal change, wishing to postpone until the socialist future the resolution of many issues, the woman question included.

In the early years of Alexander II's reign, these three approaches overlapped considerably, reinforcing one another and ensuring the acceptance of the woman question as a vital social issue. But as time went on, political reaction narrowed the range of permissible activity and fragmented support for women by dividing progressive society. Reaction started in the late 1850s with the reimposition of censorship on certain subjects and new limitations on discussions of emancipation. This was relatively mild, however, compared with what followed in February 1861 with the publication of the long-awaited emancipation edict. As the peasants saw it, the edict provided them with insufficient land and no real liberty. The land that it did grant them often was of inferior quality, and the peasants had to redeem it at a price exceeding its real market value, thus paying not only for the land they had tilled for centuries but also, indirectly, for themselves. Freed from the landlord's power, they were subject instead to their own peasant communes and were hedged with various restrictions that kept them legally separate from other citizens of Russia.

The peasants felt cheated. Some greeted the emancipation edict with uprisings, which the government brutally suppressed. Others, scorning this "false edict" that the nobility had clearly concocted, sat back and waited for the tsar's "golden edict" to declare "true" emancipation. The remainder, probably the majority, passively reconciled themselves to their fate.

Everyone on the left of the progressive spectrum found the edict disappointing, too, and subsequent stages of the "reform" era did little to restore their confidence in the government. To be sure, the tsar continued to enact legislation with a regularity that reassured those who preferred their reforms from above. In 1864 the government instituted trial by jury. Later that year it established the *zemstvo*, a form of local self-government that was popularly elected (although election procedures were carefully weighted in favor of the nobility). The *zemstvo* assumed responsibility for services such as maintenance of roads, health care, and elementary education in rural areas, and so was useful to the peasantry. But neither the *zemstvo* nor the other reforms really came to grips with Russia's greatest social problem: an impoverished, ignorant, and increasingly land-hungry peasantry. Nor did they redistribute power in any meaningful way. The *zemstvo* had little real authority, but much responsibility. The autocracy remained an autocracy, despite the desire of some liberal nobles to place constitutional restrictions on it.

The emancipation edict, inadequate though it was, appears to have exhausted the tsar's good will. His impatience with his restless people and his growing receptiveness to conservative opinion became evident almost immediately thereafter in the bloody suppression of the Bezdna peasant uprising and in the beating, arrest, and exile of peacefully demonstrating students in the fall of 1861. In 1862, a series of fires of unexplained origin swept St. Petersburg. Blaming them on leftist incendiaries, the authorities arrested several prominent radicals. In 1863, a nationalist uprising in Poland served to polarize opinion further. When the government moved to suppress the revolt, educated society rallied to the throne in a flurry of chauvinism, while a minority of radicals persisted in supporting the insurgents.

Reaction also undermined support for women attempting to change their lives. Many liberals became more cautious, and nihilism faded, while the left grew more militant and increasingly prepared to set aside the woman question to pursue the revolution, even as they intensified their efforts to recruit women to their cause. As a result, the options for rebellious women became polarized, too.

The social and political developments of the 1860s would affect not only the evolution of the woman question in Russia but also the consciousness of women in rebellion.

CHAPTER 3

SEARCHING FOR A POLITICS OF PERSONAL LIFE

In 1856, Russia entered a new era. Alexander II announced his intention to free the serfs and then encouraged his subjects to discuss the matter. A wave of jubilation swept over progressive society. After thirty years of perceived stagnation, events seemed to be moving with astonishing speed. This was springtime at last, after the long winter of Nicholas's reign, and society would surely be regenerated. The abolition of serfdom, the very basis of society, would necessitate changes on many other levels. The more optimistic anticipated not only emancipation of the serfs but also some limitations on autocracy, removal of juridical distinctions between classes, equality before the law – in short, liberalization according to the pattern provided by Western Europe.[1] Alexander himself appeared to share the perceptions, if not the enthusiasms, of the liberals. Had he not, after all, removed university quotas for commoners shortly after his accession? Had not censorship been eased, and the nobility invited to express its opinions concerning the forthcoming emancipation?

Not everyone approved, of course. The majority of landowners, for instance, having come to terms with the emancipation, fought hard to make it as favorable to themselves as possible. They, and other groups who felt that autocracy protected their interests, would resist any diffusion of political power, as well as any change in their customary mode of life. A few radicals, on the other hand, questioned whether any thoroughgoing change could be expected from above, although most of these seemed prepared to wait to see what Alexander would do.

But neither opponents on the right nor critics on the left proved capable of dampening the enthusiasm of "progressive" society. Progressive is the appropriate word here, and not only because these people tended to think of themselves that way. With no clearly elaborated political views (Indeed, where would they have acquired them?), and differing with one another sometimes sharply over the progress they wished to see, progressives nevertheless agreed that the way of life associated with serfdom must end. They wanted to see their society liberalized, and they wanted the opportunity to contribute to that liberalization however they could.

One of the ways they could do this was to live according to their principles. In the second half of the 1850s, enlightened members of the upper classes attempted to adopt more "democratic" ways: They dressed more simply, tried to rely less on servants, and tried to dispense with the formalities that governed polite society. When they attended the frequent "evenings" and "at homes," nobles who had once socialized only with people of comparable status found themselves sipping tea and eating sausage with the offspring of petty bureaucrats, the sons of merchants and of priests. In these informal settings, discussions would grow heated, as if every question had to be resolved at once and correctly, as if those who gathered there actually could determine the fate of their society. The fact that the educated still represented less than 1 percent of the population helps to explain this sense of responsibility and self-importance. So does the feeling the progressives had that they could actually do something, after all the long years of watchful waiting. It seemed up to them to live and work correctly, so as to show the way to a better future.[2]

In order to do this, they not only had to reevaluate, and sometimes discard traditions associated with serfdom; they also had to build anew. Knowledge, especially scientific knowledge, seemed to offer a firm foundation. Untainted by custom, superstition, or any traces of the discredited past, scientific method would provide a rational foundation on which to build. In the cities, progressive men and women began to attend newly opened public lectures on chemistry, botany, and biology and to invite students to give them private lessons. They bent over microscopes and took to cutting up frogs and other small creatures. Eager to learn as much as they could, they were almost as enthusiastic about teaching others. In the short-lived but popular Sunday School movement that gained official approval in 1859, educated people, some of them well-to-do women, took part in the effort to spread enlightenment among working people in the cities and their own peasants in rural areas.[3]

In some respects, the new tsar seemed to share this faith in the benefits of knowledge. In 1858, in one of his first reforms, Alexander II approved a plan for secondary schools for girls. The purpose: to improve the quality of public life by providing that "religious, moral and mental education which is required of every woman, and especially of future mothers." The new schools were to be day schools, open to girls of all estates, modeled on secondary schools for boys. The curriculum included arithmetic, geometry, physics, geography, and natural history, as well as religion, drawing, and sewing. The approach appealed to the public. The government provided the schools with only a small subsidy; for the rest, they remained dependent on contributions. The first *gimnaziia* (as the schools were called) opened in April 1858. By 1866 there were 38 of them; by 1881 there were 336, with an enrollment of 69,700.[4] A sector of the public not only had accepted the notion of girls' education but also were prepared to pay for it. And in St. Petersburg, at least, public support came from almost every social class. In 1878, well over half of the 3,675 girls attending the *gimnazii* in St. Petersburg were of noble origin, but 19 percent came from merchant families, 14.1 percent from the petty bourgeoisie, and 5 percent from the clergy.[5]

It is significant that one of the first of Alexander II's reforms affected women. Among the many issues of the day, questions concerning women and family life occupied a prominent position, reflecting changes already occurring in the lives of the propertied classes – changes that the forthcoming emancipation would serve to intensify. More and more noble families were becoming impoverished, making it harder for them to maintain unmarried daughters and other nonproductive members. The need to look for work, if only as a governess, made a girl less subject to the power of her parents and altered her relations with her family. At the same time, once the power of master over serf had been called into question, it was almost inevitable that progressive thinkers would be moved to examine other authority relations, including those between parents and children and men and women. Along with other traditional institutions, the patriarchal family came under critical scrutiny.

In 1856, the literary critic Nikolai Dobroliubov initiated the attack in an influential essay, "Realm of Darkness," in a left-wing organ, the *Contemporary*. Basing his criticism on the plays of Nikolai Ostrovskii, Dobroliubov found in the Moscow merchant families Ostrovskii depicted a world of despotism in which the powerful tyrannized over the weak and helpless. Women were particularly defenseless. "The weight of despotism in this 'realm of darkness' comes down most heavily on women," Dobroliubov wrote.[6]

Dobroliubov focused his attack on the family because he perceived that family patterns condition political behavior. "Family relationships," he wrote, "influence public activity." Because people who are subject to tyranny at home learn to renounce "the rights of their own individuality," family despotism fosters servile behavior in public life. "People brought up under such a [despotic] system cannot develop a sense of moral duty or of the true principles of honesty and justice." Although the censorship made it impossible for him to say so outright, Dobroliubov clearly implied that people raised properly would manifest the individuality and independent thought he viewed as crucial for the democratization of Russian society and politics.[7]

Other writers shared Dobroliubov's views. In the second half of the 1850s, Russians published unprecedented numbers of articles, books, and journals suggesting ways the family might be reformed and the new generation might be turned into better human beings and more responsible citizens. Progressives agreed that this would necessitate greater attention to childcare, because childhood was the most crucial stage of a person's life. Mothers of previous generations had done their job badly, such writers asserted. They had tyrannized or neglected their children; they had failed to nurture them properly. To build a better future, the present generation of mothers must mend their ways. As one writer cautioned: "A mother who thinks she can go out and have a good time when her children are small will harm them greatly without realizing it." Only a mother possessed the requisite "instinct" and "natural sympathy" to develop her child's personality properly.[8]

The new concepts of childrearing influenced parents aspiring to be progressive, and advocates of women's rights embraced them too. One of the more outspoken of them wrote that although she hated the image of the German *Hausfrau*, forever cooking, serving, and cleaning, the Germans were nevertheless superior to Russian women, who regarded marriage as a way to free themselves from the need to work, and who neglected all of their domestic duties. "Children they regard either as rather unpleasant but almost unavoidable products of conjugal life, or, at best, as charming toys," she complained.[9] Taking up the ideas of Swiss and German pedagogical theorists, people who could afford them rushed to buy educational toys, children's books, and a variety of pedagogical aids. Whereas formerly the interests of the parents had taken precedence over the well-being of the child, now the reverse appeared to become the norm. As the radical journalist N. V. Shelgunov wrote, "Mothers who had previously loved their children seemed to have come to their senses and understood for the first time what it means to love them and how one should go about it. Children became the first members of the household; they began to get the best, brightest and most spacious rooms. No one had thought of physical developments before – now it became the main object of family concern."[10]

Concern to liberalize human relationships prompted writers to examine other aspects of women's traditional role. Women must learn to take all their family responsibilities more seriously and to make themselves useful, they concluded. The most influential was N. I. Pirogov, a surgeon and pedagogue. His essay, "Questions of Life," published in 1856, aroused a flurry of interest and is sometimes credited with initiating the woman question in Russia. "Questions of Life" made a case for the improvement of women's education, but not for the sake of women themselves. Because girls would become tomorrow's mothers, Pirogov pointed out, the nation's spiritual and material well-being depended on their proper training. Besides, educated women would make true companions for their husbands, able to share more fully in male concerns and struggles. "Let the thought of educating herself for this goal, to live for the inevitable struggle and sacrifice, permeate the moral fibre of women," he wrote. Pirogov, who had just returned from the Crimean War, where he had supervised a detachment of volunteer nurses, suggested that someday women might be called on to sacrifice themselves outside the family, too.[11] Pirogov was instrumental in making women's education one of the most widely discussed issues of his day. The official plan for girls' secondary schools, presented to the tsar in 1858 and quickly approved, was based on arguments much like those of Pirogov.

Other writers went somewhat further than Pirogov. Women must become individuals in their own right and contribute something to society as well as to the family, they contended. Between 1858 and 1860, Maria Vernadskaia, who co-edited, with her husband, the *Economic Index*, wrote a series of articles in which she argued both that parents must become more attentive to their children and that women must enter the paid labor force in order to gain independence. "Mesdames. Cease to be children. Try to stand on your own two feet!" Vernadskaia exhorted her readers. Putting mothers to work would not be harmful to children, in her opinion, because mothers who did not work only wasted their days gadding about. They might as well employ their time usefully.[12]

Mikhail Mikhailov (1829–65), the son of a government official and the grandson of a former serf who had worked his way up to the nobility, elaborated these themes somewhat more realistically. In 1860 he published a lengthy article in the *Contemporary* entitled "Women, Their Education and Significance in the Family and in Society" in which he set out to prove that all flaws in the female character were socially conditioned, not innate, and could be eradicated simply by granting women absolutely the same rights as men to education and work. He assumed that childrearing (Mikhailov made no attempt to deny that every "normal" woman would want children) would require only eight to ten years of a mother's life, two years per child for the four or five children he considered the average. The rest of a woman's life could be devoted to work. Therefore, he assured his readers, the emancipation of women need not destroy the family. If men gave up their power over women and treated them as equals, this would strengthen the family and make it more durable. Mikhailov (himself a participant in an amicable ménage à trois) also advocated the freedom to divorce, so that unions would remain based on love.[13]

The very diversity of these views encouraged experimentation. During "evenings" and "at homes," debates raged over the future of marriage and the family, as well as the social role of women. In the cities, especially, all roads seemed open; whatever course a woman chose, at least some of her acquaintances would approve it.[14]

There was, however, one exception. Progressives agreed that personal happiness and family happiness were not worthwhile goals in themselves. It is true that they believed that sympathy between spouses would lead to more rewarding marriages and that improved childrearing practices would promote more intimate bonds between parents and children. Nevertheless, progressives of the 1860s were far less concerned with the individual well-being of family members than they were with the ways in which improved family relationships would benefit public life. In contrast with the middle class in industrializing Europe and America, which had begun to idealize family life, most progressive Russians found such an ideal self-centered and hopelessly bourgeois.[15] Nadezhda Khvoshchinskaia, the novelist, spoke for them in a critical essay. Family happiness, she wrote, is the "vulgar happiness of locked up houses, tidy and orderly; they seem to smile a welcome at the outsider, but they give him nothing but that smug and stupid smile. These oases are simply individual egotism united into family egotism. They are orderly, temperate, and self-satisfied – and totally self-involved." Progressive women of that and subsequent generations agreed.[16] To direct their "special talents" toward husband and children was all well and good, but women could sense that more exciting and more important things were happening elsewhere and that devotion to family, even a more egalitarian family, was no substitute for participating in public life.

Encouraged by the temper of the times, even provincial women tried to overcome their isolation and reach out to each other. In the province of Vologda, in 1859, a group of educated women began to meet separately during gatherings of the local nobility. Their rules required that they all dress simply and that there be no discrimination on the basis of economic condition – a high-minded goal, if unattainable in such a setting. Men could attend their meetings only as guests. Women in Simbirsk formed a similar group.[17] In 1860, in the province of Perm, a young teacher, E. A. Slovtsova-Kamskaia, appeared at a public benefit for a Sunday School for women and criticized the social standing afforded women. The daughter of a local official, Kamskaia had been educated in a private boarding school and had performed brilliantly at the examination for teachers at the University of Kazan. She was deeply religious and also an intellectual. Completely absorbed in reading and thinking, Kamskaia gave no thought whatever to her appearance, and she showed up at the benefit carelessly dressed, and with her hair closely cropped. Kamskaia declared to her audience: "Women in Russia have virtually no social significance . . . People value them neither as wives nor as mothers, since until now men have had complete power over them. If a wife decides to change her position in the family . . . to insist on her rights as a wife, you can safely assume that nine out of ten people will condemn her." In Kamskaia's opinion the only solution was for women to join together for mutual support. "The morally developed woman of our time suffers for every injustice borne by another woman. Feelings of envy, ambition, coquetry, the slavish desire to please men at the expense of her sisters should be alien to her. She is profoundly aware that she is primarily a female human being. Each act of kindness she performs for her sisters, she performs for herself."[18]

Women who lived in the major cities found many more opportunities for activity and for contact with each other. In 1859 they began to audit university lectures, which had just been reopened to the public. The first to attend was Natalia Korsini, half Russian, half Italian, the daughter of an architect. Simply dressed, her hair cut short, Korsini was escorted by the rector of the university, who introduced her approvingly to the roomful of men. Other women followed her example, so that within a year or so their presence at university lectures had become almost commonplace. In Kiev, one professor came to expect a considerable portion of his classroom to be occupied by ladies with shorn hair and blue eyeglasses, the costume of the "new woman."[19]

These sanctuaries of knowledge inspired in women an almost reverential feeling. "With what trepidation I entered the University, as if everything in it, even the walls themselves, inspired a feeling of awe."[20] Most of the women sought only to supplement their superficial education, but a few studied systematically and tried to take examinations. Among these were Natalia Korsini and Nadezhda Suslova, the daughter of a serf, who was to become one of Russia's first women doctors. When in 1861 the Medical Council agreed to admit women to the St. Petersburg Medical Surgery Academy, Suslova enrolled. By 1864, over sixty women were studying there.[21] By and large, their fellow students welcomed the women and treated them respectfully, and most professors calmly accepted their presence. When the Ministry of Education, revising university statutes, asked the opinion of university councils in 1861, university authorities in St. Petersburg, Kharkov, Kazan, and Kiev endorsed women students, too. Moscow and Dorpat alone dissented.[22]

The Sunday School movement provided another outlet for women's energies. It represented a chance to work for others, and it gave some women their first taste of practical activity. As one put it, the Sunday School movement was "the very first outlet for our aspirations for work, for the public good, and for contacts with the people."[23] Approved by the government in 1859, Sunday School teaching attracted a broad spectrum of the educated public. Some participants were already subject to police surveillance. Others resembled the more conventional Maria Shpilovskaia, who supported herself and her mother by translating, but who also wanted to do something for others. She established a Sunday School that enrolled around thirty girls, six to fourteen years of age, from all social classes, and taught them reading, writing, sewing, and religion. To ensure that the girls returned home promptly, Shpilovskaia kept a notebook in which she recorded the time they left the school.[24]

The Russian women's movement emerged from this progressive milieu and proved to be one of its most successful offshoots. Initially a hybrid of philanthropy and the democratic strivings of the day, it developed into a movement that lasted for decades and that could claim some credit for almost every advance in higher education for women.

The tactical abilities of the leadership had much to do with its successes. Like progressive society in general during the early years of Alexander II's reign, the women's movement included people with widely divergent and occasionally irreconcilable views. As a result, the women who led it, Maria Trubnikova, Nadezhda Stasova, and Anna Filosofova, learned to steer a careful course. No longer young, comfortably off, conventional in dress and demeanor, the three were well suited to that task. Because they belonged fully neither to the aristocratic circles into which they had been born nor to the younger generation that already challenged traditional ways, they were able to draw on the resources of the one and meet the needs of the other.

Of these three leaders, Maria Trubnikova had the most unusual background and was the least conventional. Born on January 6, 1835, Maria was the daughter of an exiled Decembrist, Vasilii Ivashev, and a Frenchwoman, Camille Ledentu, who had followed him to Siberia and married him for love. Both parents lavished attention on their first surviving child and the three who followed, but they both died young. The mother's frail constitution could not withstand the Siberian climate and the strain of bearing four children, several of them prematurely, in the space of seven years. Camille Ivasheva died in 1839, and her husband outlived her by only a year. At six, Maria was the oldest of the three surviving orphans.

Princess Ekaterina Khovanskaia, their aristocratic aunt, generously took charge of the children, raising them no differently than her own. Maria, a talented and exceptionally curious child, was permitted to study with her foster brothers when the lessons of her governess ceased to interest her. But convention dictated that she be a lady, not an intellectual; so when she turned sixteen her formal education ended, and she was introduced to society. Thereafter, she studied alone, reading in her uncle's excellent library. ·

Maria had already become something of a liberal when she married Konstantin Trubnikov in 1854 at the age of nineteen. Trubnikov at that time served in the statistical division as a provincial chancellory. Purportedly, he won her hand by quoting to her from Aleksandr Herzen, whose journalistic work while in emigration had made him the foremost critic of Russian society. The couple soon moved to St. Petersburg, where Trubnikov began working for a joint-stock company.

A few months after they moved to St. Petersburg, Maria Trubnikova gave birth to their first child. During her marriage she was to bear six more, four of whom lived. She seems to have inherited her mother's constitution, and the difficult birth of her child, combined with family responsibilities, kept her home over the next several years. However, she continued to read: Plato, Michelet, Proudhon, Kant, Saint-Simon, Lassalle, Louis Blanc, Heinrich Heine, Aleksandr Herzen, and contemporary literature both domestic and foreign. And she continued to take music and drawing lessons. Her biographers did not tell us how she managed this feat, but presumably she enjoyed the assistance of many servants. She certainly had inherited more than enough money, and the Trubnikovs lived very well indeed, keeping their own horses and carriage.

This aristocratic life did not prevent Trubnikova from manifesting certain progressive tendencies. She went about the streets unaccompanied by her servants, rode about in a cab by herself, and dressed, despite her wealth, with great simplicity. In conformity with the ideas of the period, she also found time to teach her children.

Toward the end of the 1850s, Trubnikova's home became a meetingplace for democratically minded youth. A young radical, Aleksandr Serno-Solovevich, was a frequent visitor, and he would talk to her about the European workers' movement and the first Workingmen's International. Trubnikova's sister said that these conversations transformed Maria into an evolutionary socialist, but this is difficult to reconcile with the fact that Trubnikova worked with her husband on the *Stock Market News*, a daily he had founded. In matters of personal life, Maria Trubnikova was more of a nonconformist than a rebel, unwilling to challenge conventions even on relatively trivial issues. In the 1860s, she and her children often spent summers in the country, where the girls donned boys' clothing to help around the house and garden and to climb trees and wander in meadows and forests. But as soon as their father appeared, all of the females, their mother included, rushed to change into feminine attire. She could not defy Trubnikov, a perfect despot at home, who was unrelenting about such things. "It was impossible to change father's mind, and he demanded that his wishes be met," wrote their daughter, Olga. Trying to live with her husband amicably eventually drove Maria to a nervous breakdown; only after she recovered did the two separate.[25]

More conventional was her friend and co-worker, Nadezhda Stasova. She, too, was exceptionally well-educated for the times. She was born in 1822 to the family of a court architect, who spared no expense in educating her. Perhaps she would have married and immersed herself in family life had not her fiancé jilted her to marry someone else. She was so grief-stricken that she had a breakdown, regaining her mental equilibrium only after years of suffering. Then, renouncing personal happiness, she resolved to dedicate her life to others. As she put it, "my personal grief became my happiness. I grew accustomed to it, and first transferred all my love to my family, and then to society. So it transpired that everything is for the best. . . . The idea of my very own family ceased to tempt me. I began to love the universal family [*vsemirnoi sem'e*].[26] Stasova took advantage of the opportunities for philanthropic activity that opened up toward the end of the 1850s. She participated in the St. Petersburg Society for the Improvement of the Lodgings of the Laboring Population, in hospital work for the poor, and in establishing a Sunday School for illiterate working women. Her collaboration with Trubnikova followed naturally.

Anna Pavlovna Filosofova (1837–1912), the third member of this triumvirate, shared the background as well as the inclinations of her friends. Born Diagileva, Anna received a good, if conventional, education at home, where her mother raised her strictly and her eccentric father spoiled her. At sixteen, they declared her grown up, put her in a long dress, introduced her to society, and terminated her education.

In 1855 she met and married Vladimir Filosofov, a gentle, sensitive, rather romantic young man, who matured into a conscientious bureaucrat. Soon after Anna's wedding, her mother tried to warn her about the "emptiness" of social life. "Remember," she cautioned her daughter, "there is no destiny in the world more elevated than the family."[27] The lively Anna, who enjoyed entrée into the most exclusive social circles, refused to heed that advice. Besides, such socializing could help promote her husband's career. After she met and began to collaborate with Maria Trubnikova at the end of the 1850s, Filosofova used her contacts to help circumvent official opposition to their endeavors and to gain official support. Vladimir Filosofov did not approve of his wife's work on behalf of other women, but he did not try to stop her, and he remained a devoted husband. She wrote him loving letters during the 1860s, filled with domestic details and news of their nine children, but very rarely did she mention the work that had come to absorb most of her energy and interest.[28]

None of these three women was personally rebellious, and they all retained considerable traces of their aristocratic origins. They had the *savoir vivre* and social abilities of women of the world, and they knew how to use them. Neither Stasova nor Filosofova ever adopted the simple dress so characteristic of the period. Instead of severing their connections with aristocratic circles, these women used their connections to facilitate their work on behalf of other women. This enabled the movement to score significant victories, but it also lessened the movement's appeal to the rebellious young women it aspired to assist.

Their first undertaking, the Society for Inexpensive Lodgings, resembled traditional philanthropy, but it incorporated some new elements and demonstrated a special sensitivity to the situation of impoverished women. It originated in 1859 as an effort to provide decent housing and otherwise to assist needy women in St. Petersburg. All three women acknowledged the philanthropic nature of their endeavor. It was, in the words of Trubnikova's daughter, "the only kind of social activity possible at that time," especially if one wanted official approval.[29] Still, the three acted in a principled fashion, refusing to patronize the women they assisted or to interfere with their privacy. Their project attracted considerable support, and within a few months the society had over 200 members. But even this rather modest endeavor distressed allies to their right. Some of the more old-fashioned aristocratic women found the society's approach too radical; they would insist on the traditional right of the benefactress to monitor her beneficiaries. The triumvirate refused to back down, and the organization split in two.

Trubnikova, Stasova, and Filosofova obtained official approval for what remained of their organization on February 15, 1861. The Society for Inexpensive Lodgings proposed to help the poor to stand on their own feet, without offending their sense of dignity, by providing them with inexpensive housing and respectable work. There was a sewing workshop to provide jobs for the residents, who were mainly widows and abandoned wives of petty bureaucrats and artisans. To free the women from domestic chores, the society's lodgings provided day care for small children and a communal kitchen to prepare meals. The organization kept the three women very busy. They selected the women who would live in the housing, administered the residence, instructed the children, helped to find work for the women, and organized fund-raising events to support the whole enterprise.

By the time the society gained official approval, reaction had set in, ending the optimism and unity of the earlier period and making liberals such as Trubnikova, Stasova, and Filosofova more cautious, more dependent on the "establishment," and more likely to alienate allies to the left. The impossibility of forging a broadly progressive coalition became clear in 1865, with the attempt to establish the Society for Women's Labor. The original idea belonged to Petr Lavrov, later a major radical theoretician, and his friend, Anna Engelhardt. To combat women's economic dependence on men, the two aimed to create a multifaceted organization that would find work for women, train then, and assist them financially during difficult times.[30]

Lavrov and Engelhardt, already compromised in the eyes of the authorities because of their association with radicals, could not hope to gain approval for their society. They would need respectable people to request such approval, and so they turned to Anna Filosofova, Countess Rostovtseva, and two men who would not offend official sensibilities. They obtained approval from the government on February 22, 1865. About fifty members of the society then met for the first time at Filosofova's residence. The friends of Lavrov and Engelhardt tended to be nihilists – the men with long hair, the women in simple dresses, without hats, their hair cut short. Filosofova and Rostovtseva had invited elegantly dressed ladies and such pillars of the establishment as the vaguely liberal A. V. Nikitenko, who had served as censor under Nicholas I, and who suspected "redskinned liberals" (i.e., some leftist publicists who attended) of using the society as a front for their seditious plots.[31]

The first confrontation between the two groups concerned the question of governance. The list of officers for the society, which had been drawn up beforehand, included Grand Duchess Elena Pavlovna as president and the minister of the navy, Shestakov, as vice-president, with Countess Rostovtseva chairing the proceedings. The nihilist camp opposed all of these choices, as well as a plan to include in the executive committee six men who in the opinion of the nihilists had never shown sympathy with laboring women. Led by Ekaterina Tsenina, the nihilists demanded that at least half of the governing body consist of people who actually worked, whereas their opponents attempted to prove that women workers would be unable to defend their own interests and that "their employers, so to speak," would have to do it for them. Neither group would give in, and the meeting ended with the differences unreconciled. Then the triumvirate attempted to mediate, and a compromise was finally reached. Rostovtseva was elected to preside, and two of the women from the nihilist camp were incorporated into the executive committee. But the compromise proved short-lived. Her position gave Rostovtseva the right to veto candidates to the society, and alleging that subversives aimed to take it over, she used her power to reject all candidates who did not share her views. Differences reemerged more sharply than ever, and the society collapsed.[32]

Two years later, when the triumvirate attempted to mobilize women in a campaign for advanced education, they had to contend with the same divisions. In 1867, prompted by Evgenia Konradi, they led a petition campaign to gain permission for university-level courses for women. The petition was signed by close to 400 women "from all levels of society, from nihilists as well as aristocrats." Fear of alienating the authorities caused the leadership to offend its more radical allies. A delegation was to present their petition to the Ministry of Education. When the time came to choose representatives, the organizers decided to exclude Konradi, the initiator, because she was too "excitable and tactless." Ekaterina Solodovnikova, another elected delegate, was rejected because the police had searched her apartment, and people feared her presence would compromise the campaign.

In this instance, the effort to appease harmed rather than helped the movement. Angered by her exclusion, Solodovnikova decided to make a proposal of her own, less ambitious than the original and thus more acceptable to the government. Solodovnikova had spent time training village schoolteachers, and she knew something about the inadequacies of women's education. She therefore proposed a sort of supplementary program, rather like a university preparatory course. Taking advantage of these divisions in the women's movement, Dmitrii Tolstoi, minister of education, denied the petition for university-level courses and accepted Solodovnikova's more modest proposal. In 1869, the Alarchin courses opened in St. Petersburg and the Lublian courses in Moscow. They were evening lecture courses designed as university preparation, and they had no entry requirements. There were hard feelings all around. The moderates were understandably furious. "The nihilists spoil everything for us," they complained. The nihilists were equally angry. "We don't need philanthropists or benefactresses!" they responded.[33]

In subsequent campaigns, the leaders of the women's movement relied less on forging broad-based coalitions and more on the efforts of a
trusted few. This tactic proved more successful. Their connections enabled Filosofova, Stasova, and their allies to lobby the appropriate officials. Their proper dress and refined manners quieted the conservative
opposition, and their progressive views enabled them to argue with
conviction that backward Russia desperately needed trained personnel
regardless of sex. The government proved willing to compromise. Late
in 1869 it approved public lectures on serious academic subjects for
women, the Vladimir courses. After 1870, it encouraged courses for
teachers. In 1872 it approved Courses for Learned Obstetricians, which
became the Women's Medical Courses in 1876. Finally, in 1878, the
government approved a university for women, the Bestuzhev Courses.[34]

These very real gains came at a price. Even as it made possible substantial achievements in the area of education, the approach of the women's
movement narrowed the appeal of Russian feminism. As Evgenia Konradi,
one of their critics, observed, the leaders of the women's movement
"wear blinders, and see nothing else on either side."[35] People who sought
more fundamental change came to regard the women's movement as
moderate, prepared to compromise with the authorities, prepared to
accept partial solutions. This cost the movement the support of hundreds of the very women who benefited from its successes. While gratefully acknowledging the movement's contribution, they preferred to
channel their energies elsewhere.

Moreover, in order to work within the system, the leadership had to
narrow their formulation of women's issues and thus limit the scope of
Russian feminism. When people discussed the woman question in the
late 1850s and early 1860s, they usually had in mind not only the lack of
opportunities for women but also the authoritarian family and its relationship to the social and political order. Some men and women continued to raise these issues during the second half of the 1860s. In 1867,
Evgenia Konradi even made so bold as to suggest that some men might
be more at home in the nursery or the kitchen and that some women
might be better off in their jobs.[36] But Konradi stood to the left of the
women's movement, as did other women who alluded to such issues.
Fearing to alienate their support, the moderates avoided them.

During the 1860s, people did not lose interest in the radical implica-
tions of the woman question. But it was nihilists, not feminists, who
tried to find solutions.

CHAPTER 4

DAUGHTERS AGAINST PARENTS

Ask about whatever noble family you would at that time, you always heard one and the same thing – the parents had quarreled with the children.... An epidemic seemed to seize upon the children – especially the girls – an epidemic of fleeing from the parental roof.[1]

Whereas some women organized during the early years of Alexander II's reign to reform traditional institutions, others adopted a more radical and individualistic stance. Encouraged by challenges to traditional authority and the promise of greater opportunity in public life, young women, mainly of the upper class, attempted to liberate themselves from "family despotism" in order to establish autonomous new lives. These "new women" (as Chernyshevskii, the most popular writer of their generation, dubbed them) – *nigilistki* in their opponents' opinion – aspired to live as the equals of men both publicly and privately, and toward that end they willingly dispensed with the colorful dresses, enormous crinolines, and elaborate hairdos that were the traditional trappings of femininity. Austerely garbed, their hair cut short, their eyes hidden behind blue glasses, they defiantly flouted convention. Such rebelliousness required considerable courage and optimism, as well as a certain naiveté. Although family relationships often confined women, they also provided the sort of protection and support that women had great difficulty finding elsewhere. To flee the family was to risk economic need, sexual harassment, emotional isolation, and in some cases political persecution.

This made women's quest for autonomy difficult, and it became more difficult still after political reaction set in. As society's tolerance for unconventional behavior diminished, the scope for experimentation narrowed, and women's struggle for personal freedom was increasingly treated as an attack on the social and political order. In response, many women simply abandoned that struggle and retreated into conventional arrangements; however, a few moved from personal radicalism to political opposition. Whichever course a woman chose, she usually ceased her efforts to radically restructure her private life. When political reaction crushed the nihilist subculture, it also ended the only systematic attempt by the left during this period to support female autonomy and to transform personal relationships.

Women's rebellion provided an essential ingredient in the controversial blend that contemporaries called nihilism. Neither an organized effort nor a clearly identifiable phenomenon, nihilism is difficult to define, because the meaning of the word varied considerably according to who used it. In his controversial novel *Fathers and Children* (1862), Ivan Turgenev had affixed the term *nihilist*, meaning people who reject everything, to the youth of his time, and although many of them regarded the word as a vicious distortion of their ideals, it stuck.[2] Over the next several decades, government officials, polite society, and the foreign press applied it indiscriminately to anyone who defied the existing order.

Nihilists, or "new people," as many preferred to be called, had a rather different self-perception. They rejected the existing social and cultural order, to be sure, but not merely for the sake of negation. In order for them to restructure their lives according to new and more rational principles, everything associated with the discredited era of serfdom would have to go: all authoritarian relationships, all custom and tradition, even art, insofar as it failed to serve a practical purpose. Only science, free of all traces of the past, could provide an objective foundation on which to rebuild.

These beliefs made nihilists cultural revolutionaries rather than political or social revolutionaries. Nihilism was actually profoundly individualistic. In the words of Sergei Kravchinskii, a leading activist of the 1870s, "nihilism was negation in the name of individual liberty, negation of the obligations imposed upon the individual. Nihilism was a powerful and passionate reaction, not against the political despotism, but against the moral despotism that weighs upon the private and inner life of the individual."[3]

Their concern for individual liberty led nihilists to be especially critical of the relations between the sexes and within the family, which they regarded as a mainstay of the authoritarian order. According to nihilists, the family should no longer be permitted to subordinate people to its interests or to interfere with individual aspirations, especially the aspirations of women. Because authoritarian relationships were more likely to victimize women than men, nihilists devoted considerable attention to women's problems, and during the 1860s they tried to help women by encouraging them to become autonomous and by providing alternatives to the traditional family.

In this, as well as other respects, nihilists resembled the progressives described in the preceding chapter. Although nihilists went much further, they shared with progressives a revulsion against the old order and a faith in knowledge, scientific knowledge especially, as the most reliable insurance for human progress. But the two also differed in significant ways. One was age. Nihilists, unlike progressives, were almost always young. Often students enrolled in the medical faculties (like Turgenev's Bazarov), they had little stake in the old ways and felt less compromised by serfdom than their elders, who had tolerated its existence for much of their lives. This prompted the young people to go to self-righteous extremes. Untainted by the ownership of human beings, they felt that they had the right to destroy the old world, and the purity to build a new one.

The social origins of some of them intensified these feelings. It was once believed that *raznochintsy*, that is, people of common birth, made up the majority of nihilists, but historians have proved this false.[4] Nevertheless, there can be little doubt that *raznochintsy* set the tone. As a result of liberalized admission procedures, the numbers of students from clerical, merchant, petty bourgeois, even peasant families increased in institutions of higher education after 1855. These commoners had been more narrowly educated than upper-class students and lacked their polish and familiarity with the ways of polite society. Well-born young people shared the commoners' impatience with social conventions and so adopted many plebeian ways. One can hardly blame polite society for finding nihilists coarse and rude, careless in their dress and personal hygiene, uncompromising in their views, intolerant of others, and, perhaps most difficult to endure, contemptuous of everything the older generation had learned to value.

Polite society was even more appalled by the *nigilistka*. Her dress and her habit of going about the streets unescorted, smoking in public, and asserting her rights in a variety of ways made her at least as unconventional as the men and seemed a declaration of independence and a denial of her femininity. Most *nigilistki* derived from what the Russians somewhat misleadingly called the middle classes; they were daughters of middling and impoverished nobles and of petty civil servants. Their rebellion, like the men's, was directed at "the stagnant past and all tradition," but it also involved a personal dimension that contemporaries found particularly unsettling. In the name of her own independence, the *nigilistka* not only defied those conventions of dress and demeanor that society associated with femininity but, far worse, seemed to renounce family life, a woman's most sacred calling.

To be sure, some had little choice. It is difficult to imagine how an emancipation so disappointing to the peasants could also have hurt their former owners, but many landowners perceived it that way. Nobles lost roughly half of their land, as well as their rights to free labor and dues in kind. They did receive substantial redemption payments, but most landowners used them neither for investment nor for pleasure, but to pay off their heavy debts. They found it hard to adjust to the loss of their land, and harder still to get used to paying people they had once owned.[5] However rapidly their impoverishment proceeded (historians still argue about the pace), there can be little question that most landed nobles felt the need to cut back on expenses. Poorer nobles might encourage daughters to go to work; the more well-to-do nobles proved less willing to support dependent female relatives.

But even women who could have stayed at home sometimes chose to be independent. The emancipation of the serfs gave rise to new emphasis on the value of labor. In order to be self-respecting, a person must be economically self-sufficient. These ideas affected women as well as men, and as a result, some women simply preferred working for a living to dependence on someone else. And there were other women who wanted to study, to contribute in some way to the well-being of their society, or quite simply to live as they chose.

How many *nigilistki* there were we cannot be sure. The term itself is distressingly vague and is almost invariably intended to condemn the person it refers to. Yet it is difficult to avoid, because *nigilistka*, not new woman, was the expression contemporaries used. Our sense of them, like the word itself, is impressionistic. They were the handful of women who acquired police records on account of "suspicious behavior" or "nihilist tendencies."[6] They could be found among the sixty women who attended the Medical Surgery Academy in St. Petersburg before it closed and among the 396 women who signed the petition for women's higher education in 1867. They were undoubtedly a minority of the educated women, themselves a tiny minority in Russia. Still, they were numerous enough to arouse concern about the breakdown of order, family order in particular.

Nigilistki appeared everywhere: in urban areas, where one might expect them, but also in the remotest provinces. The "new ideas" were contagious, and books, journals, people, and even schools could propagate them. Elizaveta Bervi, who became the wife of the social critic Bervi-Flerovskii, remembered how even she "experienced the spring air, and burned with the desire to act upon every good impulse" at the conventional boarding school she attended in the early 1860s. One day the headmistress burst into her classroom to announce the formation of a Sunday School for factory workers. Bervi volunteered and succeeded in teaching a working woman to read. And Bervi knew two girls, ages sixteen and fourteen, from the steppes of the South, whose family held them almost literally under lock and key for fear of "liberal influences." Nevertheless, they learned of the opening of a secondary school for girls in St. Petersburg, and they resolved to enroll. The opposition of their family did not deter them. When their mother and aunt refused to help, the girls simply fled to St. Petersburg on their own.[7]

Propagators of the new ideas encouraged such unconventional behavior by maintaining that active participation by women in society's regeneration was more than their right – it was their obligation. Like men, women must master the principles of science, chart themselves a rational course, and overcome the obstacles that family and society placed in the way of their self-development. The idea that they were serving a larger purpose legitimized women's rebellion against home and family and their strivings to participate in the world of men.

How this appeal worked in practice, and why it provoked family discord, can be seen in the life of Anna Korvin-Krukovskaia, whose transformation from an indulged daughter to a *nigilistka* has been documented in considerable detail. Anna, born in 1843, was the oldest and most favored child of a rather well-to-do noble family. Her mother, the former Liza Shubert (see Chapter 2), having experienced bitter disappointment in her marriage, sought consolation in an active social life and rarely troubled to attend to her three children. The father, a major general in the artillery, had served in Moscow, Kaluga, and then Vitebsk. He "surrounded himself with an aura of inaccessibility as a matter of principle," and after his retirement in 1858 to their provincial estate, he tried to impose his authority on his family as he once had on his soldiers.[8]

Her parents raised Anna to expect a glittering social life, but fate "played a cruel joke."[9] The emancipation, by weakening the family's economic position, deprived her of the world for which she had been prepared and "incarcerated" her, as she put it, in the provinces with nothing to occupy her. Anna found her first outlet in religion. At sixteen, she became drawn to mysticism, and she tried to live like the monks in her books. Then the son of a village priest, on holiday from school, brought her issues of the *Contemporary* and other progressive publications. Their ideas suggested a more realistic course of action. Anna simplified her dress and hairdo, refused to attend parties, and developed a passion for reading. Providing a revealing glimpse into society's expectations of upper-class women, Anna's aunt criticized her unconventional niece in a letter to her own daughter: "Anna appears only at dinner," she wrote in 1862. "The rest of the time she spends in her room, studying. She never keeps anyone company, never does needlework, never takes walks." This behavior put Anna directly into conflict with her father, and when she begged him to allow her to go to St. Petersburg to study, he angrily refused: "If you don't understand that it is the duty of every decent girl to live with her parents until she is married, then I won't even try to argue with you, you stupid child!"[10]

Anna's mother proved more sympathetic, at least in private. The mother had already suffered her own disappointments, and still had, in her own words, "bitter thoughts," and to her diary she confided, "although I don't encourage her, I understand the dreams and aspirations of youth, for which I had to suffer so much."[11] But her mother's sympathy brought Anna no closer to her goal.

Anna Korvin-Krukovskaia obtained her freedom only at the end of the 1860s, after her younger sister Sofia married and went abroad, and Anna managed to convince her parents to allow her to join the couple. In the spring of 1869 she settled in Paris, found work as a typesetter, and began to move in socialist circles. She became friendly with André Léo (pseudonym), a woman writer and propagandist of socialism and feminism, with whom she founded the Society of Struggle for the Rights of Women, and a newspaper, *Women's Rights*. She also fell in love with a militant French socialist, Victor Jaclard. She lived with him and then married him on March 27, 1871, the day before the Paris Commune was proclaimed, in order to avoid scandalizing her parents and raising obstacles to her return to Russia. During the Commune, Anna acted as secretary of the Women's Committee of Montmartre and worked for the Women's Education Commission. After the Commune fell, Anna's father used his influence to rescue Jaclard from the victorious French authorities. Anna played no further political role, settling with Jaclard into rather conventional domesticity.[12]

Few *nigilistki* became as prominent or as political as Anna Jaclard.[13] Her contacts in Paris, her husband's influence, and the events of the Commune presented Anna with opportunities not available to women who remained in Russia. But one thing Anna did share with the others: the need to struggle against parental authority in order to live according to her principles.

The desire of a young woman for independence challenged tradition and led to conflict between the generations. Accustomed to owning human property, some nobles tended to regard children as if they were serfs with no right to a will of their own. "Where did you get desires and thoughts so unlike mine?" demanded a mother of her newly assertive eighteen-year-old daughter. "How can you express ideas without my permission?" When another young woman became interested in the new ideas, her mother found her "disobedient," and their relationship deteriorated drastically. "What sort of disrespect is this!" her mother would challenge her. "Remember, you are in the presence of your elders!"[14]

According to many memoirs, by the early 1860s few mothers were as permissive as Liza Korvin-Krukovskaia. A daughter was a mother's responsibility, after all, and to allow her to take too great an interest in ideas, to dress like a *nigilistka*, or to go about the streets unescorted – to cite just a few of the innumerable ways she might violate convention – was likely to ruin the girl's chances for a proper match and a secure future. One mother, whose eldest daughter had married unhappily, refused to allow the younger sister to read books, in the conviction that "excessive reading" had destroyed the eldest daughter's happiness. "You're liable to get carried away, just like your sister," the mother warned. "Father wants you to become a capable housewife, not a blue-stocking." Most people would have agreed with the aunt of Anna Korvin-Krukovskaia when she condemned Anna's mother for her daughter's breaches of propriety: "To my mind, it is unforgiveable that Liza allows her daughter to choose such a false and dangerous path, unforgiveable that she does not take steps immediately to direct her to a different one." A daughter's lapse meant that her mother had failed.[15]

Moreover, authority over a daughter remained just about the only authority a mother could exercise after the emancipation of the serfs. As the old world crumbled before her eyes, many a mother clung to the remnants of her power by appealing to her daughter's guilt: "Your mother has never had her way her whole life. She served her relatives, she served her husband, and now you, too, will not let her carry out her will."[16] As pathetic as it was despotic, the message was clear: Daughters must subordinate themselves to the family as their mothers had done before them.

It is no wonder, then, that daughters who aspired to live according to the new ideas began to feel "incarcerated" in the family. The literary evidence suggests that the generational conflict between daughters and parents, as compared with the conflict between fathers and sons, was far more intense and tended to be more personal than ideological. Women's struggle for independence inspired several rather lengthy short stories, none of them as well known as *Fathers and Children*.

The first, *Pensionerka* (*The Boarding-School Girl*), appeared in 1860, two years before Turgenev's novel. It was written by Nadezhda D. Khvoshchinskaia, who published under a male pseudonym, and at thirty-six was by no stretch of the imagination a *nigilistka*. Khvoshchinskaia, the daughter of an extremely poor noble family, had been educated by her parents and remained close to them until they died. She felt ambivalent toward the younger generation, whom she regarded as lazy, excessively proud, and unable to live up to their ideas. Only in her idealism and love of independence did Khvoshchinskaia really resemble the *nigilistka*. She lived with her sister in an apartment in St. Petersburg, where they moved in literary circles and entertained whom they chose. Khvoshchinskaia married at the age of forty-one, shortly after the death of her beloved sister had driven her to the verge of suicide.[17]

Despite Khvoshchinskaia's ambivalence, in Lelenka, the heroine of her novella, she sketched the evolution of a *nigilistka* with remarkable sensitivity. The daughter of a provincial noble family, conventionally educated in a boarding school, Lelenka learns to acquiesce to the wishes of "papenka" and "mamenka" and to accept unquestioningly everything they do. Then a verbose intellectual by the name of Veretitsyn, on a visit from the capital, turns her head with his talk of human progress and his attacks on the old authorities. Lelenka grows increasingly critical of her parents and finally rebels against them. At the close of the story, we find her working as an artist and living on her own in the capital, where she runs into Veretitsyn. Proudly she shows him the independence she has achieved, only to hear herself compared unfavorably with another woman who has married a man she does not love for the sake of her mother and her family. Lelenka, a "new woman," believes that such sacrifice harms not only the woman but also society, because it perpetuates harmful old patterns. Better to live according to one's principles and to set an example to others. Anticipating the credo of the new woman, Lelenka declares: "I will never fall in love, never. It's stupid. . . . I swear that I will never again grant someone power over me, that I'll never serve those old, barbaric codes in word or deed. On the contrary, I say to everyone, do as I have done. Liberate yourselves, all you people with hands and a strong will! Live alone. Work, knowledge and freedom – that's what life is all about."[18]

Nadezhda Suslova's "Rasskaz v pis'makh" ("A Story in Letters"), published in the *Contemporary* in 1864, has a strikingly similar theme. But by contrast with Khvoshchinskaia, Suslova completely shared the values of her heroine. Nadezhda Suslova was born in 1843, the daughter of a former serf of the wealthy count Sheremetev. Her mother, unusually well educated for a peasant woman, taught Nadezhda to read and write. At eleven, Nadezhda went off to boarding school in Moscow, and six years later, in 1860, she moved with her family to St. Petersburg, where she came into contact with some of the leading progressives of her time. In 1861 she began to audit university lectures and to do scientific work, and she published her first scientific article a year later. Soon afterward, she transferred to the Medical Surgery Academy, where she remained until the academy closed its doors to women in 1864. By then, Suslova had been implicated in Land and Liberty, one of the earliest circles to oppose the emancipation edict of 1861, and she had attracted the attention of the police on account of her "sympathy with nihilism." Nevertheless, the authorities permitted her to go abroad to continue her studies in Zurich, and in 1867 she earned her physician's diploma.[19]

"A Story" is one of her several works. It is the tale of two sisters, the older a *nigilistka*, the younger an obedient daughter. The *nigilistka* has broken with her family and lives defiantly alone in St. Petersburg. Her sister, fearful of offending her parents, remains at home, although the parents torment her and the independent sister repeatedly offers assistance. In repayment for her self-sacrifice, the younger sister is crushed by her family and betrayed by the man she loves. By contrast, the elder flourishes.[20]

Both these women writers portray the *nigilistka* very positively as a strong and determined woman who has set aside other ties for the freedom to live according to her principles, in contrast with Turgenev's ambivalent depiction of his hero.[21] To be sure, at first glance the *nigilistka* also appears absolutely self-centered in her single-minded pursuit of her own self-interest. But a closer look reveals that this self-centeredness is not simply self-serving. By developing herself to her fullest capacity, the *nigilistka* is at the same time promoting social progress. For *nigilistki* are also new people whose independent lives and productive labor indicate the possibility of a society that is more rational, well ordered, and just.

On the other hand, these women writers portray the older generation without redeeming qualities. The parents are petty, greedy, and self-serving, despotic beneficiaries of the traditional order who consistently oppose anything that threatens it. They totally refuse to acknowledge (indeed, they do their best to crush) the separate identities and aspirations of their daughters. Neither writer displays Turgenev's subtlety or his generosity toward the older generation. The fathers in Turgenev's work cannot help what they have become, and most of them accept, even when they do not share, the strivings of the sons. The older generation, too, once attempted to live according to the ideals of their time; it is not their fault, only their misfortune, that their children have exchanged the old ideals for new ones.

The contrasting ways in which Turgenev and the two women treated the fathers in their stories reflect more than just literary talent or political preferences. The fact that family authority weighs more heavily on females than on males also accounts for the women authors' more negative portrayal of the older generation. Families expected a boy to leave home to attend school or university, and then find a job. Should he acquire views at school that differed from those of his parents, should he begin to dress oddly and behave disrespectfully – all this ordinarily took place after the young man had left home and had already acquired a measure of independence. If his parents rejected him, the young man had alternatives: student funds, student communes, and a whole subculture that had undoubtedly encouraged rebellion in the first place, as well as official avenues of advancement that could reward independent initiative. One example concerns I. M. Krasnoperov, the son of a clergyman. Krasnoperov wanted to continue his studies; his mother insisted he assume his deceased father's position as sacristan. Mother and son took their conflict to a bishop, before whom the mother tearfully pleaded her case. Children have a duty to obey their parents, she maintained. The bishop sided with the son. He confided that he, too, had once fought with his parents over the right to continue his studies, and look at the respected position his persistence had earned him! Krasnoperov remained in school.[22]

By contrast, the women of the 1860s often had to fight fiercely for the most commonplace male prerogatives. Parents reacted negatively when daughters expressed the desire to study or work, desires that the parents would have found perfectly acceptable in their sons. Exclaimed General Korvin-Krukovskii when he learned that his daughter Anna had sold a short story for publication: "First you sell your story, next you'll sell yourself!"[23] It is no wonder that a *nigilistka* sought first of all to escape her parents' authority.

To gain her freedom was by no means simple. By law, a young woman was absolutely subject to her parents' authority until she turned twenty-one, or until she married, at which point she became forever subject to her husband (men reached majority at eighteen). If a woman was of age and single, independence presented less of a problem – she could presumably dispose of herself freely.[24] Many *nigilistki*, however, were still in their teens and were unwilling to wait those few years to obtain their own papers. And if they wanted to study abroad, as Suslova had, whatever their age they needed their parents' permission.

A fortunate few, like Suslova, had their parents' support. Others struck out for freedom on their own, as did Anna Evreinova. Denied a passport, Evreinova crossed the Russian border illegally in order to enroll in a foreign university. Still others turned to principled young men for assistance and contracted for fictitious marriages. In these unconsummated unions, a man would wed a woman solely in order to liberate her from her parents. He would go through all the motions of courtship to convince the parents of the authenticity of his suit; then, after the church wedding, when the woman had become legally his, he would present his bride with a permit for separate residence, and the two would part, presumably forever. The young woman was then her own mistress.

Her struggle was by no means over, however. Liberation from family authority almost invariably brought a new set of problems. Once a young woman had her freedom, where was she to go, and what was she to do with it? Everything she had read and heard told her to head for the city, where she could find a job, or an opportunity to study. But, most important, she would find others like herself with progressive aspirations and the desire to be useful. The city usually was St. Petersburg, because that was where she could find the new people. But by moving to St. Petersburg, she had in no way solved her problems. How was she to find a job, when she had no experience of the world, no particular training, and the most superficial sort of education, and when, in addition, the state service that supported most of the men of her class was closed to her?

Her problems were intensified by the emancipation of the serfs, which forced an unprecedented number of educated women into the labor market, swelling the demand for employment but doing nothing to increase the number of jobs. According to one estimate, between 1860 and 1865 the female population of St. Petersburg grew by 45,095 (unfortunately, the sources do not tell us the social origins of these women). By 1865, approximately 100,000 women sought positions, many of which paid barely subsistence wages.[25]

Education, at least the typical education of an upper-class woman, was of little help in finding a job. The opening of secondary schools (1858) greatly benefited the daughters of the middle classes, but it actually curtailed opportunities for educated women, because even well-to-do families preferred sending their daughters to the schools rather than hiring a governess for them, and most of the schools preferred to employ men. In any case, the principled woman of the 1860s tended to resist becoming a governess or a teacher's assistant, because those positions restricted one's freedom as much as the family had done, and they were also servile and demeaning positions. But women found it difficult to locate other sorts of work.

Women who knew foreign languages tried to support themselves by translating, but the wages were low, and the supply of work was unreliable. Some did copying, sewing, or weaving; others became typesetters or clerks. In almost every case, however, the supply of workers exceeded the demand, driving wages down. Still another obstacle was the social prejudice that greeted any woman of gentle birth who wanted to work for a living. Most people regarded her with frank disbelief. And if she happened to be young and pretty, too, "they created almost insuperable obstacles for her, and it required a great deal of energy on her part not to throw up her hands."[26]

Housing proved equally difficult to obtain. It had been scarce enough before the emancipation, but the influx of peasants afterward made it virtually impossible for a woman to find a decent place to live when she worked for a mere pittance. A self-employed seamstress, for example, rarely earned more than five rubles per month, and the very cheapest housing in St. Petersburg rented for ten rubles per year, for a dark, dank basement apartment that was flooded a considerable part of the year. Ten rubles was a bargain. Most places cost at least three times as much.[27]

The economy, even in relatively advanced St. Petersburg, remained unprepared in this early period to absorb an influx of gently reared women who wished to be independent. Even if families crushed women's personalities, at least they guaranteed their members food, shelter, and a modicum of comfort. As Linda Gordon perceptively observed in *Women's Bodies, Women's Selves*, it requires considerable courage for women to abandon the institutions that protect them. This was especially so in Russia in the early 1860s, when so few economic alternatives to the family existed. In subsequent years the situation improved, as a result of the success of the women's movement in obtaining higher education for women and the willingness of the government and the private sector, pressed by the need for trained personnel, to employ them as teachers, stenographers, telegraphers, and even doctors (although never as civil servants). But in the early 1860s it remained exceedingly difficult for a woman to make her own way.

The women's movement was trying to assist these women, but some remained uneasy about the movement's politics, and in any case its efforts reached only a few. Women seeking another solution found an answer in literature. Nikolai Chernyshevskii's novel *Chto delat'* (*What Is to Be Done? Tales of New People*) proved extraordinarily influential for young men and women of this generation, because it suggested how women working together might overcome the obstacles to their independence, and also how men might assist them. Chernyshevskii, the son of a village priest, a materialist and a socialist, was an editor of the left-wing *Contemporary*. The writings of George Sand and Charles Fourier had prompted his interest in the woman question, and in matters of personal life Chernyshevskii had long tried to live according to his principles. Shortly before his marriage, he had written in his wife's album that it was the obligation of every honorable man to destroy the servile relationships between men and women, even if this meant that *"he might become a slave."*[28] Still, until Chernyshevskii's arrest in 1862, he avoided "undue emphasis" on the woman question in his published writings. Then, incarcerated in the Peter and Paul Fortress, Chernyshevskii wrote a full-length novel devoted almost entirely to elaborating solutions to the woman question that combined the essentially liberal endeavors of the women's movement, the aspirations of his *nigilistki* friends, and his own socialist convictions.

The book is difficult to read now. Its style is turgid and didactic; its characters are wooden and its plot mechanical. It seems less a piece of literature than a pamphlet in fictional form. It is difficult to imagine why it became so popular, but extraordinarily popular it became, especially among the young. It slipped past the censorship only by the merest chance. Conservatives hated it. Moderates like Elena Shtakenshneider, who had worked closely with the Society for Inexpensive Lodgings, found it electrifying and, having read it, for the first time understood what nihilism was all about.[29] The issues of the *Contemporary* in which it first appeared vanished from bookstores at once and were passed from hand to hand until they disintegrated.

The novel is about the new people (Chernyshevskii never uses the word *nihilist*), whom Chernyshevskii depicts with unflagging sympathy. The central character is Vera Pavlovna, a deeply moral young woman who escapes an unwanted marriage and her mother's persecution by marrying her brother's tutor, a young medical student by the name of Dmitrii Lopukhov. The newlyweds set themselves up in a suite, where they have separate rooms, and they exercise great care to treat each other respectfully and to avoid trespassing on each other's privacy. It is never quite clear whether or not they engage in sexual relations. When Vera Pavlovna falls in love with their best friend (whose character differs in no identifiable way from Lopukhov's), her husband feigns suicide rather than stand in the way of their happiness. At the end of the novel, the supposedly dead husband reappears, disguised as an American businessman. He befriends the new couple and winds up living communally and amicably with his former wife, her husband, and some very shadowy children.

Respect from her husband, a room of her own, personal happiness, and even sexual freedom are not enough for Vera Pavlovna. She requires economic independence, too. This she attains by organizing a sewing workshop, which she gradually transforms into a collective. She encourages the workers to share the profits and to take an active part in managing their shop. The collective works so well that the women set up a bank, start purchasing their supplies cooperatively, and then organize a commune.

This book represents the first attempt by a Russian to combine utopian socialism and feminism. Chernyshevskii conveys his socialist ideas through the collective solutions he provides for women's problems, through Vera Pavlovna's dreams of the future, and through the character of the mysterious Rakhmetov, a revolutionary ascetic who surfaces intermittently in the novel and is a harbinger of profound changes to come. Chernyshevskii's feminist message is equally powerful. We can see it in his concern for Vera Pavlovna's independence, in his sensitivity to her personal life as well as to her employment problems, and in his portrayal of her as a strong and self-motivated individual. It is true that she must depend on men at various points in the story – it is marriage that liberates her from her family and her husband's feigned suicide that frees her to marry another – but this is more a reflection of existing inequities and of Chernyshevskii's sense of men's duty toward women than the result of any prejudice on his part.

By placing women's oppression at the very heart of his novel, and by linking its solution so firmly to socialism, Chernyshevskii increased men's sensitivity to the woman question. Moreover, the apparent ease with which Chernyshevskii's new people found principled solutions to the woman question inspired others to follow their example. After the book's publication, collectives proliferated greatly. They provided an opportunity to experiment with socialism on a small scale, to build the bases of a new way of life in the very midst of the old, and at the same time to help women trying to make their own way in an inhospitable environment by substituting for the economic and emotional supports the family had provided. Unfortunately for the participants, collectives also proved far more problematic than the endeavors Chernyshevskii depicted.

One of the best-known efforts to establish a collective was undertaken by Vasilii Sleptsov. Long interested in the woman question, Sleptsov had given scientific lectures to women, helped to establish workshops for them, and raised funds for projects to help them, all this before reading *What Is to Be Done?*, which inspired a more ambitious enterprise: a commune that would develop into a producer's cooperative as well as a collective living arrangement and would be a sort of "rational family" based on shared interests and aspirations rather than blood ties.[30] But instead of becoming a rational family, the Sleptsov commune (as it came to be known) encountered the difficulties that beset almost every effort to realize Chernyshevskii's ideas.

Foremost among such difficulties were the personalities of the participants, many of whom possessed neither the self-discipline nor the willingness to make sacrifices that a collective endeavor requires. Ekaterina

Zhukovskaia (*née* Tsenina) serves as a good example, for her long and bitter struggle for autonomy had left her a fierce individualist, wary of any incursions on her hard-won freedom.

Like other *nigilistki*, Zhukovskaia had had a conventional upbringing. She was born in the provinces. Her father was an army officer whose military duties kept him from caring for his property, and her mother managed their estates and left childcare to others. The mother had little contact with Ekaterina until her daughter finished her *institut* schooling, and by then the young woman was practically grown up and had acquired ideas of her own. She wanted to set up a school for peasants, to study agronomy, but most of all to be useful. Boredom, the lack of an outlet for her energies, and clashes with her mother, who feared the harmful effects of Ekaterina's reading, all induced the young woman to seek an escape. This she found in marriage. "I had no idea of marital relations," she later remembered. "It merely seemed to me that I would love anyone who came to love me, and who would not confine my ambitions or violate my tastes." A neighbor pressed his suit, and she accepted almost at once, although her mother encouraged her to wait, and she felt absolutely no attraction to her suitor. Once engaged, she was trapped. He claimed his "right" to increasing intimacy, and when she tried to terminate the engagement, her mother refused to allow it, because a broken engagement would compromise the entire family. The wedding took place as planned, and that night the new husband raped his still sexually ignorant bride.

Instead of gaining freedom, for which she felt she had sold herself "like a prostitute," Ekaterina found herself more a prisoner than ever, helpless to resist the hated sexual advances that her marriage had legitimized. Her mother tried to comfort her: "Why didn't you tell me at once that you knew nothing about marital relations?... Well, it's really too bad he did nothing to prepare you. It's a heavy cross for a woman to bear, but there is nothing we can do about it. God arranged it that way. There is nothing for it – you must get used to it."[31]

Zhukovskaia refused to submit. After years of struggle that included a period spent working as a governess for her brother-in-law, she at last gained her freedom. She was living in St. Petersburg and barely supporting herself by translating for Stasova and Trubnikova's collective when toward the end of 1863 Vasilii Sleptsov proposed that she join the commune he was setting up. At first she declined. Hesitant to concede the slightest bit of her hard-won independence for a collective endeavor, Zhukovskaia also feared that Sleptsov, a follower of Charles Fourier, aimed to try out his mentor's ideas concerning free love. After Sleptsov assured her that communal life would be cheaper than living alone and that there would be no experiments with free love, she agreed to join.

Masha Kopteva, another woman who joined the commune, was neither so principled nor so independent as Zhukovskaia, but she would prove at least as troublesome. The child of well-to-do parents, Kopteva allowed them to support her, although she did a bit of translating, too. Elegantly dressed and rather spoiled, she was a most unlikely candidate for a collective.

Attracted by Sleptsov's ideals, the other two women participants were more prepared to make sacrifices. One was Aleksandra Markelova. Born in 1843, Markelova had run off with an artist toward the end of the 1850s, traveled abroad with him for awhile, and borne a child, finally returning to Russia with the child but without the artist. She refused her parents' offer to take her in, and instead rented an apartment where she settled with the child. It was rare for an unmarried noblewoman to keep her child in those days, and it earned her the respect of her nonconformist contemporaries. She had received a good education; she painted, played the piano, and knew several languages, which she used to support herself by translating. She also edited papers and wrote children's stories.[32]

Her friend, "Princess" Makulova, was equally independent. Born in 1840, the daughter of a minor official, she supplemented her income of 100 rubles per year by working from time to time as a governess or companion – work she hated. When she had earned enough, she rented herself a tiny room on the outskirts of the city and walked daily to a public library, where she immersed herself in reading. She pared her needs to the minimum, dressed poorly, and refused any assistance.[33]

By contrast, the male members were at least as unprepared for collective living as Zhukovskaia and Kopteva. Most of them were noblemen who had much sympathy for collective principles but little willingness to work for them. This characterization applied even to Sleptsov, the founder, who behaved both autocratically and self-indulgently when it came to his own tastes. He selected a far too luxurious apartment for the commune, and he persisted in buying flowers and serving expensive delicacies to the elegant guests he invited to visit. Sleptsov's behavior led to quarrels, and so did conflicting views about the purpose of the commune. But it was the issue of housework that finally destroyed it.

A few months after the commune was established, the servant quit. In the spirit of the time, Sleptsov and most of the others resolved to do their own cleaning and cooking. They instituted a rational system, dividing the work equally among members. Zhukovskaia, however, had not been party to the original decision and absolutely refused to do her own cleaning. She had never cleaned in her life, she declared, and was hardly prepared to start now. Instead, she hired someone to do it for her, and she resisted all pressures from the group to behave otherwise. Everyone began to follow her example; no one bothered with the work, and Sleptsov had to do it by himself. Other animosities surfaced, and the commune fell apart.[34]

Many of his contemporaries blamed Sleptsov for its collapse: His tastes were overly refined, his leadership too dictatorial, his treatment of women too courtly. Even his friends acknowledged how unsuitable he was to lead the project. But to blame it all on Sleptsov is unfair. His commune and just about every other collective endeavor during this period faced similar difficulties. One was lack of agreement among participants on what they were trying to accomplish. In the Sleptsov commune, people like Markelova and Makulova wanted to live collectively as a matter of principle, whereas Zhukovskaia, a determined individualist, remained unwilling to subordinate her own needs to those of the collective, and Kopteva, if we can trust what her contemporaries wrote, was merely silly and selfish. (In another context, Zhukovskaia appeared quite radical. It was she who spoke up for the rights of women workers at the meeting of the Society for Women's Labor and she who led the faction that protested aristocratic patronage.)

The backgrounds of the participants led to other problems. All of them came from the privileged classes, and they lacked practical experience in coping with the details of everyday living. They had no idea, for example, where to buy decent food and how to prepare it, how to keep their clothes and linen mended, their rooms tidy, their bedding fresh. This greatly complicated their attempt to "live simply," especially because many found it difficult to change their habits and way of life. In any case, the values of the society around them constantly intruded to subvert their endeavor.

Even greater problems plagued the producers' cooperatives that tried to help women to be economically independent. Such cooperatives proliferated in the early 1860s because they enabled women to avoid the exploitative enterprises that usually employed them, and yet they required no fundamental social change. Most of these cooperatives were modeled on the one in *What Is to Be Done?* Their founders regarded the novel as a blueprint to be followed literally, word for word: "It was the passionate dream of the young, women especially, to possess a copy of the book. . . . Sitting down at the table, they opened the book to the place where the collective was described, and began to discuss in detail how it should be set up."[35] In every case, they encountered unanticipated difficulties.

As was the case with the Sleptsov commune, many of these difficulties resulted from the mixed personalities of the participants and their lack of agreement on the principles they were pursuing. A sizable amount of money was needed to finance a collective: to buy sewing machines or other equipment, to rent an apartment, and to pay the salaries of two or three experienced workers for a month or so, until the participants had learned the principles of association. Financing was provided either by a well-to-do backer (which ordinarily gave her some say in the enterprise) or by collections taken up among sympathizers (who often assumed a similar right to interfere). Backers gave money for idealistic reasons, and so they often exercised their prerogatives to insist that the collectives adhere strictly to "principle." One rather successful shop was managed by a competent, experienced forty-year-old woman who was receptive to progressive ideas. However, she had arranged her sewing collective too much like an ordinary enterprise, and this troubled its backers. When the manager asked them for more seamstresses, they sent her three former prostitutes whose freedom from a brothel they had purchased. No one made an effort to train them, and all three women proved totally unsuitable. They also drove out the other workers, who feared being compromised by their presence. The enterprise collapsed.[36]

The workers themselves posed problems. The *nigilistki* who joined the collectives rarely had the skill or self-discipline to labor for eight to ten hours a day, and simple working women usually proved unresponsive, even hostile, when the principles of association were explained to them. In some cases, they simply refused to listen. "Give us our salary; you can keep the profits!" seamstresses laughingly told the proprietress of a sewing workshop that was on the verge of bankruptcy. Sometimes experienced workers seized the machinery for themselves and drove out the manager. When one case wound up in court, a disgruntled worker declared to her former employer: "You yourself always insisted that the machinery belongs to the laborer!"[37]

Precisely the same problems destroyed a laundry cooperative. It was managed by a woman who endeavored to run it in a principled fashion: She paid her workers an unusually high salary, she provided them comfortable working conditions, and she addressed them politely as "you" (*vy*), instead of by the familiar *ty* usually used by members of the upper classes when addressing their social inferiors. But instead of winning them over, her actions only made them suspicious. "They had grown accustomed to seeing every employer as a despotic exploiter," wrote the former manager. So they distrusted her, too, and refused to listen to her daily lectures on the advantages of a collective. Before she had resolved these problems, she hired several former prostitutes and paid them the same salary as the other workers. The reformed prostitutes disappeared for weeks on end, and they had a demoralizing influence on the other workers. The others began to drink, even at work, and to entertain their boyfriends. The manager finally fired them, but then she was unable to hire new workers because of the reputation her establishment had acquired. "The enterprise," she concluded, "acquired a mixed character, both philanthropic and commercial, and trying to pursue two goals, I achieved neither."[38]

The failures of collectives sparked a lively and revealing debate in the press. E. Garshina, the manager of the laundry, complained that her enterprise failed because progressive society failed to support it. No one offered to teach the women about collective principles, and people left

Garshina to handle all the details herself. The clients (liberals all!) refused to pay on time, and some never paid at all. Putting pen to paper, one of the clients took issue with her. It was the collective's fault that it failed, he rejoined. The work was poorly done, and Garshina herself was too inexperienced.[39]

Other writers posed the question of collectives from the perspective of what they could accomplish for women. In 1863, Iulii Zhukovskii, in an article dedicated to Ekaterina Tsenina, whom he was soon to marry, argued that collectives would never be able to solve the woman question. The problem, he wrote, was that the supply of seamstresses exceeded the demand for their labor, and collectives could do little to alleviate this. Only revolution would solve the problem, he implied. Still, as another writer pointed out, collectives could be very helpful to those who belonged to them.[40] The problem, however, was that they rarely lasted long enough to be helpful. The most important exception was a translating cooperative established by Stasova and Trubnikova, who attributed their success to the fact that they avoided "principle." "We already have . . . enough unfortunate examples to prove that all the collectives which arise from principle and not necessity collapse and take with them many things that could really help people," the two women observed in 1864.[41]

Zhukovskii was right to argue that collectives could provide no permanent solution to the woman question; but Stasova and Trubnikova were equally correct to charge that the failure of collectives deprived women of support they vitally needed. The collectives had tried to assist women who were struggling to maintain their independence and to live according to their principles. When collectives failed, this deprived women of options, making their struggle more difficult, and in many instances impossible.

Failures of collectives dampened enthusiasm for solving social problems within the existing order and led some people to conclude that collective endeavors, as well as efforts to assist women, must be subordinated to revolutionary struggle. People continued to read *What Is to Be Done?*, but they became less eager to adopt "the most accessible and easily fulfilled of its solutions."[42] Because housing and employment continued to be scarce, and society remained hostile to the *nigilistka*, this meant that women who aspired to independence were thrown back onto their own meager resources. The disappearance of collective institutions sometimes prompted women to resort to traditional ones. It is probably no coincidence that Ekaterina Tsenina married Iulii Zhukovskii shortly after the Sleptsov commune failed. The temptation to depend on parents or to become dependent on a husband in order to obtain emotional and financial support grew greater as efforts to provide alternatives to the family foundered.

The difficulties the *nigilistka* encountered in making her own way in the world greatly complicated her efforts to restructure her personal life.

Nihilists were deeply committed to creating the egalitarian sexual relationships that would be a crucial element in the new social order. As they saw it, men must stop treating a woman "with coarse barbarism," and women must cease to be helpless and dependent, must never "hang on the neck of a man." Both sexes must renounce romanticism as part of the discredited past. Henceforward, sexual relationships would be relationships of equals, of comrades on "an equal road to equal goals."[43] Sexual unions must be freely contracted and as easily set aside, because no one should be coerced into loving. Nihilists had little concern for the rituals of wedlock, and they simplified them as much as possible when they did not abandon them altogether.

In most cases, however, the *nigilistka* did not strive for sexual freedom as such, but for the chance to contribute to society and gain access to the public prerogatives of men. Because sexuality had imprisoned her in the past, she tried to obliterate hers as much as she could. Her austere garb, appropriate to the active and useful life to which the *nigilistka* aspired, served also to diminish her attractiveness, at least as attractiveness was conventionally construed. Neglect of personal hygiene, constant smoking, and coarse manners served much the same purpose. What they wanted from men, such women maintained, was comradeship, not courtship. They wanted to be treated as human beings, irrespective of their gender.

Value us as your comrades, your co-workers in life; people who are equal to you, to whom you can speak simply, without camouflaged excuses and without the secret desire to leave something unsaid. The insincerity of our former relations was a result of your not wishing to see us as your equals; try to discern our equality and we will try to remind you less that we are women.[44]

In *What Is to Be Done?*, Chernyshevskii had suggested an ideal balance: Vera Pavlovna found that satisfaction in work and satisfaction in personal life complemented and enhanced each other. But many nihilists had difficulty sustaining this balance. Attempts to institute equality between the sexes in matters of private life proved no more successful than efforts to form enclaves of socialism.

There were many reasons why they did not work. Sometimes they failed because the man "liberated" the wrong woman. This happened to Chernyshevskii himself. He married the lively Olga Sokratovna, promising her absolute freedom, while vowing to be perfectly faithful himself. In this fashion, he would "bend the stick" of oppression in the opposite direction, as he put it in an inscription in her album. He also intended to reeducate his wife, and he assumed that she would eventually learn to share his interests. "All I'll have to do is to develop her mind tactfully, and to engage her in serious and learned conversations," he confided to his diary. After briefly trying to please him, however, Olga Sokratovna gave up. "I threw his articles away, because their subjects do not interest me," she declared. "His life takes place in his study – what could he have to tell me about? Only about what he reads and writes, and this bores me."[45] Raised to attract men, and granted a freedom she had neither asked for nor fought for, Olga Sokratovna used it to entertain a stream of young men, some of whom became her lovers. Her husband, true to his promise, never protested.

The young nihilist N. D. Nozhin tried to liberate his sister with equally lamentable results. When she gave some sign of progressive aspirations and listened attentively to Nozhin's talk of "real life" and of science, he resolved to help her escape from their family, which in his opinion had already ruined two of their sisters. As Nozhin was terribly poor, he had to borrow about 1,000 rubles. Then, at the last moment, his sister became frightened, and Nozhin abducted her. Nozhin had hoped to take her to Switzerland, where she could enroll in courses, but they were quickly apprehended, and the young woman was safely returned to the bosom of her family.[46]

Even when a woman truly desired independence, however, she often found it difficult to keep from "hanging on the neck" of some man. When she encountered the innumerable obstacles on her path to autonomy, everything she had ever learned disinclined her to persistence and encouraged her to turn to someone else for support.

The relationship of I. A. Khudiakov and Leonilla Lebedeva is a perfect case in point. Khudiakov, the grandson of an artisan, the son of a district schoolteacher, was one of those youths of relatively humble background who became more common among the intelligentsia during this period. In 1863, when he met Lebedeva, he was busily collecting peasant folk tales and at the same time working to found a conspiratorial circle. Lebedeva, at eighteen, was already known to the police as a *nigilistka*, and she frequently visited a weaving collective.[47] Soon after meeting Lebedeva, Khudiakov learned about her terrible family situation. Her mother, "infected by worldliness...was in fact insane...although it's not the kind of insanity for which people are sent to madhouses," Khudiakov wrote his parents. One evening, Leonilla visited Khudiakov, and their friendship "became intimate."[48]

Should he marry her? Khudiakov considered carefully, taking into account her financial position, her skills, her desire to work, and her capacity to earn money. There were negative factors, too: Both had been involved with the police, and he feared to attract their suspicion. And marriage itself presented problems. "Marital relations without love are nothing but legal debauchery," Khudiakov wrote.

Marriage, by creating a family, narrows the interests of the parents....Furthermore, marriage enslaves women to men; the very idea of marriage is to make a "single flesh" of two individuals, which degrades human beings. Before marriage, a man is a person, while after it he becomes half a person....A woman, on the other hand, for the most part either becomes his slave or in turn makes him the slave of her passions.[49]

These doubts he did not confide to his parents. To them he wrote in praise of his future bride:

She sings beautifully and is intelligent, although not very educated, but she is very eager to study. She's a self-sacrificing person – without any egotism. She loves me boundlessly...and she's nothing like other young ladies. They're all dolls or very ordinary people, who resemble each other too much. This one is totally original, everything is her own, nothing is artificial.

The night before the wedding, Leonilla came to his room and offered herself to him. The following day they had a "nihilist" wedding, "without dancing or hors d'oeuvres, with three or four witnesses at the church."[50]

Khudiakov regretted his marriage almost immediately. "It can be said that my love was happy only until marriage. From the moment L. acquired rights as my wife, I was constantly not myself," he later complained. His wife's skills were not what she had led him to believe. "I tried to give my wife various tasks so as not to interrupt my literary work, but I soon stopped. Each time she made the most unforgiveable errors, and always mixed up either the names or the places, so that I quickly lost all hope for her in this respect." Her education had not prepared her for hard work or self-discipline, and she went randomly from one occupation to another. But far worse than her failure to fit his ideal of comrade-wife were her sexual demands on him: "All her energy was concentrated on the most passionate physical love. Farewell to my continence, farewell to my health!"[51]

In defense of Leonilla Lebedeva, it should be pointed out that she promptly turned over 1,000 rubles she acquired after the wedding for her husband to use for "the cause," that Khudiakov returned to Russia and left his wife alone, ailing and depressed in Geneva, where she was taking singing lessons, and that Lebedeva conducted herself admirably after his arrest in 1866. Although she was pregnant at the time, and apparently quite frightened, when the police questioned her she said nothing to compromise her husband or his friends, and she moved heaven and earth just for the chance to visit him in jail.[52] She seems to have truly loved him and to have been prepared to do almost anything for him. Like other women who were prepared exclusively for marriage and family life, Lebedeva found it more difficult than did her husband to discipline her feelings or to distance herself from her sexuality.

Even a woman who fought for and achieved autonomy sometimes found it difficult to adapt her emotions accordingly. A successful struggle against the family did not always obliterate dependency, nor did achievement in public life satisfy the desire for love and intimacy. In their zeal to transform human relations, nihilists often treated such feelings contemptuously, but that did not make the feelings disappear; it only made it harder for women to acknowledge them and to deal with them.

The experience of Sofia Kovalevskaia, Europe's first woman doctor in mathematics and first woman professor, provides a tragic example. Born Korvin-Krukovskaia in 1850 (she was the younger sister of Anna Korvin-Krukovskaia), she had displayed exceptional mathematical talent from a very early age. As she grew older, she proposed to study the subject seriously, but her father forbade her. To circumvent him, in September 1868 she arranged a fictitious marriage with V. O. Kovalevskii, a brilliant young geologist and translator. By the fall of 1869 she was studying in Heidelberg with the foremost scientists of Europe.[53]

Her marriage, still unconsummated, provided endless delight. Vladimir, her "brother," was thoughtful and attentive, totally in love with her, but without the "sickly, base passion that is usually given the name of love." They had good reasons to avoid sexual relations, as Vladimir himself observed. Having married her to free her, "it would have been like taking her by cunning." Moreover, Sofia feared pregnancy and what a child might do to her career.[54]

Even without that final intimacy, however, the emotional demands that Kovalevskaia made on her husband occasionally became burdensome. When he lived apart from her, she grew jealous of her husband's absorption in his studies and of his capacity for independence: "She began to worry him with continual demands. She would not travel alone, but he must come and fetch her and take her where she wanted to go. Just when he was busiest with his studies, he had to undertake errands for her." At the same time, Kovalevskaia produced three original works in mathematics, any one of which was fully acceptable as a doctoral dissertation, according to Professor Karl Weierstrass of the University of Berlin, her mentor. In July 1874, the University of Göttingen awarded Kovalevskaia the degrees of doctor of philosophy in mathematics and master of belles-lettres, summa cum laude, on the strength of the three works she presented.[55]

Shortly afterward, the Kovalevskiis finally consummated their marriage, more out of a sense of obligation to her parents, apparently, than from any real desire. They returned to Russia, where for the next six years Sofia tried to play the role of an ordinary wife. She put aside her unpublished doctoral dissertation and involved herself in social life, in the women's movement, and in writing, but never in mathematics, the profession for which she had trained. Only after their marriage began to break down toward the end of the 1870s did she resume her career as a mathematician. In 1880 Kovalevskaia became the first woman in Europe to occupy a university chair (in Stockholm), but this by no means resolved the personal difficulties. She spent the rest of her life torn between work and love, sometimes working productively, but painfully lonely.

Even with the best will in the world, nihilists found it exceedingly difficult to liberate women, and more difficult still to institute equality between the sexes. Their own values and habits worked against their efforts; so did the lack of economic opportunities for women and the absence of reliable sources of emotional support. The only women in a position to help were the moderate feminists, but their efforts reached only a few, and their style and tactics alienated most *nigilistki*. Struggling desperately just to get by, *nigilistki* themselves were rarely in positions from which they could systematically assist and care for each other although they sometimes shared what resources they had.[56] How were such women to deal with their emotional needs, having for the sake of their ideals cut themselves off from their parents and thus severed the ties that sustained as well as constricted them? How were they to maintain their independence in the face of innumerable obstacles to finding jobs and housing – difficulties that the nihilist subculture failed to help them overcome? In the end, many, like Zhukovskaia, Lebedeva, and the Korvin-Krukovskaia sisters, abandoned their quest for autonomy and became dependent on men for emotional or financial support.

Nihilists drew no meaningful lessons from this experience. "Vulgar" materialists, they believed that changed circumstances per se were sufficient to change human behavior. Faced with the fact that some women continued to cling to institutions that degraded them, one *nigilistka* declared with annoyance: "If the nature of woman is so vain and worthless, if her thoughts are primarily directed toward triviality, then we had better find out how to change this nature for the better."[57] Instead of seeking explanations elsewhere, when attempts to sustain an equal relationship failed, men usually blamed women, whereas women quite often blamed themselves.

To complicate matters further, whatever complexities nihilists encountered as they tried to redefine relationships between the sexes, the rest of society saw only one purpose in their activities. Nihilists, they knew, aimed to destroy the family and traditional morality, the very mainstays of the social order. Conservative writers attacked nihilists in an outpouring of fictional works that depicted the men seducing and abandoning women and the women destroying their families and sometimes themselves.[58]

To be a *nigilistka* involved real risk. The political police spied on the Sleptsov commune, reporting that it was the work of young people "of immoral and harmful character," who "repudiate all the laws of public order and do not recognize family relations or marriage, which they replace by the equal right of both sexes to intimate relations among themselves."[59] Two of the women, Markelova and Makulova, who had engaged in no illegal actions whatever, acquired police records for having "nihilist views." So did the sister of N. D. Nozhin, who had so valiantly resisted her own abduction. During the early 1860s, dozens of women drew the attention of the police for similar "crimes."[60]

The personal had become the political, not only because the new people saw their struggle to redefine human relations as part of an overall effort to construct a new order but also because the authorities, in their fashion, agreed. By defining personal struggle, that is, women's quest for independence, as a political threat, the authorities helped to ensure that it became one. Threatened with police harassment or, as repression increased, with arrest, many *nigilistki* abandoned their quest altogether. A few, however, became thoroughly radicalized by their experience. Setting aside all concern for themselves, but maintaining their moral vision, they went on to become precisely what the authorities most feared.

CHAPTER 5

THE *NIGILISTKA* AS RADICAL: AN UNEQUAL PARTNERSHIP

During the second half of the 1860s, the exodus of gently reared women out of the family sphere slowed but did not stop. The woman question continued to inspire some women; economic necessity drove others out. Increasingly, however, the concern of women rebels for themselves and for other women was intermixed with a kind of altruism that had nothing to do with women's issues. These women aspired to "serve society," to be "useful to the people," and the expectation of assisting others helped give women courage to forsake the protection of the family, to defy conventional society, and even to risk official harassment.

These women's altruism was rather naive. Few had thought systematically about how they were going to act on it, but this was hardly their fault. How could their vague moralism indicate a proper course of action, especially when none of the women had had sufficient experience with real life to make intelligent choices? Indeed, how were such women to help others, when most would have difficulty sustaining themselves? These women needed political guidance, as well as economic and sometimes emotional support, and these needs drew them into the orbit of radical organizations.

Radicalism, like nihilism, emerged in the early years of Alexander II's reign. The radical movement consisted at first of a handful of individuals who issued proclamations or joined together in such short-lived organizations as Land and Liberty, but they became more numerous as the decade progressed and reaction intensified. Toward the middle of the 1860s, some radicals began to form circles to prepare for revolution in the near future.

Radicals aimed at a social revolution, to be carried out by and for the peasantry, whom they called "the people" (*narod*). Cheated of their just share of the nation's wealth, the people would rise up and overthrow the tsar and the landlords, replacing illegitimate rule with an egalitarian social order based on the peasant commune. Radicals disagreed about the exact role peasants would play in the revolution, and they disagreed even more strongly about the role of intellectuals. Despite their differences, on one point they concurred: Social revolution, not personal liberation or political liberalization, provided the only key to a just society.

Radicals sometimes included the woman question in their critiques of social relations. For example, in 1862 Petr Zaichnevskii issued a proclamation entitled *Young Russia*, which demanded social revolution and an end to autocracy and in addition offered an extreme statement on women and the family. The proclamation called for "the complete emancipation of women...and the abolition of marriage as highly immoral and unthinkable" in a society where the sexes were equal. *Young Russia* also advocated that children be reared collectively, at society's expense. In 1863, Iulii Zhukovskii placed the woman question at the very center of leftist concerns: "The position of women is ten times worse than the position of the male workers, and the fact that people have justifiably been protesting the workers' situation for a long time, while the woman question until now...has received no serious economic interpretation, makes the situation all the worse."[1]

Nevertheless, radical activists never made the woman question a first priority. For them, the "cause" always came first. Although in theory they included the equality of women among the goals of revolution, in practice they tended to regard women themselves as potential recruits and to pay scant attention to specific women's issues. Radicals supported and even participated in cooperatives, but because these endeavors could not really resolve the woman question (as Iulii Zhukovskii had pointed out), radicals never regarded them as an end in themselves. Rather, collectives provided a way to gain converts to the cause: "a sort of lake, out of which we can haul pike."[2]

Questions of personal life, like women's issues, received short shrift from the radicals. They believed that other, more pressing, matters deserved their attention; they had no time to trouble themselves about attaining egalitarian relationships or ensuring proper treatment of women. People involved in the movement, they believed, should not "wallow in personal feelings."[3] So far as we know, radical men of the 1860s dealt with their personal lives as Khudiakov had done: by subordinating personal life almost entirely to political ends.

Most women who became involved with radical circles during this time could not or would not imitate the men, but could not challenge them, either. Concerned with women's issues, but personally insecure and emotionally vulnerable, the women were in a poor position to stand up for themselves. Instead, women's different expectations and needs often made them dependent on leftists, and some men did not hesitate to press their advantage. In the second half of the 1860s, radicals' subordination of the personal to the political could lead not only to submergence of the women question, but also to subjection of women themselves.

Conspiratorial circles first emerged from the network of legal and quasi-legal organizations that existed in Moscow and St. Petersburg.

The Ishutin circle, the best known, began to take shape in Moscow in the fall of 1863. It included about a dozen students and former students, mostly sons of village priests or men of similarly humble birth. The group dedicated itself to bringing revolution to Russia, but the members disagreed almost to the point of violence about how to achieve this. Whereas the majority advocated long-term organizing among students and workers as the best approach, an inner circle, led by Nikolai Ishutin himself, declared itself prepared to employ any means necessary to foment revolution in the near future. This group called itself "Hell" (*Ad*). At various times, its members considered robbery and murder to obtain money. They also planned terrorist acts against prominent people whom they considered enemies of the peasantry. In April 1866, a member of the inner circle, Dmitrii Karakozov, actually attempted to assassinate the tsar.

While plotting revolution, members of Ishutin's circle took advantage of their contacts with the nihilist subculture to recruit people to their cauśe. Sometimes they attempted to take over existing organizations, as they did early in 1865, when they succeeded in transforming a Mutual Aid Society established by a commune of women typesetters into a group that professed socialist aspirations. But more often, these men simply initiated new endeavors. Among these was the sewing collective of the Ivanova sisters. Established in February 1865, the Ivanovas' collective was one of several projects that women had initiated to assist other women and that radicals subverted to suit their own purposes.

Ekaterina Ivanova was the older of the two sisters, in many respects a typical *nigilistka*. Born in 1842 to an impoverished noble family, she first came to Moscow from Nizhni Novgorod in November 1864. For a while she lived with her brother Dmitrii, a member of Ishutin's circle, and earned a precarious living by sewing. Then Ishutin offered 150 rubles to help her start a collective workshop. She began a correspondence with her sister, Aleksandra (born 1844), who remained at home. In their letters, the sisters weighed against their principles the advantages and disadvantages of Ishutin's offer. Ekaterina had qualms about accepting so much money. Aleksandra reassured her, pointing out how little choice they had if they wanted to make their own way and to do some good for others. They had both rejected marriage, because it would mean dependence on a man, and neither wanted to become a governess or teacher. "Can working as a governess really be considered earning an honest living?" Aleksandra inquired in a letter. "Either teachers have to teach children things that they don't believe themselves, or they must teach them to lie, by telling them to hide their ideas from their parents for fear of punishment." Even translating was dishonest, she wrote, because people translate mostly trash that can harm their readers. "How should a woman relate to an order of things in which women cannot find honorable work?" Aleksandra asked, and concluded that if a woman recognized the chance to "move the cause even one step forward" she must devote herself to it. "To work in that direction is as necessary to her as food, as freedom, as the very conditions of life, and she'll find that her justification for using whatever means she needs, to live."[4] Ekaterina finally accepted the money, and Aleksandra moved to Moscow to help her run the collective. In return for the money they provided, the Ishutin circle received the right to use the workshop as a meetingplace and to propagandize freely among the seamstresses.

The sisters planned the collective as no mere moneymaking venture. The primary purpose of the arrangement, as the Ivanovas envisioned it, was to assist other women: to free seamstresses from dependence on their employers, from exploitative working conditions, and from the evil influence of their co-workers. These objectives were embodied in the regulations that would govern the collective, which the men helped to formulate. An elected leadership would manage the enterprise; new members would be accepted only with the approval of the other workers; if a member became ill, the collective would support her for up to three months in the hospital; profits would be divided equally among the workers.[5]

The Ivanovas succeeded in carrying out only a few of these ideals, in part because the collective was perpetually short of money. The members did live communally, sleeping in the same room and eating their meals together, and only one of them actually drew a salary. When they needed money, the others asked the sisters, who ended up managing the workshop themselves. Over the course of its existence, the workshop employed ten women, who came from a variety of backgrounds. The workers included the following: Maria Kishinets, the daughter of an official; Iulia Khlopina, the daughter of a captain; Avdotia Zavalishina, a member of the petty bourgeoisie and the lover of a member of Ishutin's circle; Ekaterina and Maria Alekseeva, two noblewomen; Maria Motkova, of peasant origin and the sister of one of the more moderate members of Ishutin's circle; and Liubov Kirillova, the Ivanovas' former peasant nurse; there were three seamstresses whose names we do not know.

The ideological basis of the workshop attracted other women, who did not become workers. Foremost among these was Maria Krylova, the only woman participant who had become radicalized prior to her contact with the Ishutin circle. Born in 1842, the daughter of an impoverished nobleman who served as a minor official, she had attended boarding school in Moscow and remained there after graduation, seeking to advance her knowledge and to live on her own. Her activities soon acquired a social character. She taught in a Sunday School and became an early advocate of free, independent lives for women, participating in a number of the associations designed to assist them, the last being the Ivanovas' workshop, which she joined because she sympathized with its goals. Unable to sew, Krylova paid on a monthly basis for her share in the commune, where she lived with the others.[6]

Maria Krylova was better informed than the other women and seems to have shared the revolutionary aspirations of the Ishutin circle. Besides participating in the commune, she helped the Ishutin circle to extend its contacts among women. She brought Ekaterina Zasulich, a young noblewoman, to the workshop, and Zasulich became a frequent visitor, attending the lectures the men offered in the evenings. Zasulich often brought her cousin, Anna Kolachevskaia, and sometimes her younger sister, Aleksandra, then employed as a teacher's assistant. (Vera Zasulich, the youngest and best known of the sisters, still attended boarding school.) Among the other women connected with the workshop were Olga Levashova, the daughter of a wealthy and aristocratic family, and her sister, Maria Zinovieva. Olga later became a member of the Russian section of the International Workingmen's Association, or First International. Anna Shabanova, who became one of Russia's first women physicians in 1878, also attended the evening lectures.

The workshop proved a greater success politically than financially. The seamstresses undercharged for their services and earned barely enough to survive. Often, the Ivanovas had to pay the workers from their own funds, and eventually they had to borrow more money from the Ishutin circle. This made no difference to the men, who wanted to spread their ideas and gain recruits to their cause, caring little about proving the viability of collective workshops.

The propaganda activity of the Ishutin circle eventually alerted the police. On April 1, 1866, Varvara Nikolaevna Kishinits, the widow of an official and the mother of one of the seamstresses, lodged a complaint against the Ivanovas' workshop. She charged that it had "corrupted the morality of young people by telling them about equality and freedom of action, and that it had destroyed family relations by recognizing no legitimate authority over individuals." The police called Maria, the daughter, to testify, and she spoke freely about the revolutionary direction of the establishment and implicated most of the people who had visited it. Many arrests followed.

Three days after Varvara Kishinits registered her complaint, a young revolutionary named Dmitrii Karakozov tried to assassinate the tsar. The authorities knew of his connection with the Ishutin circle, so that when the seamstresses testified, they had to account not only for their participation in the workshop and their contacts with radical men but also for their implication in the attempted assassination. To make matters worse, Karakozov's·shot had so frightened the government that the trial proceeded in an atmosphere bordering on hysteria. Even members of the innermost circle, the fearsome Hell, tried to divest themselves of any responsibility for Karakozov's crime. Terrified of torture, which they believed the Third Section used routinely, they gave copious testimony. One erstwhile revolutionary declared with tears in his eyes how sorry he was. If he could have foreseen where such a secret society would lead, he swore, he never would have joined it. Apparently, even Ishutin broke down and cried when they confronted him with Karakozov, and he tried to convince the court that he was not responsible for the actions of members of his circle.[7]

At best only partially informed of the circle's political aims, the seamstresses could hardly be expected to want to assume any responsibility for them. In fact, most of the women denied they knew anything at all. They had only wanted to earn a decent living, they insisted. The Ivanovas, too, claimed to be totally ignorant, but there is evidence to indicate that they knew more than they admitted. Along with Motkova and Krylova, the Ivanovas belonged to the Mutual Aid Society that had become a front organization for the Ishutin circle. D. Ivanov, their brother, was a member of Ishutin's inner circle, and so was O. A. Motkov, Aleksandra Ivanova's lover. It is unlikely that these men concealed their political convictions from women so close to them. In addition, there is the evidence of the Ivanovas' behavior while under arrest. The officer in charge reported that they clung to their convictions and had become "even bolder."[8]

Nevertheless, that the Ivanovas were more passive observers than active participants in the Ishutin circle's plotting seems clear from their subsequent behavior. While maintaining friendly relations with radical men later in the decade, the two women avoided further political involvement and maintained their original objective of assisting other women.

No such ambiguity surrounds the convictions of Maria Krylova, who provided perhaps the most courageous (if also the most foolhardy) testimony of the entire trial. Krylova freely confessed to the investigating commission that she knew of a plot aimed at revolution in Russia and that when the Ishutin circle met in the evenings they sometimes discussed preparations for it. Moreover, she made no effort to conceal from the police her sympathy with the revolution, to the extent that it would improve the position of women.[9] She had discussed with Ishutin the participation of women in the revolutionary struggle, she acknowledged, and she brought Anna Kolachevskaia to the sewing collective at his request. On account of her youth (she was twenty-four), and undoubtedly because the authorities had not yet learned to take radical women seriously, Krylova was merely put under surveillance. Karakozov was hanged, and most of the other male defendants were sentenced either to hard labor or to exile in Siberia.

The Karakozov affair was a watershed. The repression that followed intensified the process of political polarization; it served to magnify ideological distinctions, and it made unconventional behavior far riskier. Even people who had had no contact with Ishutin's circle (e.g., E. A. Garshina, the well-intentioned manager of a laundry cooperative) became subject to police harassment. As a result of all this, women in rebellion against their conventional role could count on little assistance from progressives, who grew increasingly fearful of compromising themselves, and this left women more dependent on radicals.

At the same time, as the atmosphere of reaction intensified, men became far less concerned with women's issues. Around the mid-1860s, even the moderate press began to suggest that it was not the time to think about inequities in women's rights, because a question involving both sexes had to be solved. The radical movement went underground, and in the clandestine circles of the late 1860s, the woman question received almost no attention at all. Women, who had formerly been regarded as beneficiaries of social change, now became primarily a means to an end. The left continued to recruit women, but radicals remained unconcerned about women's issues and women's status within their organizations. And that status was unquestionably secondary. Clandestine organizations tended to be tightly organized and hierarchical, and the necessity for secrecy concentrated power and information in the hands of a single person or a few individuals. Determined and occasionally unscrupulous, some of these men did not hesitate to use their recruits in an attempt to attain their revolutionary ends.

The experience of Liudmila Radetskaia illustrates the vulnerability of idealistic women who became dependent on such men and how far these men could go in using others. The child of an impoverished noble family, Radetskaia aspired to study medicine abroad after finishing boarding school. Instead, her mother betrothed her to a wealthy older man, insisting that no daughter of hers would be allowed to continue to study. To escape a loveless marriage, Radetskaia contracted for a fictitious marriage with the help of her brother. The couple lived together in Moscow, at first chastely, than as man and wife.

Under the influence of her husband and his friends, new aspirations replaced Radetskaia's original aims. After the Karakozov affair, she and her husband became the center of a commune of men and women, most of whom had previously been connected with the Ishutin circle. Their group included Maria Motkova and Elizaveta Obolenskaia, whose husband and brother had been arrested in 1866. Every evening, people would gather at their apartment to discuss the commune and its future and make plans to set up a sewing collective similar to that of the Ivanovas. Their radicalism was vaguely defined but highly enthusiastic. "None of us had any doubt that we would be able to do away with the evil reigning everywhere....We felt that we had been summoned to carry out the revolution, and that everything was permitted us, that all was possible," Radetskaia later wrote. She became "possessed by the desire to abandon myself to serving the people." Her propensity for self-sacrifice was soon put to the test. The commune began to have financial problems at the very time when their discussions touched increasingly on sacrifice for the general good, on means and ends. Because their revolution could not take place if their circle collapsed, and because they desperately needed money to keep it afloat, their leader regarded finances as the first priority. Attractive, emancipated young women, eager to do whatever they could for the good of the collective, seemed perfectly suited for this project. As the most likely candidates, the leader singled out Radetskaia (that is, his wife) and Elizaveta Obolenskaia, who had previously proclaimed her readiness "to sacrifice her family and everything that was dear to her, to sink to the very depths," in order to rescue Chernyshevskii from Siberia.[10] Her husband Leonid dissuaded Obolenskaia from making such sacrifice, but Radetskaia carried out the plan and became the mistress of a banker. A second, unnamed, woman assisted the circle in similar fashion. Most members of the group did not know the source of their newfound wealth, which their leader evidently used to no revolutionary purpose, but simply to maintain the commune. In any event, when Radetskaia became pregnant the income stopped. She was then nineteen and still sufficiently under the influence of her circle to accept their argument that "children belong to society, and it must raise them." Convinced that she must contribute her energies to improving society, and not "wallow" in personal feelings, she regretfully gave up the child.[11]

Few women were so blatantly exploited as Radetskaia, but those who became involved with radical circles toward the end of the 1860s displayed the same enthusiasm for being "of use," and almost as much naiveté, and most became just as dependent on men. Of these women, we know most about the Zasulich sisters, whose political evolution we can document in some detail, and whose experiences with radical men were in many respects typical. The three sisters were of the nobility. Ivan Zasulich, their father, served as an officer, and according to his wife, he was an intelligent and energetic man, but also a drunkard and a terrible despot in his relations with his family. Having provided himself with an heir in his firstborn, a son, he proceeded to ignore his subsequent offspring, all daughters. Ekaterina, the eldest (born 1845), he genuinely disliked. His wife felt that she lacked the ability to protect the child from his beatings, and therefore she asked her sister to raise Ekaterina. Ivan Zasulich ignored Aleksandra (born 1847), and he died when Vera (born 1849) was only three. A fourth daughter, Sofia, was born three months after her father's death. His death freed the family from his despotism, but it left them nearly destitute. He bequeathed them a small estate with forty-six serfs, not sufficient to maintain a family of four.[12]

The rebelliousness of the three older sisters was shaped by their life circumstances. In an effort to cope with her financial difficulties, the widow gave her daughters Aleksandra and Vera to wealthy relatives to raise, but even at five years of age Aleksandra was sufficiently strong-willed to get what she wanted. Sent to the home of the childless Princess

Obolenskaia, who had promised to will her estate to the girl, the home-sick Aleksandra so stubbornly insisted on returning to her mother that she was sent home after only three months. The mother, subject so long to her husband's authority, could not discipline her child. She never tried to teach the girls, either, and because there were no books in the house, Aleksandra took responsibility for her own education. During the year in which a tutor was employed to prepare her brother for school, Aleksandra sat in on the lessons and learned to read and write. Later, she improved her education by attending the classes a governess taught for the daughters of a neighboring landowner. Then her education ceased until she was eleven, when her aunt, Princess Obolenskaia, paid her tuition at a boarding school. After having had her way for so many years, Aleksandra found it difficult to adjust to all the rules and regulations. "It was hard for someone like me, who had lived free as a bird, to get used to the strict regimen of an educational institution," she remembered, and never did she cease to resent it.[13]

Not so strong-willed as Aleksandra, Vera was shy and withdrawn. She remained with her wealthy relatives, the Mikulin family, who pro-vided material comforts, a governess to teach her, and tuition for board-ing school, but this left her feeling forever the outsider, the impoverished relative. "No one ever held me, kissed me or sat me on his knee; no one called me pet names. The servants abused me."[14] Unable to confront her circumstances directly, from an early age Vera took refuge in fantasy, finding in the Gospels material for elaborate fantasies of heroism and martyrdom. Because poverty condemned her to that most mundane of female roles, the governess, her future promised to be just the opposite of her fantasies. "Had I been a boy," she later wrote, "I could have done almost anything." The revolutionary cause was ultimately to replace the religious impulse, making her "equal to a boy," and enabling her to dream of action, of deeds, of struggle. But even then she retained the moral certitudes of her earlier religiosity, as well as an urge to join "those who perished for the great cause of love."[15]

For very different reasons, the three sisters were predisposed toward rebelliousness, and that mood coincided well with the temper of their times. But, as numerous other *nigilistki* had already learned, it was not easy to satisy the desire to escape socially prescribed roles, to develop oneself intellectually, and to attain economic independence, when soci-ety offered women so very few alternatives. "What sort of work could I have found at that time – there weren't even jobs as village teachers!" Aleksandra later recalled.[16] Experiencing an "insurmountable aversion" for the profession of governess, she took a position as a teacher's assis-tant in the boarding school she had attended. Ekaterina had run away from the home of her "stupid and quarrelsome" aunt, and it is possible that she worked at the Ivanovas' collective for a while, but she, like Aleksandra, eventually had to overcome her distaste and accept work as a teacher's assistant. By then, Ekaterina had come to espouse the vague radicalism of her generation. She lived with her cousins, the Kolachevskaia sisters, attended lectures at the Ivanovas' collective, and loaned books to Aleksandra to read in the evenings after she had finished work.

Lacking any clear-cut objective, each of the sisters tried her hand at a number of things over the next few years. Aleksandra quit her job as a teacher's assistant and worked as a seamstress, then in a bindery collective. Vera, who graduated boarding school in 1867, was employed for a while as a clerk. When a friend offered Aleksandra the chance to try out a principled solution to her employment problems by providing the backing for a sewing collective, Aleksandra accepted at once. For expertise she turned to her acquaintances, the Ivanova sisters, and moved in with them in a suburb of Moscow. During the summer of 1868 the collective began to function, employing three seamstresses, the Ivanova sisters, and Ekaterina and Vera Zasulich.

But even this endeavor proved short-lived, because political concerns (or, perhaps more precisely, the men who articulated them) began to compete successfully for the sisters' attention. On weekends, young radicals from the city would visit the Ivanova sisters, and Ekaterina and Aleksandra became romantically involved with two of them: Ekaterina with Fedor Nikiforov, the illegitimate son of a petty bourgeois, a small trader who had been connected with the Ishutin circle; Aleksandra with Petr Uspenskii, a noble by birth who had been active in the radical underground for years. Aleksandra's relationship with Uspenskii shaped her political development. Although he was only a year older than she, his ideas were considerably more advanced, and he gave her books to read and explained them to her. "Under his influence, I began to think about social questions and about the position of the people," Aleksandra later wrote.[17] Compared with such weighty matters, Aleksandra's previous interests seemed trivial; so when the workshop's backer went abroad, Aleksandra abandoned the project to marry Uspenskii and live in Moscow, where he had offered to find her work. Their apartment in Moscow became a gathering place for radical youth, and almost every evening Uspenskii's friends would drop in. The two Ivanova sisters and Maria Krylova often came to visit, and Uspenskii's fifteen-year-old sister, Nadezhda, lived with them. Although the members intended at some point to work among "the people," their circle had no definite objective, and they confined themselves to self-development and to elaboration of a system of ideas.

Politically, Aleksandra followed her husband's lead, and as a result she seems to have lost her own sense of direction. She had felt herself to be the most uneducated member of her husband's circle from the first, and when she became pregnant in the winter of 1868–9, her self-doubt increased. Until then, they had lived "like students," in furnished rooms, and neither of them did housework. Now the couple had to look for an

apartment, buy furniture and dishes, and so forth. Added to these responsibilities was the fact that her pregnancy kept Aleksandra from
being as active as she felt she should be. "I was ashamed to admit that I
had a personal life and personal concerns," she wrote, expressing an
uneasiness about personal needs that would be shared by many other
women who chose political activism.[18] In the self-abnegating and somewhat insecure adult that Aleksandra became, it is difficult to find traces
of the once rebellious and self-assertive child.

After their collective fell apart, Ekaterina joined a circle in St. Petersburg that was far more militant than the Moscow group of her sister.
This group, jokingly known as the Smorgon Academy (the academy of
bears), lived communally, sharing the money they earned through writing and giving lessons. Many of the men involved had already experienced prison; the Ishutin circle provided their model, and their plans
included freeing Chernyshevskii and assassinating the tsar. The women
had less political experience. Ekaterina Zasulich and Anna Kolachevskaia
had briefly been incarcerated for their connection with the Ivanovas'
collective, but Elizaveta Tomilova, Liubov Kovdieva, and Evdokia
Kozlovskaia had no criminal records at all. Kozlovskaia, the only woman
not of noble origin (she belonged to the petty bourgeoisie), prepared
food for the group and allowed her house to be used as a meetingplace.
This was sufficient to convince the police of her utter immorality, and
their report accused her of selling herself to students in order to support
the commune. In Kozlovskaia's case, the accusation appears to have
been completely unfounded.[19]

Although Vera Zasulich had ties to this circle through her sister and
through her friend, Elizaveta Tomilova, it was her contact with Sergei
Nechaev that eventually led to her arrest and imprisonment. After the
collapse of Aleksandra's collective, Vera had come to St. Petersburg to
seek work and had found a job at a bindery collective. In her free time
she attended classes in pedagogy, where she first met Sergei Nechaev,
one of the most controversial figures of this period.

Sergei Nechaev, unlike most of the radicals of his day, was truly a
"man of the people," his father a house painter, his mother the daughter
of serfs. Only through boundless energy and determination had he
escaped his background, and he possessed a strength of will that shaped
his relationships with everyone he met. He had enrolled at the university in the fall of 1868, just as police repression began to ease and the
student movement began to revive. Several hundred people, including a
handful of women, not students but sympathizers, attended the meetings of students that took place that fall. Convinced of the imminence of
a peasant revolution, Nechaev attempted to gain control of the student
movement in order to direct it as he saw fit.

Nechaev proved absolutely unscrupulous. Any means were appropriate, in his opinion, if only they served the revolution – and it remains

difficult to distinguish between service to the revolution and service to Nechaev. If people would not follow him voluntarily, then he would adopt mystification and deceit to persuade them. Nechaev was one of the primary authors of the "Catechism of a Revolutionary," a rather grandiose document that described the appropriate behavior of the "true revolutionary."[20] Such a man, it said, should utterly dedicate his life to the revolution and have no interests, feelings, or belongings of his own. The true revolutionary would show no mercy to those he deemed enemies of the revolution. The catechism divided nonrevolutionaries into categories, each to be dealt with in a particular way. In these categories, the catechism included women. One group, the "empty-headed, the senseless, the heartless," revolutionaries should exploit in all possible ways, making them slaves. Another group, "eager, devoted and capable but not on our side because they have not yet attained a real, dispassionate and practical revolutionary consciousness," revolutionaries should induce to reveal their true sympathies, whereupon most would perish, whereas a few would become true revolutionaries. Then there was a final category: "the women who are truly ours, that is, fully devoted and comprehending our program in its entirety. We regard these as our most valuable treasure, whose *assistance* is absolutely indispensable to us" (emphasis added).[21]

One of the women Nechaev tried to recruit was Vera Zasulich. A few months after their first meeting at a pedagogy class, she ran into him at the residence of her friend Tomilova. Finding her alone, Nechaev began to elaborate his plans for revolution in Russia in the near future, and he invited her to join "the cause." Zasulich had trouble sharing his optimism, but it was her first real conversation about revolution, and she desperately wanted to be of service. She ended by agreeing to let him use her address, but Nechaev evidently remained unsatisfied. A few minutes later, totally without warning, Nechaev announced: "I have fallen in love with you." Zasulich sensed something false in the declaration and politely disclaimed any interest. Later she came to the conclusion that he genuinely needed her help and had declared himself in order to recruit her, after it had become clear that political reasoning alone would not convince her to join him. According to Zasulich, he was then involved with several women.[22] She saw him for the last time several days later.

In September 1869, Nechaev settled in Moscow. With the help of his friend, Petr Uspenskii, he quickly succeeded in founding an organization and putting himself firmly in command. When one of his followers, Ivan Ivanov, appeared to challenge his authority, Nechaev accused Ivanov of being a turncoat and had him murdered at the end of November. Less than a month later, Nechaev went abroad, leaving his co-conspirators to fend for themselves. The police discovered Ivanov's body and soon picked up the trail. Before the end of the year they had rounded up over 100 people who had been connected in one way or another with Nechaev.

When they arrested people in connection with the "Nechaev affair," the police cast their net widely. Among those they rounded up before the trial in 1871 were the three Zasulich sisters and fourteen other female suspects. Of these seventeen women, seven were of noble origin, two were daughters of military officers, three belonged to families of bureaucrats, four derived from the petty bourgeoisie, and one, Maria Motkova, was a peasant.

Trial records and other biographical data suggest that these women (all politically naive, and at best only partially informed about the aims of Nechaev and his organization) had been manipulated by Nechaev or his comrades.[23] For example, Iulia Boborykina (born 1844, the wife of a lieutenant) had had no previous contact with radical circles, but someone had asked her to convey a letter to Nechaev in Geneva, and because she was already planning a trip abroad in order to study medicine, she agreed. Elizaveta Beliaeva (born 1843), "a simple, sweet girl" from a poor petty bourgeois family, was somewhat more seriously involved.[24] Beliaeva had accepted money from Nechaev to attend the newly opened Alarchin courses for women in St. Petersburg, so as "to get to know the students" and introduce Nechaev to them. Nechaev also planned a trip abroad for her and induced her to obtain a passport, although he never told her the purpose of the trip. A third defendant, the noblewoman Ekaterina Likhutina (born 1845), Nechaev saw "alone in her room a number of times," and then he presented her with a scarf. Letters she received from him implicated her in his secret society. A fourth, Varvara Aleksandrovskaia (born 1833), was the wife of a bureaucrat. In 1869 she had traveled with Nechaev to Geneva, where he gave her a "large number of printed proclamations, instructing her to deliver them...to students," which she did. Despite her willingness to inform on Nechaev, Aleksandrovskaia received the most severe sentence of any woman at the trial: exile to Siberia.

Of the women defendants, all but one attempted to dissociate themselves completely from Nechaev's plans for revolution in Russia. Vera Zasulich persistently denied ever having participated in any sort of conspiracy. "I never even considered plotting against the sacred person of the tsar," she asserted.[25] Boborykina testified that she had been told "some confusing things about a society." Beliaeva insisted that no one had informed her why she was to travel abroad and that she never really understood the goals of the organization. Likhutina claimed to know nothing of Nechaev's affairs. Aleksandrovskaia insisted rather disingenuously that she had submitted to Nechaev "unconsciously" (bessoznatel'no), only after he alluded in passing to the "danger" of not carrying out his society's orders, and in order to become an informer for the police. He never let her know the purpose of their trip, she maintained, and not until they were on their way did Nechaev tell her that the society aimed at a "people's revolt." Given our information about Nechaev's methods, there is every reason to believe that he kept these women in ignorance. The court certainly believed them: Only three women, including Vera Zasulich, were sentenced. The rest, her sisters among them, were soon released from prison or acquitted.[26]

The one woman defendant to acknowledge having consciously contributed to the revolutionary movement was Anna Dementeeva. Her story illustrates the altruism that prompted such women to act in the face of difficult circumstances. But it also shows how a male radical could divert from her purpose even a woman who was perfectly certain about what she wanted to accomplish. Dementeeva was the illegitimate child of an officer and a woman of the petty bourgeoisie. Her mother had died when she was very young, leaving her in the care of a stepfather, with whom she did not get along. From her earliest years, economic need had dominated her existence. As a high school student she took in sewing, and when she finished school she was destined to become a governess. But reading, and perhaps her friendship with Petr Tkachev, one of the prominent radical publicists of this period (who later became her husband), led her to reject that fate. Instead, she resolved to dedicate herself to helping other women.[27] Because she identified lack of employment opportunities as a major source of women's secondary status, Dementeeva adopted the popular solution and planned to establish a cooperative workshop. She wanted to begin with a printing press, then expand into other areas. But presses cost money, and although Dementeeva had a small inheritance, at nineteen she was too young to get her hands on it. So, with Tkachev's help, she tried to arrange a fictitious marriage in order to obtain the money as a dowry. It is not clear why Tkachev did not marry her himself, but in any case they approached a number of men, all of whom proved unsuitable. Nevertheless, they eventually collected enough money by other means for a down payment on a press. Then, in March 1869, there was a wave of student uprisings, followed by massive arrests. Tkachev considered it imperative to arouse the public by informing people of the reasons for student unrest, and he proposed to Dementeeva that they use her press to print a proclamation he had written for this purpose. Dementeeva readily assented. Together, they printed and distributed the proclamation, entitled "To Society." Both were arrested shortly thereafter, and plans for a collective came to an abrupt end.

They appeared before the court two years later. Tkachev, already compromised because he had worked closely with Nechaev, denied everything, maintaining that he had not written the proclamation and that he knew nothing about its publication. Dementeeva testified more bravely, if also more foolishly. After briefly denying responsibility, she then claimed credit not only for having written and printed the proclamation but also for sending some copies to editors and for distributing the rest herself. She had lied at first, she said, because Tkachev had laughed at the proclamation and had not wanted students to know that they had been defended by a woman, who had no right to act on their behalf.[28] But Tkachev refused to allow her to protect him and wound up acknowledging that he had written the proclamation himself.

Actually, Dementeeva had directed most of her testimony to the woman question, not the proclamation. By using her speech to the court as a means to enlighten the public on women's condition, she became one of the first defendants in Russia to transform the courtroom into a political forum. "I believe that the position of the educated woman is intolerably difficult," she declared. "Their work is the most thankless. They labor from 9 in the morning till 9 at night for a pitiable wage. This is because women have no opportunities, they can only teach. And because so many need jobs, wages are lowered. Even their education works against them. It makes them unfit to be stenographers or to do any sort of work." She concluded with an appeal to improve existing facilities and to expand educational opportunities for women.[29]

This speech generated a good deal of public sympathy for Dementeeva, but it did not save her from punishment. The court condemned Dementeeva to four months further confinement, then sent her into exile. In 1873 she and Tkachev finally married, and they lived together briefly before he fled abroad. After strenuous efforts, she obtained permission to join him in Switzerland, but she had to agree never to return to Russia. She and Tkachev remained together only a few months longer, then separated on account of marital difficulties. Even when they cohabited, Dementeeva seems to have played no role in Tkachev's political work.[30]

Dementeeva proved more determined and outspoken than the other women defendants in the Nechaev trial. Nevertheless, she shared with them a somewhat naive altruism and an involvement with political activity that essentially derived from her association with a man. As was the case with most of the others, too, Dementeeva's commitment to radicalism proved short-lived. The radical circles of the late 1860s provided few women recruits to the far more extensive movement of the 1870s. Of all the women arrested, only four remained active, and only Vera Zasulich and Maria Krylova played visible roles during the following decade.

In the second half of the 1860s, rebellion against traditional roles often brought women into contact with the left. Many of these women resembled the Ivanova sisters, the Zasuliches, or Anna Dementeeva, in that they were moving from nihilism to radicalism. The woman question inspired them, but so did a desire for other kinds of social change. Initially, and often most concretely, they expressed their idealism in efforts to assist other women. At some point, either their own ideals or male acquaintances brought them into contact with radical circles. None of the women thus involved, not even Maria Krylova, ever played more than a peripheral role, and despite their primary concern for the woman question, never did their participation make it a priority for the movement.

Women who became involved with radical circles during the late 1860s were in a poor position to defend their own interests. Almost all of them were dependent on men – economically, because jobs were scarce, emotionally, because many were sexually involved with the men who recruited them, and intellectually, because at that time women lacked the education and political sophistication of men. Most radical men had attended the universities and academies of Moscow and St. Petersburg, whereas the women, at best, had graduated from boarding school or high school. Because they lacked the opportunity for study and often the proper training for intellectual self-discipline, the women's political ideas remained undeveloped. And even those women who had managed to supplement their education still felt great timidity about expressing ideas in the presence of men. Moreover, women's altruism, the almost desperate need of some to be of service to "the cause," made them highly vulnerable to manipulation by men like Nechaev. For all these reasons, no woman had influence or authority in the movements of the 1860s.[31]

Nevertheless, the sheer numbers of women connected with radical organizations could not fail to impress observers on the right. In a report on the student movement of 1869, a member of the Third Section condemned all new developments that favored women, even attempts to provide them jobs and education. These, he wrote, undermined everything sacred to women, the family, religion, and femininity itself, replacing them with the "emancipated woman," with her cropped hair, blue glasses, and sloppy dress, who refused to use a comb or soap, and who lived in "common law marriage with a subject of the opposite sex, or with several of them." He found all such women politically suspect, and he recommended that even those still peripheral to the movement be placed under surveillance.[32]

This strengthened the left's conviction that women should subsume their own cause into the broader revolutionary movement. If authorities suspected all aspects of women's rebellion, radicals reasoned, then women could truly free themselves only by helping to do away with the entire existing order. Abroad, the anarchist Mikhail Bakunin paid special attention to the needs of women in postrevolutionary society. Not only was he careful to spell out that such things as liberty, universal suffrage, and access to education were the rights of "men and women" alike, but also he called for complete equality of the sexes, for abolition of legal marriage, and for a social stipend for women who were pregnant, nursing, or raising their children.[33] In Russia, by contrast, pamphlets addressed to women in the late 1860s and early 1870s summoned them to join the larger revolutionary struggle, but tended to ignore issues of special relevance to women. Nowhere is this more evident than in a pamphlet entitled "To Women from the Russian Revolutionary Society" (*Ot russkago revoliutsionnogo obshchestva k zhenshchinam*), which appeared in 1871 and was the last document of the period to be addressed to women as a particular group.

The pamphlet began with a devastating indictment of the treatment of women in past times. Women have always been completely subordinated to men in law, it declared, because men create civil law with only their own interests in mind and allocate to women only the positions of concubine and cook. Despite all their efforts, women have been unable to liberate themselves, and even the most talented woman has always been considered inferior to the most stupid of men. Schools leave women ignorant and fail even to equip them to fulfill their one special role in life, motherhood. The pamphlet went on to discuss the efforts of the *nigilistki* of the sixties. It praised them for trying to earn their own living and to free themselves from tradition, and it blamed their failures on the government. "They won't let you study and they won't let you earn a living in associations." But what else could be expected of exploiters? the pamphlet rhetorically inquired. It then proceeded to point out that only social revolution could provide the solution: "Only a revolution that abolishes exploitation will give you a chance for a human existence. Your cause is indissoluably linked to that of the working class."[34]

The radical generation of the late 1860s had absorbed the woman question into the cause of working people to such an extent that the goals of the revolution, as set forth in the pamphlet, offered nothing whatsoever of special interest to women. It called for a loose, federative type of government, but said not a word about marriage, the family, or childrearing, or about employment or training for women. Thus read the last radical document in the 1870s to address itself specifically to women. The woman question had ceased to be a theoretical concern.

PART III

CHOOSING A PUBLIC COMMITMENT

INTRODUCTION TO PART III

At the end of the 1860s, expanding educational opportunities dramatically increased the number of women seeking alternatives to a family-centered existence. High schools for girls proliferated; the Alarchin and Lublian courses, evening lectures for women, opened in 1869, followed by the Vladimir lecture courses in 1870, and, in 1872, Courses for Learned Obstetricians, which in 1876 became Women's Medical Courses. Women who remained dissatisfied with these made their way to Zurich, where in 1867 Nadezhda Suslova had earned her degree in medicine, inspiring dozens to follow her example. For women who aspired to be more than wives and mothers, the opportunity to gain an education provided a legitimate objective. The nihilist generation of the 1860s had regarded knowledge, especially scientific knowledge, as the soundest foundation for a new society, and their younger sisters of the next generation shared that enthusiasm. The newly opened educational institutions motivated women to overcome the obstacles that their families placed before them, and in some instances the new schools provided more direct help in removing those obstacles, because some parents (or husbands) began to see education as an acceptable pursuit for women.

Many women students held social aspirations that served to justify their desire for education: Their knowledge would make them useful to "the people." Despite their rejection of the conventional female role, such women continued to perceive themselves much as had the women of the preceding generation: as moral beings with a special capacity for self-sacrifice. What made the new generation different was that they wanted to exercise such qualities for the good of society as a whole, and they refused to allow "parental egotism" to deter them. A determination to act according to this self-image eventually led a minority of women from pursuit of knowledge to revolution. School exposed them to new people and different ways of thinking. Already disposed to critical thought as a result of their struggle against family authority, many women merged readily into a student community increasingly receptive to socialist ideas. A significant minority of these women would join radical circles and evolve into dedicated activists.

The new radical community that emerged early in the 1870s provided a sympathetic milieu. The members of this new generation were populists, who believed that the peasantry was oppressed by the existing social and economic conditions and was inherently socialist by virtue of its communal way of life. Motivated by a consciousness of their duty to "the people," they aspired to share their knowledge with the people and point the way to revolution. Populists tried to be egalitarian in their practice, and they were particularly scrupulous in their treatment of women, assisting women's struggles for autonomy and, in their circles, treating women respectfully and as equals.

Women, like men, joined populist circles because of shared ideals, but many of the women also found in these closely knit, egalitarian groups an emotional substitute for the family ties they had given up, and this gave added intensity to the women's political commitment. Between 1873 and 1877, several hundred young women affiliated with populist groups and went "to the people" to share the peasants' life and spread socialist ideas. After they joined the movement, women found it much more difficult than men to return to "normal life." Once they abandoned school, normal life could offer nothing more than taking shelter in their families of origin, or becoming someone's wife, and someone else's mother. Women's fate thus became linked with the fate of the movement.

In 1875, the populist movement reached an impasse. The first spontaneous, uncoordinated campaign "to the people" had ended disastrously. The people proved less accessible than radicals had anticipated, and in any case the authorities rarely allowed propagandists time to sink roots in the countryside. By the end of 1874, the police had rounded up thousands, and until their trials in 1877, many of these people rotted in fortresses and prisons, where some became fatally ill, went mad, or took their own lives. Populist activity subsided; those still at liberty sought to assist their imprisoned comrades and to regroup. The political trials of 1877 ended this period of relative quiet. In its treatment of the defendants at the trials (first the trial of the Fifty, then the trial of the 193), the government proved to be as arbitrary as it was punitive. After having kept them in prison for two to three years, the authorities dealt harsh sentences to the defendants in the trial of the Fifty, then released many of the 193 in a gesture of magnanimity. Instead of restraining the movement, as the authorities had hoped, this treatment served to foster it and to increase hostility toward the autocracy. The trials provided the populist radicals with a forum from which to propagate their ideas; in addition, a number of radicals who had previously been strangers were provided an opportunity to meet and share their ideas. After the close of the trial of the 193, in January 1878, St. Petersburg became alive with activity as radicals attempted to redefine their goals and to regroup. Despite their failures, few populists were ready to abandon the idea of going to the people, although increasingly they began to emphasize long-term projects in which they would first develop their contacts and only then reveal their ideas.

A small minority, however, had begun to advocate a different set of tactics altogether. In July 1877, Trepov, the governor-general of St. Petersburg, had ordered the brutal beating of A. Bogoliubov, a political prisoner, for his failure to remove his cap in the governor's presence. Twenty-four hours after the close of the trial of the 193, Vera Zasulich, acting from a sense of moral outrage against this violation of human rights, had drawn a revolver and shot and wounded Trepov before a roomful of witnesses. At her trial in 1878, Zasulich explained: "I waited for some response, but everyone remained silent. . . . There was nothing to stop Trepov, or someone just as powerful as he from repeating the same violence again and again. . . . At that point I resolved, even if it cost my life, to prove that no one who abused a human being that way could be sure of getting away with it."[1]

When Vera Zasulich shot at Governor-General Trepov, she inadvertently put terrorism on the agenda. The proponents of terrorism argued that peasant revolution would never occur so long as autocracy remained in command and its officials continued to intimidate the people. In their opinion, a successful assassination campaign against the tsar and other prominent representatives of officialdom would root out oppression at its source and provide inspiration for popular activity. At the very least, it would extract concessions from the government in the direction of civil liberties, which would certainly make the work of propagandists much easier. At first only a handful of people, the advocates of terrorism gained adherents as the behavior of the authorities lent force to their arguments. After the trials had ended, persecution of populists continued, and even the most patient found work among the people exceedingly difficult because of harassment by local officials. In the summer of 1879, radical leaders met twice to discuss the issue of tactics, and Land and Liberty, their largest organization, split into two factions: the People's Will and Black Repartition. Black Repartition, which clung to the old propagandist program, was stillborn. Frustrated in their attempts to go to the people, most activists eventually went over to the People's Will.

Women, who were a substantial minority in the radical movement of the 1870s, accounted for between one-fourth and one-third of the forty or so people who led the People's Will. Their involvement, like that of the men, brought daily risks to life and liberty, even as it gave them the satisfaction of acting directly on their highest ideals. But, as most radicals were aware, women's participation was qualitatively different from that of the men. First, women's emotional ties to the radical subculture tended to be more intense, because radical circles provided a substitute for the family connections women had sundered. Second, more than most male radicals, women displayed a moral absolutism that evolved from values they had acquired in the family – a moral absolutism all the more unrelenting because radical women had renounced the institutions that might have channeled their idealism into more conventional outlets.

That women's rebellion usually originated in the family and was shaped by values and perceptions acquired there proved to be crucial to the evolution of women's activity and thought.

CHAPTER 6

FROM FEMINISM TO RADICALISM

At the very time that the "men of the 60s" abandoned the woman question, another generation of women raised it again, only to interpret it in their own manner and then to set it aside. In 1869, the opening of advanced courses in Moscow and St. Petersburg gave women new reason to challenge traditional roles. The courses offered a sense of purpose, as well as a chance to develop their ideas, to hundreds of women eager to escape the confines of home and family, women with similar aspirations to knowledge. During the fall and winter of 1869–70, circles and discussion groups sprang up all over St. Petersburg as women took advantage of the opportunity for intellectual exchange with members of their own sex. Initially, most women wanted to talk about issues that were directly related to the circumstances of their lives: Their discussions focused on the relationships between parents and children, and men and women, and the right of women to autonomy – in short, the woman question. Some women eventually progressed from the woman question to broader social issues as they tried to understand the poverty of the peasantry and urban workers and the sources of the vast inequities they could see all around them. A handful of women, unconcerned with the woman question, had addressed these issues from the first.

Their new freedom broadened women's intellectual horizons and presented them with some new choices. Most had come to school intending to acquire knowledge both for its own sake and to prepare themselves for meaningful work. The woman question initially seemed most relevant to their needs, because it encouraged them to seek autonomy, to develop themselves, and to work for the well-being of society as a whole. Most women continued to hold these objectives, and they became teachers, midwives, and medical practitioners, thereby acquiring a measure of independence at the same time they were providing services to the people. A minority, however, came to view these objectives as too limited. Their reading and thinking, their contact with populist ideas, and often their propensity to conceptualize issues in moral terms prompted such women to join radical groups and to engage in illegal activities, at the risk of both personal freedom and intellectual gains. Thus, the women

109

students of the late 1860s and early 1870s composed a sort of critical mass, from whose midst would emerge some of the most dedicated revolutionaries of the 1870s.

In the fall of 1869, women from all over Russia poured into St. Petersburg to attend the newly opened Alarchin courses. From six to nine o'clock each evening, over 200 women filled the halls of the Alarchin high school, where some of the most outstanding professors delivered lectures. Although the program aimed only at supplementing women's superficial education and conferred no degree, so great was the enthusiasm it generated – and so low the overall quality of women's education – that graduates of teachers' courses (the most advanced then available to women) joined graduates of high schools and boarding schools as students. Their social origins were as diverse as their educational backgrounds. Alongside noblewomen sat the offspring of civil servants, of merchants, of priests, and of shopkeepers, their differences effectively concealed by the simple dark dresses that had become the uniform of their generation. Among the women attending these lectures were Sofia Perovskaia, Aleksandra Kornilova, and Elizaveta Koval'skaia. From diverse backgrounds, hungry for knowledge, and inspired by the woman question, these three seemed in almost every respect representative of that new generation. What made them different did not become evident until later, after all three had progressed from feminism to radicalism under the influence of populist ideas.

Sofia Perovskaia was fifteen years old when she first heard of the opening of the Alarchin courses. Living at her family's estate in the Crimea, she had been reading voraciously but haphazardly in her grandfather's library, and she welcomed the opportunity for systematic study. Because the family was about to move to St. Petersburg anyway, the timing could not have been better. Varvara Stepanovna, Sofia's mother, was almost as enthusiastic as her duaghter; so the only obstacle was her father, who disapproved of anything unconventional. The scion of an old aristocratic family, Lev Nikolaevich Perovskii had already occupied a series of powerful positions, serving as vice-governor of Pskov and Tavrida provinces, then as governor of St. Petersburg until 1866, when he had been relieved of this post after Karakozov tried to assassinate Tsar Alexander II. He had always had a difficult relationship with Sofia, his fourth child and second daughter. A despotic and ambitious man, Lev Nikolaevich valued political power and the entrée into aristocratic circles it provided. He was extremely critical of his wife, whom Sofia practically worshipped. Raised in the provinces, of relatively modest background and poorly educated, Varvara Stepanovna infuriated her husband because of her shyness and provincialism and because she preferred domestic duties to social life. As his career advanced, their relationship became increasingly strained. When Perovskii criticized his wife, the young Sofia invariably took her mother's part.

The relationship between her parents shaped the way that Sofia perceived the world. Gentle and long-suffering, the mother found strength to endure by living according to her convictions. She provided her daughter with an image of moral integrity that Sofia would strive to uphold and that she would project onto everyone she perceived as being oppressed. As Sofia's good friend, Vera Figner, put it, "in the difficult atmosphere of her famiy, Sofia L'vovna began to love humanity, to love the suffering as she loved her suffering mother." By contrast, her father's rude, occasionally brutal behavior left Sofia with a lasting antagonism toward him and a tendency to distrust all men.[1]

Sofia's education reflected the vicissitudes of the family's circumstances. Until she was twelve, tutors and a German governess instructed her; then Lev Nikolaevich lost his post, leaving the family without income and deeply in debt. Varvara Stepanovna had devised a study plan for her youngest daughter, but had to abandon it for lack of funds. (The boys had been sent to high schools, and Maria, born 1847, to an *institut*, much against her mother's wishes.) At their small estate in the Crimea, where mother and daughters retreated in 1866, Sofia was free to read as she chose. Her older brother Vasilii helped to channel her interests. Summers, he would visit the country, bringing progressive books and articles that he and his sister would read and discuss in their mother's presence, works by Chernyshevskii and Dobroliubov, as well as Büchner's materialist classic, *Force and Matter*. On the basis of these readings and her own limited experience, Sofia at fifteen had become an advocate of women (*zhenskii patriot*), prepared to dedicate her life to the struggle for women's rights.[2]

Aleksandra Kornilova, another student at the Alarchin courses, similarly learned her politics at home. Only two generations removed from the peasantry, the Kornilov family were Old Believers, and they lived modestly but well on the proceeds of a flourishing trade in porcelain. The mother had died of cholera in 1853, six weeks after the birth of Aleksandra, her seventh child in ten years of marriage. According to his daughter, Ivan Kornilov did not remarry because he was unwilling to impose a stepmother on his children. Kornilov was a remarkably progressive man, an exception to the customary conservatism of the Russian merchantry, and he permitted his children an unusual degree of freedom. His only son Aleksandr was a full-fledged nihilist who had a powerful influence on the whole family because of his personal behavior and his merciless criticism of all superstition and prejudice. His younger sisters followed his lead. In 1866, Vera, then seventeen, enrolled in a teacher training course, an act that seems unobjectionable enough now, but that at the time was considered "rather indecent." She made friends there and brought them home and introduced them to her sisters, Nadezhda, Liubov, and Aleksandra. She also took her sisters with her to the gatherings that had become a characteristic feature of progressive society. In smoke-filled rooms, crowds of young people fortified by endless cups of tea engaged in heated debates over every imaginable subject – philosophy, psychology, political economy, and so forth. These gatherings lasted far into the night, but their father never tried to stop his daughters from going about unescorted in the evening. "I can't hire four governesses for them," he would laughingly tell their aunt, who was appalled by their "nihilist" appearance. Aleksandra had occasional conflicts with the authorities of her high school, which almost prevented her from gaining a first prize at graduation.[3]

Although scarcely older than Perovskaia and Kornilova, Elizaveta Koval'skaia had already done some organizing by the time she became a student at the Alarchin courses. Koval'skaia (born Sol'ntseva) came from Kharkov, in the south of Russia, where she had been born a peasant, the illegitimate child of a noble father and a serf mother. Various dates, 1849, 1850, and 1852, are given for her birth. She spent her early years as a serf, self-conscious about her illegitimacy and all too aware of her precarious position. "I was tormented by nightmares: I dreamt that they were selling me," she later remembered. That her father could sell her mother, but not the reverse, seemed to her particularly unjust, and this combination of sexual and class oppression left a lasting impression. Only when she reached seven did her father agree to register her mother and her as free citizens. (Osip Aptekman, a comrade, wrote that it was Elizaveta herself who somehow convinced him.) Sol'ntsev subsequently made her his heir and tried to transform her into a lady, but neither freedom nor wealth could erase the lessons of those early years. After a struggle with her father, she enrolled in a high school, where a friend introduced her to the literature of the 1860s, and where she organized a study circle, first of girls and then of both sexes. Participants concentrated on social issues, but they also studied the natural sciences, astronomy, physics, and other branches of knowledge. Chernyshevskii was one of their favorite writers – particularly his novel *What Is to Be Done?*, because of its exploration of the woman question. Her father died shortly after she graduated, and Elizaveta used the property he left her to set up free courses for women seeking higher education, as well as a school for women workers. In her classes she always placed special emphasis on the woman question. These activities eventually attracted the attention of the police, who closed the school. At that point Elizaveta decided to go to St. Petersburg to attend the Alarchin courses. Before she left, she married Iakov Koval'skii, another teacher.[4]

The women who attended the Alarchin courses in 1869–70 joined a student community in a state of flux. The broad-ranging debates and the endless evening meetings attended by hundreds of young people bear witness to the ferment of the times. In St. Petersburg, Nechaev attracted no following. Instead, socially conscious students were evolving in the direction of peaceful propaganda. Various circles were to precipitate out of the student subculture over the next several years. The most important of these was the circle surrounding Mark Natanson and Vasillii Aleksandrov, although it was subsequently named after Nikolai Chaikovskii. In 1869–70, however, it remained a group of medical students who lived communally, shared resources, and discussed ways they could best serve the people. The Chaikovskii circle became complete only in 1871, when the men's circle merged with a group of women students from the Alarchin courses.

Between 1869 and 1871, these women had been quite differently engaged. Soon after the Alarchin courses opened, women began to gather in discussion groups in apartments around the city. These meetings, from which men were invariably excluded, became so numerous and so frequent that one participant commented that a person barely had time to go from one to another. Although they touched on political and social themes in passing, the woman question always remained the center of their debates.

By the woman question, these women usually meant female autonomy and the right to share the public prerogatives and responsibilities of men – a right that, by implication, derived from the special moral qualities that women might contribute to a larger cause. As Aleksandra Kornilova put it, her friends were "trying to liberate themselves from the stagnant past and all tradition, from the family and from the marital authority that had enslaved them, and prevented them from entering the broad path of self-development and work for the good of society."[5] The element of altruism led women to downplay personal relationships as an obstacle to the larger goals they had set themselves, rather than reevaluate them. Marriage, with its endless childbearing and household responsibilities, came in for special criticism. In the absence of effective contraception, free love could provide no alternative to marriage, and thus the subject of free love never arose. Instead, some simply rejected sexuality, courtship, and marriage. Aleksandra Kornilova recalled: "I had not the slightest inclination to marry anyone at that time. I despised ladies' men [and] I pitied the students who were mothers, absorbed by childcare and petty household concerns. Courtship seemed either ridiculous or coarse to me."[6] Perovskaia shared her views. In 1870, when the Franco-Prussian War broke out, Perovskaia sided with the Germans, according to her friend Aleksandra, because she found the French frivolous and overly inclined toward love affairs. According to Perovskaia, when marriage did take place, the woman should be around thirty. Earlier manifestations of sexual maturity she attributed to the artificial stimuli of urban life.[7]

The memoirs of other women of the period demonstrate a similar tendency to subordinate personal life to social concerns. The existing memoirs tell us much about social involvement, but almost nothing about relationships with men, even when those relationships were evidently intense and loving. Koval'skaia, who devoted only a sentence or so to her husband, was typical. To these women, romantic involvement constituted danger, not only the very concrete danger of being overwhelmed by petty household tasks but also the more abstract danger of being defined and constrained once again by family relationships. It seems as if they feared that to discuss sexual love in their writings was not only to be traditionally feminine but also to equate personal life and social commitment, and this the women were scarcely prepared to do.

With new opportunities before them, these women sought to escape from family relationships, not to redefine them. It was the public sphere, not the private sphere, that mattered. They wanted independence, which to them meant the freedom men had to act in the interests of society as a whole. Knowledge would provide the key to that. As Kornilova put it, "Knowledge alone could liberate a woman from material and intellectual enslavement."[8] More than just a means to economic independence, knowledge would gain them freedom from men's tutelage, would indicate the proper path of action.

The desire to understand things for themselves gave a special intensity to women's groups. Elizaveta Koval'skaia left us a description of one of their meetings held at the residence of the Kornilovs. As she entered, Aleksandra came to greet her at the door. "She was short and strongly built, with close-cropped hair and she wore an outfit that seemed almost to have become the uniform for advocates of the 'woman question': a Russian blouse, cinched with a leather belt, and a short, dark skirt. In general, she looked more like a young boy than a girl." Kornilova greeted the newcomers warmly and led them into a large room, where about twenty women were conversing animatedly. A few sat quietly, listening. So many women were smoking that she found it hard to breathe. Kornilova returned to an evidently unfinished argument, leaving Koval'skaia and a friend to make their own way in the new surroundings. The medical student who had brought them left at once, without setting foot into the room, because the meeting consisted exclusively of women. Koval'skaia quickly became absorbed by an argument between a tall, stately blonde and a short brunette – Sofia Perovskaia. Perovskaia's appearance, that of a young girl, almost a child, made a strong impression on her. Her plain costume set her apart from the others, and she was obviously totally oblivious to her appearance. She had a broad, high forehead and gray-blue eyes that indicated a kind of stubborn inflexibility. Her whole demeanor expressed distrust. When she was silent, her small, childlike mouth remained tightly shut, as if she feared saying something superfluous. Perovskaia and the other woman were arguing whether or not men's and women's circles should remain separate. The blonde insisted that there was no reason to keep them divided; Perovskaia contended that joint meetings would be harmful, because "men, as the more educated, would undoubtedly make it difficult for women to think independently."[9] The majority agreed with Perovskaia.

This issue of joint meetings was important, with a practical aspect as well as a psychological dimension. As they had in the late 1860s, radical concerns sometimes conflicted directly with women's needs, especially the needs of women students. The very presence of women in lecture halls constituted a significant victory, and that made it difficult for them to support the activities of radical male students, whose protests promised women nothing but could provide the government an excuse to destroy women's recent gains. When student riots erupted in Moscow in 1869, some women students asked the men to end the riots, concerned that the ensuing repressions would involve closure of women's lectures. The identical problem arose in St. Petersburg. In March 1869, a woman student wrote to a friend:

Things are terrible here in Petersburg. The students of the medical academy have started rioting and the result, of course, is that the medical academy is closed.... Sixty students have been arrested and many have already been exiled to far-off places. But what is worst for us is that women who were allowed into the academy will of course be kicked out again.[10]

Elizaveta Beliaeva was enlisted by Nechaev in 1869 to recruit for his organization at the Alarchin courses, but she had no success at all.

Sometimes there were differences between the educational interests of men and women. In Kharkov, for example, disagreements arose when women's study circles first merged with men's circles in the winter of 1866–7. "The men wanted only to study science, while we were drawn to questions of real life [*zhivoi zhizni*]," remembered Koval'skaia.[11]

In addition, fear of male dominance led some women to see the presence of men as a genuine threat to their autonomy. This was all the more true because women often remained very sensitive to male expectations. In a male-dominated society, it was natural for women to want acceptance by men they respected, to want to fit into men's notion of what women should be. The problem was not only that men would try to take over women's groups but also that women would be tempted to acquiesce. To all this, separate circles provided the most straightforward solution.

After 1869, women who wanted to could exclude men, because they had become somewhat less dependent on men. New educational institutions – the products of feminist victories – provided meetingplaces and stimulus for thought. Moreover, a growing minority of women had fought free of their families and had begun to live on their own. Women's networks – still few and fragile and concentrated in urban areas – existed to provide support. And a few women, mainly teachers, had begun to attain positions from which they could influence others.[12]

These women spoke primarily, but not exclusively, of women's issues. Many had come to see the woman question as one facet of a larger critique, inseparable from other social questions. Their concern with women's issues almost inexorably led them farther afield in search of answers. When she taught the women workers of Kharkov, Koval'skaia quickly learned that passionate agitation on the woman question was not enough. Her students would become aroused, but she could provide them with no program for action, for, as she put it, "I myself had no idea how injustice could be righted."[13] She eventually found her answer in socialist revolution.

The need for a more comprehensive world view led Perovskaia and Kornilova in the same direction. In the spring of 1870, a professor at the Forestry Institute offered to teach qualitative analysis to interested students. Perovskaia (whose parents had gone abroad), Aleksandra Kornilova, and a couple of other students took advantage of his offer and settled in Lesnyi, a suburb of St. Petersburg, for the summer. Kornilova and Perovskaia had become close friends, and they talked endlessly in the evenings as they wandered in the park. To protect themselves from unpleasant encounters with soldiers stationed nearby, they disguised themselves in men's clothing, which they borrowed from Perovskaia's brother Vasilii. Their gender obviously remained a problem, and the woman question continued to dominate their conversations, but other issues also claimed their attention. That summer they read *The Situation of the Working Class in Russia*, by F. Bervi-Flerovskii, and *The Proletariat in France* and *On Associations*, by M. Mikhailov.[14]

They nevertheless continued to avoid men after they returned to St. Petersburg. A translation of Karl Marx's *Das Kapital* had recently been published in a journal, and Vasilii Aleksandrov, a medical student, suggested that he, Perovskaia, Kornilova, and a few of their friends form a group to study it. Both Perovskaia and Kornilova refused, because, as Kornilova put it, "very few people were capable of understanding Marx, and we didn't want to take on faith, from somebody else's words, a philosophy we could not study ourselves."[15] Instead, they formed a group exclusively of women in order to study the more accessible *On Political Economy*, by John Stuart Mill, with commentaries by Chernyshevskii. They intended this circle to grow into a more active group, and so they chose their membership with unusual care. On the basis of her work in Kharkov, Koval'skaia was one of the few people asked to join. "This circle is destined to become another with different goals," Perovskaia announced rather portentously at their first meeting. She took her studying very seriously. She would stop thoughtfully at each idea, develop it, and raise objections, first to Mill, then to Chernyshevskii. It was obvious that she enjoyed the intellectual challenge of such analysis.[16]

Formal studies continued to claim a sizable share of their time. Besides attending the Alarchin courses, Perovskaia, Kornilova, and two of

Kornilova's sisters joined a circle of about a dozen women who studied geometry with a professor of mathematics. It turned out that Perovskaia was highly gifted mathematically, and she considered enrolling in the engineering division of the Technological Institute, which her brother told her would admit women.

They all began to live the lives of students, attending classes, meetings, study groups, benefits, and so forth, and many of them became increasingly estranged from their families. Koval'skaia already lived on her own (we do not know what had become of her husband). Ivan Kornilov allowed his daughters to do as they pleased (although Vera had contracted for a fictitious marriage to escape their "bourgeois existence"). Sofia Perovskaia, however, felt very restricted. Although she remained close to her mother, her relationship with her father had further deteriorated. He threatened to lock her in the house, and he forbade her friends to visit. That was a declaration of war. Rather than submit, Perovskaia began to stay with various friends. She was only seventeen, however, and she possessed no identity papers of her own. Several days after Sofia left home, her mother visited the Kornilovs in search of her. "Children have a duty to obey their parents," Varvara Stepanovna argued, as she asked for information about her daughter. Kornilova stood up for Sofia. "She has a right to disobey her father," she maintained, "once he resorts to force and takes away her chance to study," the key to her liberation. In the name of the individual's right to freedom, Kornilova refused to betray her friend. A few days later, Lev Perovskii called in the police, but they failed to locate his daughter. Sofia grew tired of evading the police, and with the help of friends she fled to Kiev, where she remained for several months, until combined pressure from his wife and son forced Lev Perovskii to capitulate. But after he gave his daughter her own papers, Perovskii became so enraged that he refused to allow her into his house, and mother and daughter, who remained devoted to each other, had to visit in secret.[17]

This sort of confrontation was something new. Women had, of course, fled their families before, but Perovskaia had defied her father openly, thereby avoiding the subterfuge necessary in a fictitious marriage and any consequent dependence on a man. Her woman friends defended her, concealed her, and arranged for her escape. Perovskaia thus proved her independence of her father, as well as men in general. In her own eyes, a stage of struggle, the struggle for autonomy, had ended. She was free to devote herself to serving society. The question was how to go about it.

A group of male students at the School of Medicine were considering the same question. On Vulfovskii Street, fifteen of them lived communally, two per room, sharing their every kopek and dining mainly on horsemeat: The commune would purchase a horse, and a veterinary student would slaughter it in the courtyard. They stored the meat in a shed and shared it with other communes. When they ran out of food, one of them would go out and catch a dog or cat, and everyone would eat again.[18] They took turns cleaning and cooking. Their political activity centered on their fellow students, and in the fall of 1870 they decided to extend their contacts to women. Two of the men, Mark Natanson and Vasilii Aleksandrov, took to visiting the Kornilov home, but the women remained shy of them. Natanson was kind, but patronizing, and Kornilova, conscious of his "superior knowledge and development," could never quite relax in his presence. Still, timidity did not prevent her and Perovskaia from paying a visit to his commune, ostensibly on an errand, but also out of curiosity about one of the communes that had become such a fixture of student life. The visit proved even more exciting than antici- pated. They found a policeman at the gate and two soldiers in the kitchen, letting everyone in and no one out. Evidently there was going to be a search. The police were on the lookout for Vasilii Aleksandrov, but someone had slipped out a window and warned him to stay away. Everyone was in an excellent mood. They drank tea and dined on horsemeat and whiled away the time in singing and in the animated discussions so typical of the times. All of this struck the two women as being strange and interesting.

Soon after that visit, Vasilii Aleksandrov proposed to Kornilova. Threat- ened with exile, he was preparing to go abroad to set up a printing press, and he wanted her to assist him in his work. This would be a "rational marriage," he explained, for which both partners would re- quire special intellectual and moral preparation. Kornilova, unimpressed, refused him, although she kept quiet about the fact that she did not find him very attractive personally.[19] Her women friends heartily approved her refusal. Neither Perovskaia nor Kornilova repeated their visit to the commune, and until the close of the school year they associated only with the students at the Alarchin courses.

Some of their friends disapproved of this exclusivity by the women's group. Aleksandra Obodovskaia, for one, held herself aloof at the women's meetings. Born in 1848 to a merchant family from Simbirsk, she had attended high school in St. Petersburg. Obodovskaia was somewhat older than the other members of her circle, and she was already in- volved in conspiratorial work. Olga Schleissner was another advocate of joint projects. Schleissner was born in 1850, the daughter of a nobleman from Orel. She had graduated from an elite boarding school in St. Pe- tersburg and then enrolled in the Alarchin courses. Her contacts with radical circles were extensive. Schleissner lived in the same building as the Vulfovskii commune and was considered a member. She moved easily in that milieu. Koval'skaia once accompanied her to a crowded meeting, where they were the only women present.[20]

Schleissner acted as a sort of liaison between men and women stu- dents. Involved both politically and romantically with Mark Natanson, she willingly assisted in his efforts to establish a circle parallel with his own. The Kornilova sisters and their friends seemed likely candidates; so Schleissner gathered information about them that she supplied to Natanson, argued with them over separatism, and tried in various ways to strengthen the links between men and women students. It was she who had sent Perovskaia and Kornilova on their errand to the Vulfovskii commune.

Perovskaia and Kornilova, gravitating steadily leftward, proved responsive to these efforts. At the end of the spring term they astounded their friends by reversing their previous stance on separatism. Koval'skaia learned about it from a member of a women's circle, who dropped in one day and, obviously upset, told her: "Imagine! Kornilova and Perovskaia, who have always spoken against uniting with men's circles, have themselves entered a men's circle." A meeting was held at Koval'skaia's residence to confront them. The two women came late. Kornilova's manner was relaxed, even a bit defiant, but Perovskaia seemed embarrassed and depressed, if also ready to defend herself. Everyone leveled accusations at them, but a woman who later became a lawyer led the attack. When she was finished, Kornilova took the defense with the enthusiasm characteristic of her, but no one found her particularly convincing. Perovskaia, on the other hand, refused to defend herself at all. She replied simply: "We are not going to explain anything to you." Then she rose and walked out with Kornilova. Neither Koval'skaia nor her friends ever found a satisfactory explanation for the shift.[21]

The reason for these women's sudden affiliation with a men's group was that in terms of their interpretation of the woman question, separatism had served its purpose. In the opinion of Perovskaia, Kornilova, and many of their friends, the woman question addressed the disadvantages they faced as individuals, but it led to no solution for the social inequities that increasingly dominated their discussions and that had come to trouble them just as much. Their talks in isolation from men had helped the women to free themselves from "the stagnant past and all tradition," which included subservience to men, and to raise their own consciousness, but once their consciousness had been raised, separatism seemed only to cut women off from male efforts to organize around the broader social issues that concerned both sexes. So, in the face of the "injustice reigning everywhere," women reduced the woman question to its simplest component, autonomy, and made that a means to another purpose. Instead of an end in itself, autonomy became a necessary precondition for serving society as a whole. As a result, when they allied with men, women accepted not only a political perspective but also a particular self-definition that, despite their newly won independence, still incorporated important elements of the traditional feminine ideal.

Nevertheless, it is no coincidence that Perovskaia joined a men's circle only after establishing her independence from her father. By struggling successfully against him, confronting him woman to man, so to speak, she had won her place in the larger world. However, rather than remaining on her own, Perovskaia, like other women in her position, chose instead to enter a different sort of family, replacing the emotional ties she had set aside with new ones based on shared interests and ideals.[22] Kornilova, as in so many other things, followed her friend. "Sonia [Sofia] possessed much greater abilities, and I became subject to her influence," she remembered.[23] The political development of other women followed the same general pattern: Success in their struggle for autonomy freed them to act on their altruistic impulses and thus led them to set aside the woman question, that is, their individual cause, for the sake of membership in a surrogate family and for socialism, the cause of others.

The character of the men of the Chaikovskii circle, with whom these women affiliated, proved important to their evolution. Rejecting the methods of men like Nechaev, Natanson and his friends based their alliance on trust and on shared moral principles, on comradeship and egalitarian relations. Formally, they had ceased to be interested in the woman question. It was impossible to separate it from the emancipation of the working class as a whole, Aleksandrov once argued during a student debate. Once they had solved the labor question, the woman question would automatically solve itself.[24] Nevertheless, these beliefs did not prevent the men from raising and using the woman question. Unlike the women, who set aside all issues that concerned them personally when they joined the radical movement, the men of the Chaikovskii circle incorporated the woman question into their efforts to organize factory workers. Discussions of women's role, of the family, even of the position of children helped to instill a revolutionary perspective.[25] The men also participated willingly in efforts to liberate women from "family despotism." They prized all individuals prepared to serve the cause, women especially; so among the tasks they set themselves was the task to free women. This was, in their view, comparable to freeing a political prisoner, a comparison that gave such attempts a certain romantic quality.

Although it took place a year after Perovskaia and Kornilova affiliated with the men, the marriage of Larissa Chemodanova and Sergei Sinegub is an excellent case in point. Chemodanova, sixteen, was a student at a diocese school in Viatka, where Anna Kuvshinskaia, her teacher, had already sown the seeds of rebellion. The daughter of a village priest, Chemodanova wanted to continue her studies and devote herself to serving the people. This her family strictly forbade. They made her a virtual prisoner in her home, and after she once attempted to flee, they tightened surveillance on her and prepared to marry her off by force. She appealed to Kuvshinskaia, who wrote to a member of the Chaikovskii circle for help. Rescue would have to come quickly, the letter warned, because Chemodanova had sworn she would kill herself rather than live under such circumstances. The group decided to arrange a fictitious marriage with Sergei Sinegub, whom they chose because his noble birth would make him an attractive son-in-law. They then rented a carriage and a horse, so that Sinegub could arrive in style at the home of Vasilii Chemodanov. Pretending to be the secret lover of Larissa, Sinegub paid her court until the father agreed to let them wed. They spent another month behaving as if affianced. But Sinegub actually fell in love with Chemodanova, a situation that the ethics of his group forced him to conceal. Following the wedding, he brought his bride to St. Petersburg and delivered her to a women's commune. They began to live together as man and wife only after another year, when Sinegub discovered that she also loved him.[26]

These young men who placed such emphasis on moral behavior had been sensitized by the ideas of the 1860s to issues of importance to women. During the courtship and marriage, Sinegub displayed the sort of tact and delicacy that made him and his friends fit associates for young women seeking autonomy yet also eager to be socially useful. Unlike Nechaev and other men of the 1860s, these men could be trusted not to exploit or betray women.

In the spring of 1871, Natanson's group decided to expand its activities by organizing a self-development circle for the summer, and they invited selected men and women students. After school ended, Olga Schleissner, Aleksandra Obodovskaia, Sofia Perovskaia, Liubov and Aleksandra Kornilova, Nadezhda Skvortsova (another student at the Alarchin courses), Mark Natanson, and a number of other men, seventeen people in all, moved into two neighboring cottages at a summer resort. Koval'skaia, who had had to go south for her health, did not take part. The group set out to define the tasks at hand. Someone, probably Natanson, had already worked out a systematic study program of physiology, psychology, and political economy. Natanson led their discussions, thereby justifying some of the women's earlier fears. "He turned our attention to details and made us draw conclusions from what we had read," Kornilova remembered. "It took us a while to notice that the conclusions did not emerge from our heated debates, that Natanson had prepared them beforehand, and that he was leading us in a direction that he himself had charted." Still insecure intellectually and committed to working with men, the women did not protest. When Kornilova's turn came to summarize a chapter of John Stuart Mill, she felt like a student at an exam, unsure of what she knew, although she answered the test rather well.[27] The group also engaged in mutual criticism in order to get to know one another better and to work out their differences in preparation for practical activities.[28]

Even these relatively harmless endeavors did not escape the attention of the authorities. Soon after they had settled into the cottages, the police swooped down and arrested one man, Nikolai Chaikovskii, and summoned the rest to the Third Section on the following day. The interrogation yielded nothing incriminating. Chaikovskii was soon released, and the group resumed its activities. Of greater import was the Nechaev trial, which began that summer. The trial was public, and newspapers published detailed accounts. The group followed it with great interest. Nechaev's program, his organization, which required its members to adhere blindly to an unknown center, as well as the story of Ivanov's murder, repelled them all. The trial reinforced their desire to base their own organization on close friendship, mutual trust, equality, and, most of all, high moral standards. It might well have served to make the women more wary, too.

By the end of August, they had chosen as their political work "the cause of the book" (*knizhnoe delo*). They would acquire and distribute books, at low prices, to libraries and to other circles that the group would help to establish. Soon after that decision, Nadezhda Skvortsova and four of the men left the group.[29] The rest made their headquarters in an apartment on Kabinetskaia Street. Vera Griboedova (Kornilova) registered as the mistress of the house; Natanson, Chaikovskii, two other men, and Olga Schleissner lived there too. Over the next few years, a number of other men and women joined the group. Among the women were Anna Kuvshinskaia, who had been fired from her teaching job for "nihilist tendencies," and Larissa Chemodanova, whom she had helped to free.

Until its demise in 1874, the Chaikovskii circle engaged in a variety of activities, all aimed at fulfilling the debt that intellectuals felt they owed the people. During the winter of 1871–2 the cause of the book flourished, supplied by a printing press run by Vasilii Aleksandrov in Zurich and by some publishers and booksellers who sold them books at discounts of 30 to 50 percent. They distributed the books to provincial circles, together with reading lists to serve as guidelines for self-education. They had managed to establish links in thirty-seven provinces when the government cracked down on them, warning bookstores not to traffic with them and confiscating their books. In any case, many of the group had grown dissatisfied with work that was limited of necessity to the educated.

Women were among the first to move closer to the people. In the late spring of 1872, Aleksandra Obodovskaia taught in a village school in Tver and then briefly conducted propaganda among the peasantry. Perovskaia assisted a village schoolteacher in Samara, experiencing both the pleasures and the problems of work outside the capitals. Her presence in the village immediately attracted attention, for she dressed in a blouse cinched with a leather belt, a short, dark skirt, and boots. She looked very different from the local women. She acted differently, too, going for long walks alone in the woods, and occasionally sleeping there. Warned by her students that the boys of the village thought her a witch and boasted that they would murder her, she only laughed. In the words of someone who knew her that summer, she was in her Rakhmetov phase (after the ascetic hero of Chernyshevskii's novel *What Is to Be Done?*), eating milk with kasha, sleeping on a straw pillow, and rowing herself back and forth across the river.[30]

At that very time, according to the letters she wrote to Obodovskaia in Tver, she was deeply dissatisfied and depressed by her work, which brought her no closer to the lives of the people and provided no basis for political action: "I've had such a bad case of the blues these days it's been impossible for me to get involved in anything. . . . Meanwhile, everything around me is so painfully boring, even the schoolteachers, because they're so sad themselves." Provincial stagnation was far worse than she had imagined. "All around, Aleksandra Iakovlevna, you can sense the reek of a deep, deadly sleep. Nowhere do you see people working and living active and intelligent lives. It's the same everywhere, both in the cities and in the villages. And the peasants struggle on from day to day, having no more thoughts than a dead machine." A feeling of helplessness overwhelmed her. "You feel that the only way out of the situation is to try and shake people like these teachers out of their sleep, to try and help them break out of their situation. But I have neither the knowledge nor the ability for this. Whatever one tries, one cannot carry off. . . . Now I understand why the people who go out to the provinces alone gradually lose their spark and wind up being altogether worthless." She appealed to Obodovskaia to join her. "We can take a place together and devote ourselves to medical work, law and studying."

A month later, nothing had changed. "Mostly I read now; more than ever, I feel the need of knowledge but otherwise the situation is really terrible. All you see around you is the kingdom of sleep." Knowledge seemed to her the only solution. "Different people are struggling but their efforts are always wasted, it seems to me, and I think it's because they have so little knowledge of existing conditions and of theory as well that they can't come to the right conclusion once and for all about what must be done." Yet knowledge by itself was not enough. "Inactivity, staying alone between four walls all day long, shuffling books, talking with one person and another – it brings me to such a state of apathy and mental dullness that I can't get into any book, and everything, from myself to everybody and everything around me, disgusts me."

Occasionally the frustration of being unable to act directly on her ideals became almost unbearable:

Sometimes you want so badly to do something besides reading books and talking that your condition simply becomes abnormal – you run from corner to corner, or roam the woods, and then you sink into the deepest apathy. It's imperative for me to work – in part even physically, for five, six hours daily; then my theoretical work goes better, too.

Here, undoubtedly, lies the key to the activities remarked by her friend. Perovskaia's experience was typical: "All the letters I've been getting indicate a really foul situation – everywhere people are struggling and nothing comes of it."[31]

At the end of August, her commitment to the peasantry unshaken, Perovskaia took a different tack: She departed for the countryside, after having taken a few lessons in vaccinating from a local *zemstvo* doctor. With a few instruments and a certificate testifying to her right to vaccinate, she at last went to the people. In her eagerness to learn how they lived, she chose to share their life as much as possible. She went on foot around the neighboring villages, stopping at each one for a few days to vaccinate its residents. She slept and ate with the inhabitants of the first hut she chanced upon, and the lack of comforts to which she had grown accustomed in childhood seemed to bother her not at all. At first Perovskaia had trouble convincing the peasants to accept her help; they believed smallpox was a sin, a sign of the devil. It took her a long time to convince mothers of the usefulness of vaccination, but she learned to gain their trust by bringing candy for the children. As she acquired confidence, she began to dispense propaganda, trying to shake their faith in the tsar. She also distributed revolutionary literature to those who could read.[32] Her vaccination work completed, she started to help out in a local school.

The following spring, she rejoined her comrades in St. Petersburg, where they had begun to settle in various sections of the city, organizing schools in apartments and propagandizing among workers in the evenings and on holidays. Perovskaia shared a small room on the outskirts of the city with Leonid Shishko, another member of the group, and with him ran a school for workers. She also took charge of correspondence with prisoners in the Peter and Paul Fortress, which she conducted with the help of a policeman someone had bribed. In addition to political work, Perovskaia assumed the role of housekeeper for her apartment, dragging buckets of water from the Neva, serving as cook, and keeping house.

Larissa Chemodanova, Anna Kuvshinskaia, and Aleksandra Kornilova also took part in organizing factory workers. Kornilova, recently returned from studying women's diseases in Austria, read aloud to workers and talked to them about the Viennese Social Democratic movement.

All these efforts proved short-lived. Arrests soon destroyed the group, and by the spring of 1874 everyone had been imprisoned. Some, including Kornilova, Perovskaia, and Schleissner, were to resume activity later in the decade, but the Chaikovskii circle as such had come to an end.

The Chaikovskii circle contributed to the Russian radical movement by its ethical tone as much as by its activities. Petr Kropotkin, its best-known member, later remembered: "Never did I meet elsewhere such a collection of morally superior men and women as the score of persons whose acquaintance I made at the first meeting of the circle of Chaikovskii.

I still feel proud of having been received into that family."[33] As was the case with any family, to be complete it required women. But only women of a certain sort. Convinced that they could influence others by their own principled behavior, the members of the group aspired to purity and total self-sacrifice, and because the men (like other members of their society) presumed that women already possessed these qualities, they expected their women to behave in certain ways, and the women usually did so. The Chaikovskii women were "the purest embodiment of the ideal, limitlessly devoted and self-sacrificing women who have so often inspired our poets and novelists," wrote Petr Lavrov, whose ideas helped to shape the generation of the 1870s.[34]

The men's expectations coincided almost perfectly with the women's own moral self-perception. This facilitated the women's participation in radical activities and gave the women a kind of power. For example, it is likely that the women intensified the group's moral fervor. "The feminine influence on the masculine element gave the membership such a moral character," wrote one historian of populism.[35] The women were certainly demanding. True to their denial of traditional feminine roles, they would tolerate no flirtation or sexual advances. Perovskaia, "a rigorist from head to toe, strict, stubborn and consistent," introduced a particularly strong note of asceticism. Quick to criticize any breach of their ethical code, she once accused a member of being a ladies' man. On another occasion, she attacked a comrade who claimed to be a rigorist but who allowed himself extra expenditures for clothing. As a result, he was expelled from the group.[36] By embracing a high moral code, the women gained a special influence in a group that valued such qualities greatly.

But they paid a price. The moral ideal they embraced excluded such personal satisfactions as intimacy and sexual love. Moreover, in order to join the Chaikovskii circle, they set aside the woman question, and professional aspirations sooner or later gave way to political work. Some of the women tried to combine the two: Kornilova, for example, studied midwifery in Vienna and women's diseases in St. Petersburg before devoting her time completely to organizing. For a while, Kuvshinskaia attended the Courses for Learned Obstetricians newly opened in St. Petersburg. In 1873, Olga Schleissner earned a degree in midwifery, but she never practiced. Perovskaia, released on bail soon after her arrest, trained as a medical aide and worked in a hospital until 1877, when she, too, resumed full-time political work.

Abandoning the woman question meant that women's issues first became subordinated to the struggle of the whole working class and then were forgotten altogether. So far as we know, women radicals never exercised their influence in mixed circles on behalf of women as a group. Even when they organized, radical women rarely focused on their peasant and worker sisters. And of woman-oriented issues – of marriage and the family, equality of education, the right of women to be treated with dignity – they rarely spoke at all.

The pattern would repeat itself in years to follow, when many altruistic and intelligent women felt that they had no choice but to move from the woman question to radicalism. It is difficult not to agree with them. The woman question led to no solution to the inequities that pervaded Russian society, and whatever their disabilities, educated women were, after all, highly privileged in comparison with peasants and workers. Moreover, their experience with women's groups had lasting results. It left them free of many traditional constraints on women, and it gave them some confidence in their own ideas, as well as a sense of sisterhood that remained even after separatism was abandoned. Their male comrades, affected by the same ideas, treated women respectfully and as equals. Acknowledging the difficulties that women experienced in carrying out propaganda activities, men and women alike agreed that women radicals should be granted no special dispensations: "Let the women who could go to the people like the men, in peasant clothes and as best they could avoid the unpleasantness connected with belonging to the fair sex."[37]

Nevertheless, women's battles were far from won – battles for education and individual autonomy, but also battles in the more personal realm of love, sex, and marriage. Perhaps the time was not ripe for struggle in those areas, but when the left subsumed the woman question within the question of the working class as a whole, populism ceased to deal creatively with those personal issues. Never, as a movement, would it return to them again.

CHAPTER 7

HEROINES AND MARTYRS

Nowhere did Russian women's desire for knowledge lead more surely to radicalism than in Zurich, Switzerland. In the early 1870s, the Swiss canton of Zurich sheltered the largest and most politically active emigré colony in all of Western Europe. Zurich had long been a haven for leftists, and at the end of the 1860s the ranks of the Russian contingent were swelled by an influx of young men who had been involved in the student uprisings of 1869. Then came women, attracted by the University of Zurich, which allowed them to enroll on an equal basis with men. By 1873, the colony included more than 300 people, 104 of them women.

In many respects these women resembled their sisters in St. Petersburg. Like the women studying at the Alarchin courses, the Zurich women wanted to serve their society, and they sought knowledge both as a key to autonomy and as the best way to prepare themselves. But unlike the Alarchin students, the Zurich women pursued professional training; most had their parents' approval to travel abroad, and some had their parents' financial support.

Their comparatively privileged status affected these women's ideas. Having avoided the struggle against "family despotism," most Zurich women felt less need than the Alarchin students to develop critiques of the family and personal life. "Generally speaking, as a group the female students abroad were not advocates of the woman question and smiled at any mention of it," wrote Vera Figner, who studied in Zurich during this time. "We came without thought of pioneering or trying to solve the woman question. We didn't think it needed solution. It was a thing of the past; the principle of equality between men and women had been achieved in the sixties."[1] Social rather than personal questions engaged many of them from the first.

The Zurich experience transformed this social awareness into political opposition. Enjoying their new freedom, these women took advantage of opportunities to familiarize themselves with Western European socialist movements and thought. The emigré community fostered these women's political development. So did the women's circles, which drew

127

particularly close in the unfamiliar surroundings, and which enabled the more strong-minded to exercise considerable influence.

These unique circumstances resulted in a greater degree of radicalism among women students in Zurich than among women studying anywhere else. Over 60 percent of the women who traveled to Zurich would later acquire police records, many for quite serious crimes. Of these, the women of the Fritsche group became the best known and most influential.

The Fritsche group consisted of fourteen women, all under twenty, who met in Zurich and quickly became united by intense bonds of personal friendship and shared political conviction. Young and inexperienced, they acknowledged as their leader Sofia Bardina, no older than the rest, but considerably more mature both personally and politically. With Bardina at their head, the women participated in the life of the colony, visited socialist meetings, and engaged in a comprehensive study of socialist literature and thought. These experiences channeled the women's altruism, gave it a political focus, and indicated the appropriate course of action.

The Zurich experience, crucial to the members' political development, was shared with other women of the emigré colony; what made the Fritsche group unique among the women radicals of the 1870s was the fact that their political consciousness was forged in a group made up exclusively of women. Therefore, examination of the Fritsche group not only reveals much about the influence of Zurich and its emigré colony on the genesis of women's radicalism but also throws into unusually sharp relief some of the special characteristics of women of the radical intelligentsia.

It is Vera Figner, a relative latecomer to the group, who tells us most about it. Figner's memoirs provide a remarkably frank account not only of her own personal development but also of the influence of Zurich, its emigré colony, and the Fritsche group on the making of a revolutionary. She was born in 1852, the first child of relatively prosperous noble parents, who provided her with a sense of authority relations that never ceased to color her perceptions. Her father, Nikolai Aleksandrovich Figner, was by no means as influential as Lev Nikolaevich Perovskii, but he shared a number of Perovskii's traits, particularly a willingness to exercise in quite arbitrary fashion the patriarchal power he enjoyed by law and custom:

Father punished us cruelly and unmercifully. No trifle got past him; we were to hide nothing from father; he demanded unflagging honesty from us and mother was our example. Her heart sank knowing the results of our little crimes, but did not conceal one aspect of our behavior from father. He only stopped beating us girls after he almost maimed me when I was six because of a prank while crossing the Volga on a ferryboat.[2]

However much she wanted to, Ekaterina Khristoforovna Figner, his wife, did not dare to defend the children – indeed, she so feared her husband that she would not even hold them or play with them. Instead, fortified by her strong religious faith and her reading of *Lives of the Saints*, which provided models of endurance, she tried to temper his despotism by subordinating her own will to his and sacrificing herself endlessly for others. In this she succeeded. Vera wrote that "we had the happiness of spending our childhood years in an atmosphere that was full of purity, without domestic scenes, struggles or strife. Only mother's extraordinary tact and amazing restraint performed this daily miracle."[3]

Vera's peasant nurse provided the children with a very different experience of human relationships. Figner discussed more fully than other woman memoirists the relationships between peasants and noble children, and her account provides a clue as to why so many of the latter subsequently came to worship the former. According to Figner, in this rather typical noble family, where mother as well as father maintained a considerable distance from the children, the peasant nurse became for them the single source of affection. Only the nurse loved and caressed the children, and only she permitted herself to be loved and caressed in turn. Her room, which Nikolai Aleksandrovich never entered, became a refuge, a place where the children could pour out their sorrows, where they could express their feelings: "In that deadly barracks atmosphere, the only bright spot, the only comfort and consolation was nurse."[4]

The emancipation of the serfs shook this hierarchical little world to its roots. Vera was nine when it happened, and she mainly noticed the effects on those closest to her: her mother's fury at two maids for leaving, her father's decreasing despotism. The emancipation had an enormous impact on her father, who became a peace mediator to implement the terms of the emancipation and help settle disputes between landlords and peasants. Vera often encountered crowds of peasants waiting to see her father in the corridors of their home. Nikolai Aleksandrovich began to dress differently, too, looking rather like a nihilist in his red shirt, wide pants, and high boots. He even adopted certain radical ideas. Much later, he told his daughter that "if the serfs hadn't been liberated and they had revolted, I would have led them."[5] In her memoirs, Vera explained this dramatic change in her father by attributing it to the profound social transformation that made the slave equal to the master and eroded the moral and economic bases of the old order. Vera's mother, who had "grown stronger morally," also exercised a beneficial influence on Nikolai Aleksandrovich, Vera wrote. As a result, her father ceased to be so despotic, and the atmosphere at home changed markedly.[6]

Two years after the emancipation, Vera entered the Rodionovskii Institute in Kazan, where reforms had modified but not ended the traditional practice of secluding students, and where intellectual curiosity was not encouraged, despite more stress on intelligence and ability, and less on appearances and social graces. When Vera graduated at sixteen, she was playful, but rather childish and frail, and as she later

observed critically, she was quite ignorant of the way that people actually lived.

Her real education Vera owed to her mother. Ekaterina Khristoforovna,
who had received only the most superficial education at home, had
managed against overwhelming odds to acquire a love of learning, and
she passed that on to her daughter after Vera left school, encouraging
the young woman to read foreign languages, and giving her progressive
publications: *Notes of the Fatherland*, the *Contemporary*, the *Word*. Despite
(or perhaps because of) this encouragement, within a few months of
returning to her family's provincial estate, Vera began to grow restless.
"After being enclosed within the four walls of my boarding school," she
remembered, "I was bursting with a joyful feeling of freedom.... This
excess of joy, this heightened emotional state demanded action. I found
it unthinkable that I might live without making some mark upon the
world."[7] The dull routine of provincial life – visits, meals, cards, a little
business – could hardly satisfy her hunger for life. Desiring a larger
sphere than the domestic, she had exactly three options: She could
become an actress, a teacher, or a physician. She chose the third after
reading in the journal *The Cause* an account of Nadezhda Suslova's successful studies in Zurich. She decided she would also go to Zurich.[8]

In order to go to Zurich, however, Vera needed her father's permission. Although her mother fully approved of Vera's plans, legally she
was powerless to help, and Nikolai Aleksandrovich, while assuring his
daughter that she had the capacity to achieve her goals, nevertheless
refused to give her the papers she needed. So instead of going to Zurich,
Vera accompanied her father to Kazan, where he introduced her to society, a tested method of dealing with restless daughters, but in Vera's case
it failed to work: "After drinking at the cup of worldly pleasures, and
even getting a bit drunk, I again asked father to let me go and do what *I*
wanted."[9] Again, he refused. By then, however, Vera had found another
way to get what she wanted. Taking advantage of an opportunity to
marry a man over whom she would have some control, Vera succeeded
in escaping her father, over whom she had no control at all. In Kazan,
Aleksei Viktorovich Fillipov, a young candidate in law who served as a
legal investigator, had fallen in love with her. He pressed his suit, and on
October 18, 1870, they were married. Vera had little difficulty convincing
her infatuated new husband to resign his position in the service and go
abroad to study medicine with her.[10] For the next two years she prepared
herself, in her own word, "fanatically," learning mathematics, physics,
German, and Latin. In order to save money, the couple lived separately:
He continued to work in Kazan, while she remained at her mother's
house in the country and set aside his entire salary for the trip. She used
her dowry and wedding gifts to cover expenses, and by the time they
departed, she had pared their material possessions to a minimum. Her
younger sister Lidia (born 1853) accompanied them.

When she left for Zurich, Vera thought she knew what she wanted from life. As she wrote to a friend, "Aleksei will leave his service to become a *zemstvo* doctor, and I'll set up a hospital and open a school or a workshop. It's wonderful!... Economic independence, formation of my mind, and the need to be useful – that is, useful to others – these are the three goals of my existence."[11] She intended to devote herself whole-heartedly to her studies and planned "to refuse all pleasures and amusements, even the most innocent, so as not to lose a moment of precious time."[12]

The Zurich experience challenged Vera's conception of her future and forced her to reevaluate her ideas. The three arrived in Zurich shortly after the start of the spring semester, 1872, and immediately came into contact with the emigré colony. They could hardly avoid it, because Russian students sat beside them in their classes and in the cafeteria, and on the streets they were easily recognizable – the women with their short hair, dark dresses, and blue glasses, the men with their long hair, red shirts, and careless dress. Most lived on the Oberstrasse, located near the Polytechnic. They existed, especially the women, as most Russian students did – that is, on very little. "Tea and bread, some milk and a little slice of meat cooked over a spirit lamp, amidst animated discussion of the latest news from the socialist world or the last book read – that was their regular fare. Those who had more money than was needed for such a mode of living gave it for the common cause."[13] The center of the emigré community was the Russian library. Founded by Mikhail Sazhin, an adherent of the anarchist Mikhail Bakunin, the library housed a treasury of revolutionary literature. Together with works on history, political economy, and the major social questions of the day, it included all the illegal literature published in Russian and all the leading works of Western European socialism. The "old-timers" who established it intended the library not only for their own use but also to radicalize the students arriving in ever-increasing numbers, and in this they proved very successful. The library, a place where they could speak and read their native tongue, acted as a sort of magnet, and all the Russians gathered there, even those who never became politically active.[14]

Lidia became friendly with other women students almost at once, but Vera found her new world intimidating as well as compelling. Most of the men had been politically active for years, and those women who had arrived earlier and had become caught up in the political life of the colony had soon learned to speak their language: "Everyone else who had arrived in Zurich before me seemed so learned and intelligent. They didn't doubt: they affirmed."[15] It took Figner some time to overcome her insecurity and strike up a conversation with Sofia Bardina, who sat next to her during mineralogy lectures and was to have a decisive influence on her development.

Bardina, like Figner, was of noble birth. She was born in 1853 in the province of Tambov in south central Russia. Her father served as a police officer and was something of a despot, and his daughter always felt closest to her mother, a kind and gentle soul. The daughter of a merchant, Sofia's mother spent her days in housekeeping and childcare. She was terrified of her husband, to whom she strictly subordinated herself, addressing him invariably by name and patronymic – none of which prevented her from getting her way much of the time. Like the Figners, Sofia first learned about authority relations and the efficacy of self-sacrifice at home.[16]

After attending boarding school in Tambov, Sofia went to Moscow to continue her education, and there she encountered radical ideas that reinforced her desire for knowledge. Because it was still impossible for a woman to earn an advanced degree in Russia, she resolved to go abroad. When Vera first met her, Sofia was studying agronomy, with the intention of improving the farming methods on an estate her parents owned in Tver. Bardina soon transferred to the Medical Faculty.

It was not politics, but rather a dilemma she shared with other women, that convinced Vera to attend her first meeting. A few days after their initial conversation, Bardina invited Vera to a gathering of women students planned for the same evening. The women proposed to establish a circle for women only, so that they could learn to think logically. "At meetings with men," Bardina explained, "women usually keep quiet; we feel shy and so we don't say anything. But maybe with practice we'll learn to develop our thoughts logically, and then we won't be afraid to speak in public. A women's circle would be a place where we could learn."[17] Men were to be excluded, because, as one of the more militant members put it, "in our opinion, even the most stupid man would try to gain the upper hand over women." Concerned to develop themselves as fully as possible, most of these women found masculine authority to be a threat to their fragile sense of self. Others responded differently. Generally older and more moderate, they insisted at the first meeting that men should be admitted: "They found it ridiculous that women should be afraid in the presence of men, and thought it would be both more natural and more expedient to form a joint self-education circle without fear of masculine competition."[18] Having gained the opportunity to study, they evidently considered their struggles over. They were drowned out by the majority, who insisted that initially only women students be admitted.

In the sense that the Zurich women felt a strong psychological need to exclude men in order to learn to think for themselves, they were repeating the experience of the women of St. Petersburg. But whereas the form seems similar, the content differed significantly. In St. Petersburg, women students discussed almost exclusively matters relating to their experience as women; in Zurich, by contrast, political issues absorbed and divided women from the first. For example, the first topic for discussion was suicide, an odd choice for a group of youthful pioneers in women's education.[19] The question was whether or not suicide should be regarded as psychologically abnormal, but in keeping with the spirit of the times, the speaker also tried to place the problem in a social context. After arguing at length that every suicide was the product of psychic disorder, she concluded that in the final analysis "suicide must be categorized with syphilis, prostitution and crimes against property." All arise from social conditions, from poverty and from powerlessness. To get rid of suicide and all social ills, the existing order must be destroyed and replaced with a new and just order. She exhorted her listeners to study the diseased social structure of Russia as they studied medicine and to consider the measures necessary to cure it.[20] The second paper, given by Varvara Aleksandrova, was more explicitly political. Aleksandrova, born in 1852 to a wealthy Moscow merchant, had come to Zurich to study medicine. She chose as her topic the peasant rebellion of Stenka Razin, whose destructive fury had terrorized members of the upper classes in 1670 and 1671. Totally idealizing Razin's personality, the paper evoked heated debate as the members divided over the question of science and civilization: Did science and civilization yield benefits to humanity, or did they merely oppress the majority of the people? The meeting grew chaotic, people shouted at one another, and the chairwoman proved totally unable to maintain order.

Such political differences soon destroyed these women's fragile unity, but during its brief existence, their group served the important purpose of enabling a number of like-minded individuals to get to know one another and form circles more suited to their needs. One such group was the Fritsche circle. It included Sofia Bardina, Vera and Lidia Figner, Varvara Aleksandrova, Vera and Olga Liubatovich, Beta Kaminskaia, Evgenia, Maria, and Nadezhda Subbotina, Dora Aptekman, and Anna Khorzhevskaia. If Ekaterina Tumanova, a more peripheral member, is added, the group numbers fourteen. Sofia Bardina became their acknowledged leader.[21]

Bardina had encountered two of the members of the circle, the Liubatovich sisters, while all three were living in Moscow. Olga, born in 1854, and Vera, born in 1856, were the daughters of a political refugee from Montenegro. They spent their childhood in comfortable surroundings, their father being the owner of a prospering brick factory in Moscow province. Their mother, the daughter of the owner of a gold mine, died when the sisters were teenagers. Very well educated for the times (Olga wrote that "she had studied in the best French boarding school in Moscow and had spent time in the company of a number of writers at the home of one of her school friends"), the mother undoubtedly influenced her daughters' desire to study. Her education may also have left her dissatisfied with the restricted life of women. Her daughter Olga certainly felt that way at a very early age. As a child, she had prayed to God for hours on end that He might make her into a boy. The opportunity for higher education provided another way to escape conventional femininity. Olga was eighteen when she traveled with Bardina to Zurich. Vera Liubatovich, only sixteen, followed her sister soon after, leaving high school after three years without completing her studies. Both sisters enrolled in the Medical Faculty.[22]

Beta Kaminskaia, later a close friend of Olga Liubatovich, came from quite a different background. She was born in 1854 to a well-to-do Jewish merchant. Her mother died soon after, and her father, though loving, left her very much to herself. Beta used her almost limitless freedom to read widely, which left her feeling isolated and different from the people around her. Eventually she came to terms with her loneliness and resolved to devote herself to science. After first refusing her, her father permitted her to go to Zurich. There she finally found people who thought as she did. A friend described her as a "passionate, impulsive Southerner, as fervent as a medieval prophetess."[23]

Like Kaminskaia, Dora Aptekman was a Jew, born in 1852 to a petty bourgeois family in Kharkov in the Ukraine. While attending a girls' high school, she came under the influence of her cousin, Osip Aptekman, subsequently a major populist leader. "To get to know our unknown life, to see how village people lived," she decided to become a physician.[24] Her parents raised no opposition to her chosen profession, and in 1872 she went to Zurich.

Thanks to their mother, the Subbotina sisters received genuine support for their studies. The mother, Sofia Subbotina, had received a superficial education, but supplemented it by stealing books from her father's study, locking herself up at night and reading by candlelight. At twenty-two she married a candidate in law, who died six years later, leaving her a widow of twenty-nine with a substantial estate and three young girls to raise: Evgenia, born in 1853, Maria, born in 1854, and Nadezhda, born in 1855. Assisted by a governess, Sofia Subbotina taught her daughters Russian, geography, religion, mathematics, French, and music. She herself never stopped learning, reading Rousseau, Voltaire, and Montesquieu and subscribing to progressive journals.[25]

The three girls attended a high school in Moscow that their mother chose on account of its comprehensive science program. During her last year there, Evgenia decided to pursue professional training, because that seemed to her the perfect way to combine her desire for education with the social concerns she had learned primarily from her mother – that is, she would gain the knowledge she needed to serve the people. Her mother proved very sympathetic, providing money for Evgenia to travel, permitting Maria to leave school and go with her, and in addition supporting Anna Toporkova, a friend of her daughters from school, and offering to support Ekaterina Anserova, still another friend. Anserova, the daughter of a village priest, was forbidden by her parents to go, but Toporkova, born in Moscow in 1854 to the wife of a silversmith, accepted the offer and studied with the Subbotinas abroad. In Zurich, Evgenia enrolled in the Natural Science Faculty, and Maria Subbotina and Toporkova entered medical school. About a year later, Nadezhda Subbotina arrived in Zurich accompanied by her mother.

Ekaterina Tumanova and Aleksandra Khorzhevskaia, friends of the Fritsche circle in Zurich, officially joined the circle only after its members had returned to Russia. We know little about them besides their birth dates and social origins. Khorzhevskaia was born in 1852 to a noble family in the province of Kherson. She was educated at home and arrived in Zurich in 1872. Tumanova, the daughter of a wealthy official, was born in 1855 in Tavrida province and attended high school in Odessa.

Despite differences in educational backgrounds and social origins, the members of the group had much in common. Most striking was their youth. Vera Liubatovich was sixteen when she joined the group, and none of its members were older than twenty. Most had gone to Zurich straight from the confining walls of boarding school or high school and had only the vaguest ideas about real conditions in their homeland. Whereas most other women of their age and class had to struggle to gain the right to an education, many of their group enjoyed an unusual level of parental support, sometimes from their fathers, more often from their mothers. Of them all, only Vera Figner had had to marry to gain the freedom to travel abroad. However they may have felt about their daughters' ambitions, the fathers of the other women (except the Subbotinas) had at the very least approved of their travel, because without a father's permission, it was impossible to obtain a passport. Sofia Subbotina had encouraged and even paid for her daughters to go to Zurich. Vera Figner's mother had contributed money, too, and in the fall of 1872 she organized a fund-raising drive on behalf of women studying in Zurich.[26] As a result, these women rarely referred to family despotism, and when they did, they meant the power of the father, never the mother. Because they were relatively free to pursue professional training, the woman question, even when construed as women's struggle for autonomy, never mattered very much to them.

They did care a lot about professional training, however, because it promised both an opportunity to develop themselves and a legitimate outlet for their aspirations. Even so, professional training was not their only goal. Many of these women had learned the moral worth of selflessness in their families, from reading religious works and often from their mothers; others had somehow absorbed it from the culture. As a result, these women tended to conceive of professional training as a means to the end of serving the people.

The Fritsche group intensified these women's altruistic impulses and helped to transform their embryonic political consciousness into a comprehensive revolutionary ideology. It served as both a study group and a warm and protective family, and with the exception of "auntie" Bardina, its members acted like sisters, which many of them actually were. To outsiders, too, they seemed to be a family, which is how they struck Ivan Dzhabadari, later an affiliate of the group, when he first met them in 1874:

We had just sat down when the other, more timid girls surrounded their "auntie" like children; one sat on one side and seized her waist; a third leaned her whole body across the arm of the sofa and seized her shoulder with both hands, and a fourth tried to place herself as close as possible to "auntie". But Bardina, realizing that she was threatened with suffocation, freed herself from these tight embraces and shouted jokingly at her friends "What the devil! They simply won't let me say a word to people!" They all laughed, but didn't change their positions; we laughed too. It reminded us of a picture of childhood.[27]

A surrogate family meant a lot to them. They were, after all, very young and very far from home. And for all the freedom and opportunity Zurich offered them, these women always felt like strangers there. The people of Zurich did not approve of the young Russian women its universities attracted. Nadezhda Suslova, the first woman to arrive, had behaved in exemplary fashion, and even she had had difficulties. Many of those who followed her created more problems by being openly contemptuous of Swiss values, by smoking in public, by perpetually attending meetings, and by going about the streets unescorted.

It was inevitable that they should encounter such difficulties, because having defied convention at home, Russian women students were scarcely likely to conform to convention in another and even more restrictive form elsewhere. For although it is true that Russian radicals rather indiscriminately used the word *bourgeois* to condemn values and behaviors of which they disapproved, these women nevertheless had good reason to perceive that, in some ways, Swiss bourgeois expectations of behavior, feminine behavior especially, were even more limiting than the restrictions imposed on them by authoritarian Russia. Vera Figner wrote of Zurich: "I must tell you that Switzerland is the most bourgeois place in the world, in the sense of reverence for convention, propriety and external appearances." Maria Subbotina echoed her friend's judgment. "In despotic Russia, life is easier," she wrote. "There is no such depressing atmosphere of routine and habit as in free Switzerland." Even Rosalie Idelson, the librarian of the Russian library, and by no means among the most radical of the Russian women in Zurich, wrote to a friend in the most scathing terms about the local youth: "Don't look to them for anything fresh and alive – it's a useless task!" She accused them of being petty bourgeois philistines, overspecialized in their studies and completely given over to abstract philosophizing. Everyone, monarchists

and republicans alike, displayed the same "philistine-bourgeois characteristics; the same callousness, the same desperate ignorance, the same
impenetrable rigidity, the same implacable hatred for anything new."
According to Idelson, women students had a particularly difficult time
in this setting: "Republican students, imbibing all the delights of Dutch
morality with their mother's milk, are not yet ready to part with their
precious ideal of woman – an obedient, industrious servant, tidy cook,
solicitous nurse, wetnurse, fecund she-cow and so forth. As you know,
all these delightful qualities are usually implied by the sonorous and
silly word femininity."[28]

Sofia Bardina, the most mature and most politically developed member of the group, seemed best able to maneuver in these alien surroundings. If any of them behaved too outrageously, there was always "auntie"
Bardina to set things right. "Thanks to her marvelous capacity to conceal
her confusion, even in the case of a total fiasco she could come out the
victor," Figner remembered. "If there was a problem in the kitchen we
hid behind her back; competent and well-spoken, she generously acted
as our perpetual delegate."[29] Her qualities made Bardina a natural leader:

Her sober, sarcastic mind could not stand sentimentality, while her strict and
critical attitude to herself and to others prevented that limitless idealization that
serves as the basis of any thoroughly exalted friendship. Among those green
youths, Bardina seemed much older and more serious than her years, and they
therefore treated her with a measure of respect. She had no special friend in the
circle, because she shared attachments fairly and therefore equally. This naturally increased her over-all influence.[30]

So did the fact that many of her group had regarded their mothers as the
sources of moral authority, which predisposed these young women to
accept a woman's leadership.

Bardina's participation in the activities of the emigré colony also enhanced her position in the Fritsche group. When opposition to the ad-
ministration of the Russian library arose in the fall of 1872, for example,
Bardina was among its leaders. The insurgents resented the fact that the
founders of the library, a group numbering around 20, controlled the
selection of books for readers, who numbered over 100. In the book of
announcements that lay in the reading room, Bardina wrote an article
expressing the general dissatisfaction and demanding that readers, who
already had "equal obligations," be given "equal rights." The leadership
refused to yield; so the insurgents walked out and established their own
library. The Subbotina sisters contributed most of the money to buy the
house for it, and many of the Fritsche group settled on the top floor.[31]
Downstairs, people offered lectures on various subjects. Although women
predominated in the audience, Bardina was the only woman among the
lecturers. During the course of 1873 she spoke on "The Split in the First
International" and on "Socialist Theory." Others, all men, spoke on

"Anarchy and Its Relationship to Contemporary Political Movements,"
"Parties in France from 1787 to 1797," and so forth.[32]

It was Sofia Bardina who played the most immediate role in Vera
Figner's radicalization. Figner had arrived in Zurich determined to devote herself entirely to her studies: "I was enormously enthusiastic – you
could almost say fanatical – about my future profession." Her political
ideas were liberal, and she was motivated by a desire to help others.
"People who are educated and – like me – born to well-to-do families
ought to share my natural desire to assist the poor." She planned at
some future date to help the peasants buy horses and build huts, and as
a doctor she intended to cure people afflicted with various diseases.
Political structures concerned her not at all, nor did fundamental social
change. Her contact with the emigré colony shattered her beliefs: "Like a
bolt from the blue it hit me that I, who was virtually fresh from school
and inspired by the finest aspirations towards science and goodness, I,
at the age of 19 was already an exploiter and my mother and uncle and
all my relatives were all greedy, mercenary exploiters: They belonged to
a privileged minority under whose oppression the masses, the proletariat were born, suffered and died."[33]

She turned to Bardina in her confusion, and Bardina explained how
the system worked. Because they lived off of the taxes that the toiling
masses paid, every government servant (and, in Russia, practically everyone who was educated worked for the government) exploited the
people. "If you were a minister or a professor, a forester or a judge, a
peace mediator or a zemstvo doctor, you lived at the people's expense, in
luxury or at least in comfort," Bardina demonstrated calmly. "You engaged in very pleasant and respectable intellectual pursuits, while the
people, who fed everyone and paid for everything, bent their backs,
went hungry and lived in perpetual need and ignorance." To accept this
argument would necessitate major changes in Figner's life. For one thing,
Figner's need to behave in conformity with her principles would require
her to abandon her inherited status: "If it was all true, then I would have
to renounce my position, for it would be unthinkable to recognize that
you are the cause of others' suffering and still retain your privileges and
enjoy your advantages."[34] For another, she would have to separate from
her husband, who did not share these beliefs. Figner seems almost to
have welcomed the latter prospect, because the couple had been having
problems since their arrival in Zurich. Vera remembered: "I had been
troubled by the fact that I had to take the initiative in everything and that
I could not see in him a man larger than myself, who could have a
positive influence on me." Their interaction with the emigré colony
exacerbated these socially imposed expectations:

An abyss opened between my husband and me as soon as we came into contact
with different people and new questions. He joined with the older, more con-

servative people while I merged wholly with the extremists. At every meeting, on every question, I sharply opposed him.

The more politically conscious Vera became, the more burdensome became the relationship, so that she could think only of how to break things off: "He blocked my path in everything and like a Chinese wall, cut me off from people with whom I agreed." Finally, she left him. "Our relations," Vera explained, "became repulsive to me."[35]

So far as we know, Figner never became involved in another sexual relationship. She sought freedom to develop and act on her new ideas, rather than to express herself personally or sexually. After she left Aleksei, Figner moved into the top floor of the new library building, where the rest of the Fritsche group had settled, and engaged with them in an intensive course of study. The women were preparing themselves for action. To keep up with the contemporary workers' movement, the women read and discussed socialist news. They systematically read the socialist theorists in historical sequence, then studied national movements and revolutions. A man who worked with them a few years later was struck by the unusually high level of their political development: "They were the most prepared for revolutionary activity of any of the people I'd met, men as well as women."

Political interests did not detract from their formal studies. With the same earnestness they attended lectures and studied medical texts. "We valued our anatomy lectures highly, work in the anatomical theatre in particular," Figner recalled, "and we never missed a physiology lecture." As a rule, Figner remarked, the women studied harder than the men. Bardina took the lead in this, as in every other sphere of the circle's activity:

[She] insisted on the need for serious theoretical and professional preparation for our future activity. She read a lot herself, drew up "papers" as one does in self-education circles, and at the same time she eagerly followed her lectures, first in the Polyteknikum...and then at the University where she had transferred to the Medical Faculty after deciding that medical training was more appropriate for settling among the people.

For the moment, at least, professional aspirations and the desire to serve the people were not in conflict.[36]

Their ignorance of conditions at home made it easier to pursue both goals at once. It was European theories and European conditions that they studied. They did not sign up for the lectures on "Russian Emigration and the Russian Emigré Press," "The Student Movement in Russia," or "The Reform of February 1861 and the Disorders that Followed" when they were offered at the Russian library, preferring instead to hear about revolutionary history and organizations. When workers struck in Zurich, many of the Fritsche group contributed to their fund. Lacking knowledge of their native land, they assumed that they could learn about their own workers by observing those abroad. "I didn't regard the workers' movement I knew as a product of Western European life. I assumed that the same teachers would be valid for any time or place," Vera Figner explained at her trial in 1884. The Fritsche group took every opportunity to acquaint themselves with the Western European movement. They often attended meetings of the International Workingmen's Association, both the Marxist and the anarchist wings. In the fall of 1872, the struggle between Marx and Bakunin for control of the organization had finally led to its breakup, but the Fritsche group ignored the finality of the rift. To them, Figner remembered, "the appearance of unity remained."[37]

Nevertheless, these women preferred Bakunin's ideas to Marx's when it came time to think about their own course of action.[38] The insurgent library possessed a German edition of *Das Kapital*. Neither the Liubatovich sisters nor Beta Kaminskaia borrowed the book, but Bardina probably did, because, according to Figner, Bardina carefully explained Marx's labor theory of value to her as they walked the corridors of the Russian library house. When the Fritsche group studied the socialist theorists, they very probably assigned Bardina, their most politically sophisticated member, to read and explicate Marx. Still, it is unlikely that all the Fritsche circle understood Marx "very well," as Ivan Dzhabadari claimed.[39] Moreover, whatever contribution Marx may have made to their theoretical development, when it came time to plan what they were actually going to do, it was Bakunin who seemed to these women to be more relevant. After all, he was a Russian by birth and knew Russian conditions. Yet he also cut a figure in the West, having spent much of the time since his escape from Siberian exile in European radical circles. More than any other radical of his time, Bakunin seemed to straddle both worlds – Russia and the West.

Moreover, his ideas may have held special appeal for women such as those of the Fritsche group. In his various blueprints for a new society, Bakunin was unusually scrupulous about the position of women. All the liberties he carefully enumerated were to be enjoyed by "men and women" alike. Legal marriage would be abolished, children would be raised communally, and women would receive all the social and political benefits of the new order.[40] The Fritsche group spent time with Bakunin in Zurich and were familiar with his ideas, and it is likely that they influenced the women in his favor.

But Bakunin appealed not only to women's residual concern with women's issues; more important, he touched off their moral fervor by insisting that knowledge would only widen the gap between the upper classes and the people and that students should abandon their studies to go foment revolution in the countryside.

The longer they lived in Zurich, the more convincing became Bakunin's call to action. Everything these women learned in the West seemed to testify to the imminence of revolution. The Paris Commune of 1871, though abortive, had shown that workers could run their own city. Many workers attended the meetings of the International. And when the women looked homeward, there, too, they found encouragement:

We looked hopefully to the Russian people. There had been great popular explosions in the past: There was Razin, Pugachev and the revolt of the Haidamaks [a book about the Haidamaks was one of the most popular in the Russian library]. In fact, from the outset the entire history of serfdom had been the history of popular protest. In the most recent past, peasant riots had occurred sporadically throughout the first half of the nineteenth century. And hadn't the tsar himself said, before he emancipated the serfs, It is better to free the serfs from above, than to wait for them to free themselves from below? . . . Bakunin also claimed that revolution was imminent, and that their very position made workers and peasants into socialists and revolutionaries.[41]

But if the Fritsche group truly believed in imminent revolution, shouldn't they abandon their studies and hasten home to participate in it? Their growing radicalism created a painful conflict for the women that the moral absolutism of the group served to exacerbate. Despising the moderation that seemed the essence of bourgeois conventionality, the women vied with one another as to who had the most revolutionary fervor, choosing, inevitably, foreigners and men as their models: "The Fritsche had the most extreme views, and as if showing off for each other, we all chose as heroes the most irreconcileable leaders of the great French revolution. Some were attracted by Robespierre, while others would be satisfied with no less than the 'Friend of the People' Marat, who demanded millions of heads." The group was not monolithic. Still, they asked a lot of themselves and of each other. Maria Subbotina, ill with pneumonia, refused to heed a doctor's advice to go south for six months. She had no right to spend so much money on herself, she declared. "The asceticism of some, requiring denial of all the goods of the earth, approached the fantastic. One day, Bardina carelessly admitted that she liked strawberries and cream and was teased by the group to which she belonged. From that day on Vera Liubatovich, with perfect sincerity, began to consider her a 'bourgeois'."[42] At some point, the women also agreed to renounce sexual relations.

Their values contained a religious element that heightened the tendency to extremism. "Jesus taught that self-sacrifice is the most supreme act of which man is capable," wrote Vera Figner, remembering how much she and her classmates had been influenced by the Gospels. "It was the most authoritative source we knew, not only because we had grown used to seeing it as a holy book in childhood, but because of its inner spiritual beauty."[43] Even after they had ceased to be religious, they retained religious ideals.

The religious element strengthened the appeal to action. To the comfortable existence of the educated it contrasted life among the people. It would be a life of toil and struggle, perhaps, but one that would conform to their highest ideals. Figner wrote: "All the work that a physician does began to seem simply egotistical. None of it would demand spiritual strain or struggle with myself, nor would it elevate me." Viewed from this perspective, medical training lost its value. "If I helped the peasants by working as a physician I would endure neither filth, nor deprivation nor suffering; and I would fail to live up to my ideal."[44]

This way of thinking had its darker side. "Despite our absolute certainty of the masses' revolutionary mood and readiness to act, despite our belief in the proximity of social revolution and its ultimate victory over the entire existing order, we made a strange distinction between our own fates and the radiant prospects of revolution," Figner remembered later. "About ourselves we were always pessimistic; we would all perish; they would persecute us, lock us up, send us into exile and hard labor." Under certain circumstances, this willingness to accept martyrdom became the active pursuit of it. A sad perversion of Figner's idealism echoed in the ravings of Beta Kaminskaia, released from prison in 1877, after she had lost her mind in solitary confinement. "The goal of a socialist's life is death," she told Figner then.

Only through death is socialist propaganda possible; only then is it most effective. What can you say to workers about socialism? What can they make of all our talks, lessons, and explanations? These are absolutely worthless. . . . Perishing is another matter altogether. Should an arrest occur at the factory, the whole place would be in an uproar. Thousands of workers would know about it and immediately ask: arrested – for what? What sort of man have they arrested? What books did he have? What speeches did he make? People will start talking and hundreds and thousands of workers become interested.[45]

The growing tendency toward self-sacrifice notwithstanding, the Fritsche group continued their medical studies until forced to abandon them. The prospect of a legitimate outlet for their moral aspirations served at least temporarily to keep those aspirations under control. Only when the government blocked even legitimate outlets did these women turn to radical action. As Vera Figner wrote, "if it were not for the persecution I am not at all certain I would have become a socialist at that time."[46] Ultimately, it was government harassment that fully unleashed women's moral absolutism.

Officials at home had long disapproved of Russian women studying abroad. In 1872, after Ekaterina Khristoforovna Figner raised money to assist the women in Zurich, local officials compelled her to return the funds to the donors. In Zurich, rumors persisted that if women students returned to Russia to visit, their passports would be confiscated. In 1873, a confidential circular, listing "suspicious characters," warned district officials that those on the list must not be permitted to teach school. Forty-four of the suspicious women had studied in Zurich. Many had acquired no police record at all, despite the zealous efforts of agents planted in the colony to uncover their radical activities.[47]

Matters reached a critical point on May 22, 1873, when the *Government Herald* published a decree ordering women students to leave Zurich. Women who continued to attend lectures after January 1, 1874, it warned, "will not be admitted to any occupation the permission for which is dependent on the government, or to any examination or Russian institute of learning." The decree accused the Zurich women of neglecting their studies for radical politics and free love – the two inevitably linked in governmental minds: "The undignified behavior of the Russian women has aroused the indignation of the inhabitants, and even the proprietors of boarding houses accept them unwillingly. Some of these girls have fallen so deep that they are making a special study of the branch of obstetrics which in all countries is punished by criminal law and despised by honest people." Because Courses for Learned Obstetricians had recently opened in St. Petersburg, the decree declared that young women who continued to study in Zurich would automatically be suspect.[48]

The women in Zurich were incensed. Not only did the decree force them to end their studies prematurely, it libeled them as well. The Swiss reacted sympathetically on the whole. Professors were outraged, university officials met, and on June 8 the entire university senate convened to discuss the problem, although it took no meaningful action. Some people, however, began to regard the women differently: "It reached a point where foreigners began to treat us as prostitutes. With utter seriousness they would tell us that we'd earn more in dissipated Paris than in frugal Switzerland."[49] Although they soon realized that they could study elsewhere in Europe, the women in Zurich did not want to let the insults go unchallenged. They wanted to protest publicly, in print.

A general meeting was called, for women students only. Even the students who generally did not attend meetings, the "placid-liberal bourgeois" faction, as Figner called them, appeared. But their differences proved insurmountable. The older women, closer to completing their studies and with more to lose, tried to demonstrate the futility and danger of a public protest. Following an angry debate, they announced that if the younger women protested in print, they would sign their names to a counterprotest. Because this would have completely discredited a public statement, no one took action. Some evidently did not take the government's threat seriously, because three of the women who were enrolled in the Medical Faculty and three in the Philosophical Faculty continued to study in Zurich for several years after the government ordered them to leave, and two (one in each faculty) managed to earn their degrees.[50] The Fritsche group, however, departed Zurich angrily. They felt betrayed by the government, and this strengthened their determination to overthrow it.

Before they left, they drew up a program to formalize their group, hitherto based on friendship and shared interests. Anarchist in orientation, the program was copied word for word from the Bakunist Swiss (Jura) Section of the International. Nowhere did it consider that conditions in Russia might differ from those in the West. But, as Vera Figner aptly put it:

Could anyone really have expected us to understand our native land? We were all young, fresh from boarding school when we went abroad and settled in a free country – an environment totally alien to Russia – as if it were our natural element. Everything we saw, heard or learned about Western European conditions and attitudes we interpreted as being totally applicable to Russian life – to the Russian village, to the Russian factory, to the Volga peasant and Ivanovo-Voznesensk. The initial program... reflected our total estrangement from everything native, everything Russian.

Steeped in the literature of Western Europe, they chose to organize industrial workers, not peasants. Still, agrarian revolution remained their eventual goal. Factory work in Russia was seasonal, they reasoned; so the workers they organized would spread socialist ideas to the peasants when they returned to the villages at harvest time. They also chose a mode of action appropriate to the conditions in Russia. In order to conduct propaganda successfully among the people, the Fritsche group resolved to "take to plain living" – to engage in physical labor, to drink, eat, and dress as the people did, "renouncing all the habits and needs of the cultured classes."[51] Manual labor alone could preserve them from the danger of exploiting others. No longer did they speak of doing cultural work among the people or of becoming *zemstvo* doctors.

Nevertheless, almost every one of them tried for a while to continue her education, as did the majority of other women medical students who had become politically involved in Zurich. In order to complete their training, eight went to Bern, two to Paris, and one to Philadelphia, whereas five enrolled in the St. Petersburg courses as the government had intended. Six more contented themselves with becoming midwives.[52] At first, the Fritsche group seemed to follow a similar pattern. Bardina, Lidia Figner, Varvara Aleksandrova, and Maria and Evgenia Subbotina went to Paris and enrolled at the Sorbonne; Beta Kaminskaia, the Liubatovich sisters, Anna Khorzhevskaia, Anna Toporkova, Vera Figner, and Dora Aptekman moved to Bern. Only Ekaterina Tumanova returned immediately to Russia, but she, too, attempted to complete her training, enrolling in midwifery courses in St. Petersburg.

The women who continued their medical studies in Paris faced greater hardships than they had in Zurich. Students paid higher fees there and had to purchase their own microscopes and equipment. The women had very little left for room and board, and someone who knew them at the time estimated that they lived on one-third less than a simple Parisian worker. One of the rooms in their apartment had no ventilation, and they took turns sleeping in it. Called in to treat one of them, a French doctor warned that they would simply waste away if they continued to live under such conditions.[53]

Although separated from the emigré colony, the Fritsche group maintained their commitment to revolution. In Paris they got to know a worker named Fesenko, and through him they learned about the nationalist movement in Serbia, whereupon they appointed Vera Figner to go to Serbia to help the local forces in the interest of international solidarity. When she refused, Maria Subbotina and the Liubatovich sisters left school to go in her place. The rest were soon faced, once again, with intervention by the Russian government, which forced them to leave the Sorbonne. By this time, their money was running out, and the women feared entering a third university, sure that their government would force them out once more. If these women felt singled out for persecution, they were probably correct, because three other women who had gone to Paris from Zurich were permitted to complete their studies. Abandoning hope for a medical degree, Aleksandrova, Bardina, and Lidia Figner went to Geneva to enroll in midwifery courses, and Evgenia Subbotina studied sociology and economics. They were joined by Aleksandra Khorzhevskaia and Beta Kaminskaia, both of whom left Bern voluntarily.

In Geneva, these women decided to affiliate with a group of Georgian men whom they had encountered earlier in Paris. Two of the men, I. S. Dzhabadari and Mikhail Chikoidze, had traveled abroad in order to learn the blacksmith trade, in preparation for going to work with the people. The third, Aleksandr Tsitsianov, they met at a conference of Transcaucasians, where the three of them had been among a small minority advocating alliance with revolutionary Russians. Returning to a café after one of the meetings, the men encountered two young Russian women, utter strangers, who asked to borrow 500 francs. After some hesitation, Dzhabadari gave the money to the women and was rewarded by an enormous smile from Varvara Aleksandrova, who had just joined the two strangers, and whom he knew from Paris. They invited him to visit them that very evening. When he arrived, he found seven or eight women in a crowded room. To him they seemed very fresh and young – like a family. After the usual formalities had ended, they began to talk of Russia, of recent arrests, and of the need to replace those captured. It soon became clear that they were as eager to return to Russia as he. The conversation then turned to questions of ends and means. All of them concurred on the necessity of organization, but they feared centralization. They were reacting against Nechaev's example and had been influenced by anarchism, renouncing any authority, whether in the family,

church, or government. They concluded that if the members of an organization are truly committed to liberty, there can be no place in it for
people who want to dominate. There were other issues that needed
resolution, but because the desire to return was uppermost in all their
minds, they shelved negotiations until a future meeting in Russia. They
did agree to merge, however, and to call themselves the Pan Russian
Socialist Revolutionary Organization (PRSRO), with Moscow, where their
comrades had already been captured, the center of their activity.[54] But
before the union could be considered final, they had to obtain the agreement of the remaining Fritsche group.

By that time, only Vera Figner and Dora Aptekman remained in Bern.
The colony there was far smaller than at Zurich and far less political. So
long as the Liubatovich sisters, Kaminskaia, and Toporkova had remained,
it had been possible to meet daily for readings and debates. But the
others soon left, and neither Aptekman nor Figner was able to generate
enough support for another Russian library. In Bern, Figner noted, the
students were more well-to-do than in Zurich, and they apparently
lacked the social conscience that had led to her own radicalization. Equally
important, in the absence of a radical emigré colony, there was nothing
to foster the political development of the students in Bern. Eight other
women who had acquired police records in Zurich managed to complete
their medical studies in Bern, and several served courageously in the
Russo-Turkish War.[55] The apolitical Bern milieu failed to satisfy the other
members of the Fritsche group, but Figner and Aptekman settled into
their work. This time, the government left them to their books.

Dzhabadari arrived in November 1874 to obtain their agreement to the
merger. Figner and Aptekman willingly consented, but neither wanted
to abandon her studies to join the group in Russia. Figner subsequently
explained her reluctance in terms of her revulsion against a worker's life
and her desire for professional training:

I could see clearly all the beauty of my friends' consistency and sincerity, and I
knew they would be doing the very best sort of work. It tormented me that I
couldn't bring myself to do it too, that I didn't want to become a worker. For so
many years I had longed to go to the university; I had been studying so long,
and the idea of being a doctor had become so much a part of me. Now even after
my plans...had been replaced by the goals of a socialist propagandist, I still
wanted the trappings of a doctor's life. A worker's life was horrible, inconceiv-
able to me![56]

But to Nikolai Morozov, passing through Bern at that time, she gave a
somewhat different explanation. "Almost all my close friends at the
courses in Bern have recently left for Russia to become factory workers
and conduct socialist propaganda," she told him, "but I couldn't make
up my mind to join them, even though I wanted to very much." "Why?"
he asked. She replied:

I'm too attracted to science. Besides, don't you think people should be consistent above all, and finish what they start? We came here to study. If we abandon school midway through and if of 100 girls who enrolled in Swiss universities only a few finish, then won't we give our enemies a chance to say: "Experience has demonstrated that women are neither suitable nor capable of higher education." That's the main reason I'm not leaving. I've begun one thing and won't leave it for another, even if the other is more important.[57]

Both accounts were written long after the events they describe. Figner's account stresses the selfishness of her impulses; Morozov's account stresses her sensitivity to the position of women. If, as seems likely, both reflect parts of the truth, then the version that Figner chose to tell us reveals something about how her later radicalism came to color her memories. Aptekan, who left no account of her feelings, remained with Figner in Bern. She continued to maintain her connections with radicals in Zurich, but for the next two years neither woman communicated with their friends.

By December 1874, the rest of the Fritsche group had returned to Russia. Besides these twelve, the new organization included the three Georgians from Geneva, as well as Georgii Zhdanovich, who had come with Dzhabadari to Moscow, a few revolutionaries who had avoided the first wave of arrests, about ten workers recruited by Dzhabadari the previous October, and four or five others, former students. In all, the group numbered about thirty.[58] Having postponed action for so long, the women wanted to begin work at once. A number of the men in the factories had already begun to organize, and it seemed to the women that they would be able to extend their influence to new factories and for the first time involve women workers.

The men of their group did not want them to enter factories. "We were sorry to abandon young girls who had never in their lives come near a factory to these difficult conditions, which overwhelmed even many women workers," Dzhabadari remembered. Unable to overcome his uneasiness – "I was so frightened by the mysterious world of the factory, with its unknown horrors" – Dzhabadari went himself to inspect the place where the women would work and arranged for trusted workers to be present to ensure their safety. When that first arrangement fell through, Dzhabadari and his friends insisted on meeting the workers who would take charge of the women at a second factory. Only then would the men consent to their starting work. The women never knew of these arrangements, although they were perfectly aware that the men did not like the idea of the women doing factory labor.[59]

The educated men were quite reluctant to enter factories themselves. They probably shared Dzhabadari's distaste for factory conditions and his belief that workers (of which the organization could boast ten new recruits) were best suited to organize other workers. Instead of doing factory labor, male intellectuals of the PRSRO involved themselves with organizational affairs and propaganda among the educated.

No such compunction restrained the women. Having abandoned the professional goals that might have channeled their idealism, they manifested a special fervor and eagerness to sacrifice themselves that the men did not share. Moreover, convinced by their Zurich experience of the necessity of plain living, of engaging in physical labor, drinking, eating, and dressing like the people, they were scornful of hardship and unconcerned with personal well-being. Even their fears – appropriate enough under the circumstances – did not deter them. Beta Kaminskaia started work first. The night before, she and Evgenia Subbotina took one room in a hotel, Dzhabadari and Grachevskii another. All night, Kaminskaia and Subbotina remained awake, Subbotina arranging Kaminskaia's clothing for the following day, fussing over her "as if for her wedding." At three in the morning, Dzhabadari heard a knock at the door. "Take her quickly, gentlemen!" Subbotina whispered hastily. She embraced Kaminskaia and began to cry. "Why are you crying?" Dzhabadari asked Subbotina in amazement. "Oh gentlemen, you don't know how hard it will be for her," she replied. "If it's so hard, why should she go?" Dzhabadari asked in surprise. Beta hurried to the door in silence and they hurried after her.[60] That first week, Grachevskii, disguised as Kaminskaia's brother, visited her daily at the factory, and on Saturday evening he brought her home in a cab. Her friends greeted her as if she had been gone for years.

The men had not exaggerated the perils of factory labor. The work was backbreaking and dirty. The days were long, and often the women had to sleep in dormitories – filthy, stifling, and vermin-ridden – and could not escape to the sanctuary of home at night. Kaminskaia had a very difficult time. She worked first at a factory where rags were sewn together. About sixty workers, mainly women, sat on a damp and filthy floor, breathing air perpetually filled with dust, because the exit provided the only ventilation. Work began at 4 a.m. and continued until 8 p.m., with a fifteen-minute break for breakfast and a two-hour break for dinner, which ordinarily consisted of black bread and salted cucumbers, eaten right there in the shop. After work, women had to do additional labor, cleaning the workshops and dormitories where they slept, washing the floor, and carrying wood and water for the foremen and stewards. They had to wash the men's bed linen at the river and perform other services, too. Exhausted at the end of their long day, the women workers were uninterested in talk of revolution. After three weeks of trying to reach them, Kaminskaia quit and went to a cloth factory that employed about 1,000 people of both sexes. She found life there even harder. She had to be on her feet, working intensively, fourteen hours a day and carry heavy bales of cloth on her back. She worked a different shift every week. She would grow so exhausted that she would have to excuse herself to go to the outhouse in order to catch a few moments sleep on a floor that was filthy with sewage.[61] Kaminskaia still failed to make any progress with the women workers. She found them quarrelsome, jealous, and possessive of their men. Finally, she resolved to break factory rules and go to the men's dormitory, where, thanks to her persistence, she succeeded in forming a small workers' circle.

A few weeks after Kaminskaia began, Sofia Bardina and Olga Liubatovich also started work. Like Kaminskaia, Bardina had no success with her women co-workers. "She found them deaf to propaganda, which bounced off them like peas off a wall," as one of her biographers put it. "It was absolutely impossible to get them interested in anything besides clothes, lovers and gossip." But she managed to make her way to the men's quarters, where she read aloud to ever larger numbers of listeners. Her demeanor protected her from the sexual overtures occasionally endured by her friends, and her literacy she explained by saying that she was an Old Believer, a sect in which literate women were common. A foreman soon discovered her reading sessions, however, and she had to leave the factory.[62]

Despite the men's resolve to allow no more than three women to work in factories (one wonders about Dzhabadari's use of the word *allow*), Vera Liubatovich and Lidia Figner soon began working too. They all ran enormous risks. On days off, for example, the women had to take their revolutionary literature with them, concealed in their knapsacks. If they left such material in the barracks, it might be found in a search. But carrying it brought its own dangers, because the women were searched whenever they left the factory. Lidia Figner was almost caught when a guard tried to detain her, and she had to quit work after only two weeks.[63] Their efforts bore fruit, however. According to Dzhabadari, within two months the combined efforts of the organizers resulted in workers' circles in twenty factories and workshops in the Moscow area.

The group had postponed formalizing its status in order to concentrate on action, but in early February, Dzhabadari assumed responsibility for drafting a set of rules. He began by studying the regulations the Fritsche group had drawn up, which he found full of moral fervor, but lacking in concern for the practicalities of struggle. After he had drafted a new set of regulations, the entire circle convened to consider it. Bardina, Kaminskaia, Lidia Figner, the Liubatovich sisters, Aleksandrova, Evgenia Subbotina, and Anna Khorzhevskaia all attended the discussions, which lasted several days. According to A. Lukashevich, who also attended the meetings, the Fritsche group disagreed with the men on a number of practical matters. Of them all, Lukashevich found Vera Liubatovich, the youngest, to be the most passionate dissenter.

One particular issue over which the men and women clashed was celibacy. Despite the fact that Bardina and Olga Liubatovich had apparently acquired fiancés, as a group the women had resolved to renounce sexual relations altogether for the sake of the struggle. At one point, Varvara Aleksandrova expressed a desire to marry a physician, but an ascetic one who would teach her "only medicine." The men did not share the women's eagerness to subordinate the personal to the political: "Among women, asceticism had reached such an extreme that they tried to make celibacy obligatory for all members. The men fought this ardently, and over-ruled the women."[64]

There were other disagreements over theoretical and organizational issues. They began by discussing the scope of their program. Was it appropriate, someone asked, for revolutionaries to work out the details for the socialist future? Bardina, Dzhabadari, and others said no. Because they believed the revolution was decades away, their task was to undermine the old order; to those lucky enough to be there at the time of the revolution would fall the task of creating the new order. Besides, their views of socialism differed so markedly that an attempt to delineate the future would only lead to argument. Because unity was by far the more pressing need, they should postpone detailing the future. Their immediate demands were for civil liberties: freedom of speech and assembly, equality before the law, without distinction of sex or nationality, and so on.

They also agreed on matters of principle: So as to exert maximum influence, revolutionaries must adhere to the strictest ethical standards in every area of their lives. Certain aspects of Dzhabadari's program, however, were so controversial that they appointed a commission, consisting of Lukashevich, Zhdanovich, and Bardina, to redraft it. Over the protests of Dzhabadari, the commission inserted a clause requiring each member to become a factory worker. In the interest of strategy, Dzhabadari had insisted that it was better to have workers organize workers and intellectuals organize intellectuals. He had warned that women doing factory work might attract the attention of the authorities and endanger the entire organization. The future would prove him correct, but the women, filled with moral fervor and the urge to self-sacrifice, refused to heed his warning. The requirement was included in the program. The regulations reflected the fervor and idealism of the Fritsche group in other ways, too. For members of the PRSRO, revolutionary activity was to take precedence over love and friendship, over every aspect of life. "Everybody must be prepared to sever personal ties for the sake of revolution," the rules read. Nobody could possess personal property. No one could move except with the permission of the organization. The group demanded single-minded devotion of its members. In return, it gave them freedom of activity and absolute equality. Fear of Nechaevism remained sufficiently strong during the early 1870s that participants in this first attempt at a disciplined organization carefully guarded against centralized authority.[65]

Even before it could act on the basis of its new program, the PRSRO suffered its first defeats. The mistress of a worker, suspicious of the time he spent with two women organizers, went to the police. Dzhabadari somehow got warning of their arrival, but on April 4, before the group had finished liquidating their headquarters, the police appeared and arrested Bardina, Kaminskaia, Dzhabadari, Lukashevich, Chikoidze, and four workers.

The loss was debilitating, but efforts continued. Prince Tsitsianov and Vera Liubatovich assumed administrative duties in Moscow, and everyone else fanned out among the industrial centers of Russia. With perhaps a touch of exaggeration, Evgenia Subbotina wrote of her success with workers in Moscow:

I established connections with twenty factories and arranged meetings with workers in the forests or taverns. My efforts were quite successful. Workers travelled from afar to hear the "wise woman who can explain everything"; but I also heard them say: "Lead us! We will destroy the factory!"...I wanted to organize the more capable and mature workers into study groups, but my arrest destroyed my plans.[66]

Olga Liubatovich went to Odessa and then to Tula. Khorzhevskaia went first to Odessa, then to the Caucasus, and finally settled in Kiev. Toporkova, Lidia Figner, Varvara Aleksandrova, and the workers Agapov and Barinov went to Ivanovo-Voznesensk, where Tumanova later joined them. In Ivanovo-Voznesensk the group rented a small apartment and established themselves as a work collective. They slept in the same room, wore simple clothing, and went barefoot, so as to resemble ordinary workers. Toporkova kept house, and Lidia Figner administered their fund, made up of the wages they pooled. The women soon found jobs at a textile factory, under typically appalling circumstances.[67] They came plentifully supplied with illegal literature, which they read aloud and distributed among their co-workers. But before they could build an organization, the police, vigilant because of the growing number of organizers, swooped down and arrested everyone. In an attempt to protect her friends, Lidia Figner claimed that the large supply of revolutionary literature found in the apartment belonged to her.[68]

Their downfall resulted partly from their mode of operation. Evgenia Subbotina had tried to warn them about their failure to observe the most basic precautions. "You're heading rapidly for ruin," she wrote. "You'll make no impact on Ivanovo-Voznesensk, and you'll hurt the entire cause dreadfully. You're being even more careless than the people in Moscow."[69] In their eagerness to reach the workers, the women distributed illegal literature with little regard for the reliability of the recipient; they kept such literature in factories and in homes and carried it on their persons; they risked expulsion by entering the men's barracks to read. All this inevitably aroused suspicion. Nor did the organizational center take much care regarding their conspiratorial practices. In the apartment of Tsitsianov and Vera Liubatovich, people came and went as they pleased. By September 1875, the entire organization was in prison.

Their trial did not take place until February 1877, two years and six months after their arrest. By then, their lengthy incarceration under foul prison conditions had exacted a dreadful toll. Beta Kaminskaia lost her mind after two or three months. Confined to a mental hospital, she was released into her father's custody after he paid 5,000 rubles to the police. When she had regained her health somewhat, she made an unsuccessful attempt to go to the peasantry, then tried to join her friends at their trial in St. Petersburg. Her father prevented her. Distraught, she poisoned herself with matches, dying a slow, painful death and calling for her friends in her last moments. Her obituary, written by Sofia Bardina and Olga Liubatovich while they were still in prison together, and based on a letter sent by a female relative who had witnessed Kaminskaia's death, ends as follows:

"There are no letters?" she asked her father. . . . "Tell me what will become of them. . . . And I will die!" Her father tried to comfort her, saying she would get well and live. Although she could barely understand what was being said to her, and what answers she gave, hearing her father's last words she convulsively pressed his hand and in a terrible dispirited voice cried: "For what? Without a goal, without a cause . . . without my people . . . no, I can't live. But where are they, where are they all?! Lidia, Olga!" She was dead by morning.[70]

Prison shattered the health of Maria Subbotina, too. She refused to succumb to prison discipline and earned herself a term in a punishment cell for trying to stop the beating of a fellow prisoner. The cell, near a stove, was almost unbearably hot, except for a constant, freezing cross draft. She began to spit blood and tried unsuccessfully to kill herself by burning herself alive. In 1876 she was released from prison on the verge of death from tuberculosis. Instead of taking time to recover, she went to work to help those still incarcerated, making bed linen, collecting books and money for them, and easing their lot as best she could. Anna Toporkova also tried to poison herself with matches. A male defendant, Georgievskii, attempted to kill himself by hitting his head against a wall.[71]

The government had planned the trial of the Fifty to discredit revolutionaries, but succeeded in doing exactly the opposite. Both lawyers and defendants knew that they could not expect a fair trial; so the basis of the defense was not to emphasize trying to save the defendants' lives but to explain the ethical bases for the defendants' actions. The trial proved a landmark in the revolutionary movement – the first time a judicial platform was used intentionally to propagate revolutionary views. The fact that sixteen of the defendants were women, all of them young (ages twenty-one to twenty-five), could not have been more helpful. In fact, one of the lawyers got so carried away that he actually began to praise the defendants as women who "refused to pine away at home and instead tried to create a broader sphere of activity for themselves by expending their energies in unparalleled self-abnegation." As would be the case in all political trials of that period, the defendants emerged as the conscience of their society. The fact that these women had abandoned lives of wealth and comfort to live like workers impressed observers enormously; so did their moral fervor and readiness for self-sacrifice. "They are Saints!" proclaimed those who attended the proceedings. Peters, the prosecutor, who showed the defendants no mercy during the trial, was nevertheless touched by them. In a letter of March 13, 1887, he wrote of the "moral suffering" brought on by the necessity to pronounce harsh sentences according to the letter of the law.[72]

At various points during the trial the defendants assumed a more aggressive stance. They protested the prison conditions. Several became so troublesome that they provoked the judge and had to be ejected from the court. Others succeeded in articulating the views for which they were being tried. The high points of the trial were the speeches of Petr Alekseev, a worker, and Sofia Bardina. Bardina's speech, written collectively by all the defendants, was a powerful statement of the movement's goals, as well as a ringing challenge to the government. In systematic fashion, it answered every accusation leveled by the prosecution. To the charge that she and her comrades had undermined the state, Bardina replied that the government would be responsible for its own downfall. She and her comrades were not cruel and violent revolutionaries – quite the contrary, she asserted. If their ideals could be realized without violent revolution, all of them would be much happier. It was not they, but historical circumstances, that made revolution necessary. According to Vera Figner, Bardina was allowed to continue only because she spoke so calmly and quietly "with such tact that even Peters, the fierce prosecutor, only tried to stop her once. She spoke with the sort of rationality and conviction she had had in Zurich."[73] Her calm disappeared only when she concluded:

I do not ask mercy of you and do not desire it. You may persecute us as you wish, but I am profoundly convinced that a broad movement such as ours, which has already existed for so many years and which obviously was evoked by the very spirit of the times, cannot be stopped by any repressive measures. It can be suppressed for a while, but it will burst forth again, which always happens after a reaction of this kind; so it will continue until our ideas triumph. I am also convinced that the day will come when even our slothful and sleepy society will awaken and become shamed that for so long it permitted itself to be trampled upon with impunity, that it allowed its brothers and sisters and daughters to be torn away from it and destroyed for expressing their beliefs freely. And then it will take revenge for our destruction! Persecute us – you have material strength for a while, gentlemen, but we have moral strength, the strength of ideas – and ideas, alas! you cannot pierce with bayonets![74]

The defendants in the trial of the Fifty received harsh sentences. Bardina, the Liubatovich sisters, Aleksandrova, Khorzhevskaia, Lidia Figner, and nine of the men were condemned to five to ten years hard labor. Others were exiled or banished to distant regions. Overcoming the resistance of the women, who were reluctant to ask for favors from a government they despised, and who in any case had no great desire to mitigate their own suffering, their lawyers managed to convince them to appeal for clemency, and their sentences were commuted to Siberian exile.[75] For all but a few, the trial marked the end of their participation in the movement.

Nevertheless, their influence proved substantial. Educated society responded very sympathetically to the women defendants in the trial of the Fifty. Although they had become revolutionaries, these women still manifested characteristics that struck people as compellingly feminine. By virtue of their "high moral qualities, and boundless devotion and self-sacrifice," many felt that they represented what was best in Russian womanhood. According to Vera Figner, several well-placed individuals offered to help them financially. Their attorney contributed 900 rubles toward the needs of the defendants. Even people who did not share their ideas could not help but admire their altruism.[76]

The women in the trial of the Fifty also provided an attractive model for subsequent generations. Wrote E. Salova, who was just entering her teens when the trial took place, these women "left a deep and powerful impression, which for several of us led to serious consequences. . . . I resolved to follow the same path as the women of the Fifty trial."[77]

By the late 1870s, that path had become clear. Official persecution and the limited range of permissible activities made that path narrow and hard. A person who truly aspired to serve the people would have to abandon all other ambitions and drives, all hope for personal happiness and well-being. This was certainly not to everyone's taste. But some people found that such total commitment "elevated the individual, and freed him [sic] from anything commonplace," as Vera Figner later put it. "A person felt more keenly that an ideal lived, and ought to live within him [sic]."[78]

Women who had been steeped in religion during childhood and who had learned the virtues of self-sacrifice at mother's knee proved particularly susceptible to this sort of thinking, and those in the Fritsche group may well have been more susceptible than most, because they had arrived at a radical consciousness in an exclusively female circle, where the members' fervor served to reinforce the tendency toward extremism. But this was a difference in degree rather than kind, because the propensity to self-sacrifice prompted most women who joined the revolutionary movement and made them its most devoted adherents. The presence of such women did more than enrich the movement's forces. The women's moral fervor, their "spiritual beauty," earned populists the sympathy of a sector of the educated public. The quality of their participation increased the movement's legitimacy in the eyes of society, and so helped it gain support, financing, and recruits.

It also contributed to the creation of a sort of mythology, which defined the revolutionary woman as limitlessly devoted and endlessly self-sacrificing, a martyr-heroine. A myth with enormous appeal to women as well as men of the left, it would remain alive in every subsequent revolutionary movement and war.

CHAPTER 8

FINDING A LEGITIMATE OUTLET

It won't do you much good to be a physician. You'll wind up setting aside the revolution in order to deaden the pain of the people around you. Imagine for just one moment the Russian village: picked clean, cold and hungry. You won't have a moment left for propaganda.[1]

The ethical vision that so often inspired women's quest for knowledge did not lead inexorably to revolution. Only a minority of women students engaged in illegal activities, and fewer still made revolution a full-time career. Differences in personality provide only a partial explanation for this. Not all women found devoted self-sacrifice to their taste, but even many of those who did chose to make their sacrifices in ways that were politically acceptable to the authorities. In determining the expressions of women's idealism, objective circumstances often proved as important as personal inclination.

A comparison of the women studying medicine in Zurich with those attending the Women's Medical Courses in St. Petersburg illustrates this point well. Between 1872 and 1881, 796 women attended the courses in St. Petersburg.[2] Only a minority of these students, approximately 10 percent, became involved with the police, and only a fraction of those abandoned medical school for full-time political activity. In Zurich, of the ninety-three women studying medicine between 1871 and 1873, forty-three acquired police records, twenty-seven for relatively serious activities.

In both cases, the desire to escape the narrow confines of traditional femininity, to attain a responsible position in a man's world, and at the same time to be of service to society led women to medical school and differentiated them from their more conventional peers. Constraints on the St. Petersburg students, however, were far greater. From the first, the authorities closely monitored the women's behavior and explicitly connected the women's lack of political involvement with the future of the courses, and thus opportunities for other women. Therefore, although their altruism and willingness to challenge the traditional sexual order and defy convention linked women medical students in St. Petersburg with their counterparts studying in Zurich, the circumstances of their professional training set the St. Petersburg students apart and held the majority of them back from the full-time commitment to radical politics to which their heightened social consciousness might otherwise have led.

Women had been pressing for medical education since the early 1860s, prompted by the nihilist faith in science, their desire to serve society, and their wish for independent professional status. When the Medical Surgical Academy was closed to them in 1864, those who could afford to do so traveled abroad to study, whereas women without means (like four of the defendants in the Nechaev trial) became midwives, for which the requirements were comparatively low and the training of relatively short duration. Women with aspirations to medical training remained unsatisfied with the Alarchin and Lublian courses that opened in 1869. They found the lectures superficial, and they attended only the mathematics and physics classes required for advanced education.[3]

Women's undiminished interest in medical training kept the debate alive. So did the efforts of the women's movement, as well as growing progressive support. Toward the end of the 1860s, some members of the medical establishment began to lend equipment to women and admit them to their lectures, laboratories, and anatomical theaters. Convinced that women would make able practitioners, three medical professors approached the authorities to ask that they establish formal medical training for women. To counter the arguments of the opposition that the female sex, "by virtue of the peculiarities of its makeup and its intellectual and spiritual capabilities," would be unable to pursue higher education,[4] proponents pointed out that women's self-sacrifice, their tolerance and patience at the sickbed – "those feminine qualities that require no proof" – naturally suited women for medicine. To bar women from medical school, they contended, was to risk greater damage to women's well-being than would result from admitting them. The professors reminded their listeners that many women had already gone abroad to study medicine, but "with the help of a foreign morality."[5] This was a transparent reference to Zurich, where women were absorbing radical politics as well as anatomy lessons.[6]

One of the most convincing arguments, however, proved to be the government's own urgent needs. People were dying for lack of qualified medical care. According to one contemporary authority, "fifty percent of Russian children die before the age of two. Innumerable mothers perish in the towns and villages, sacrificed to the incapacity or ignorance of those who assist at birth." Although we know of no reliable surveys of maternal deaths during childbirth, the figures on infant mortality are borne out by a survey of Moscow province for the years 1869–79 showing that of 1,000 newborns, 519 died in the first year.[7] Well-trained midwives (or "learned obstetricians") seemed to be an answer. Even the chief of gendarmes concurred, finding that midwifery, unlike medicine, was perfectly suitable for the female sex.[8] Dmitrii Miliutin, the minister of war, also favored such a solution. Miliutin was a firm advocate of women's medical training, and his support was a crucial factor in the establishment of the courses. In 1870 he came out in favor of "correct, systematic training of midwives in the major branches of medicine, of the sort that only a school for physicians could provide." Having had far better training than ordinary midwives, the graduates of the projected courses would also be prepared to treat female and childhood diseases, as well as syphilis in women and children. A donation of 50,000 rubles by Lidia Rodstvennaia, a noblewoman with aspirations of her own to higher education, overcame the final obstacle, and in June 1872 the *Government Herald* (*Pravitel'stvennyi Vestnik*) announced the opening of Courses for Learned Obstetricians at the Medical Surgery Academy in St. Petersburg the following autumn, under the auspices of the Ministry of War.[9]

The decision was a compromise; the government had withheld support for full medical training for women. The school would open on an experimental basis only. The training would last four years, and its scope would be narrower than that of the regular medical courses, which lasted five years. Moreover, the very title, Courses for Learned Obstetricians, seemed an affront to women who wanted to be physicians. People were aware of the uncertain future of the school. Vera Figner, who for that very reason decided to remain studying in Zurich, recalled in 1884: "The women's academy in St. Petersburg had already been opened, but from the first it showed the same sickliness that characterizes it today."[10]

Still, the announcement in the *Government Herald* set off a wave of activity, with women hastening to prepare themselves for the entrance examinations. With unnecessary vagueness, the instructions read that applicants were to be tested on all subjects taught in women's secondary schools, "in conformity with the rules established for men." Rumors flourished. Wrote one candidate: "I heard from someone that...they want women to fail and so prove the flimsiness of their aspirations and the good sense of their opponents. There are (already!) around 400 applications, and only 70 vacancies!" Newspapers increased the anxiety by estimating the number of applicants to be around 500. The president of the Academy of Medicine, trying to inject a note of calm, achieved just the opposite effect by assuring applicants that the examinations would be easy. To women, this suggested that the quality of the courses would be lowered. Many of the 130 applicants in fact found the examinations easy and the examiners somewhat patronizing.[11]

In general, the eighty-nine women who passed came from more humble backgrounds than their counterparts who studied in Zurich. Only four of the St. Petersburg students belonged to the hereditary nobility. The majority were clustered in the middle ranks of society, and ten

Wife or daughter of	St. Petersburg (1872)[12]	Zurich (1872-3)
Privileged		
Noble	4	14
Civil servant	30	7
Merchant and honorary citizen	8	9 (6 Jews)
Military officer	17	3
Clergy	9	3
Free professional	6	1
Doctor or student	4	1
Nonprivileged		
Petty bourgeoisie (*meshchanstvo*)	6 (4 Jews)	3 (2 Jews)
Lower official	3	0
Peasant	1	0
Craftsman	0	1
Foreigner	1	1
Unknown	0	27
Total	89	70

derived from nonprivileged strata. In subsequent classes, the percentage of women from nonprivileged strata slowly but steadily increased. In large part, this increase resulted from the influx of Jewish women, almost one-third of the classes of 1878 and 1879. (Jews were barred from teaching; so medical school provided escape from their severely restricted lives and a passport out of the Pale.) A comparison with the backgrounds of the women studying medicine in Zurich during the same period suggests that most women who could manage it preferred to study abroad, where they suffered no restrictions and could pursue the same program as men. Complete statistics for Zurich are lacking, but memoirs, biographies, and arrest records provide a partial picture of the ninety-two women studying there in 1872–3.

It is not surprising that a high percentage of the women who went to Zurich came from wealthy noble families or were the daughters of well-to-do merchants, because it was expensive to travel and live abroad, and it placed additional demands on parental tolerance. In Zurich, the one representative of the laboring classes was Anna Toporkova, the daughter of a silversmith, whose education was paid for by the well-to-do Sofia Subbotina, at the request of her daughters, Anna's friends.

In contrast, the students in St. Petersburg tended to be far less well off, and their families far more conventional. It is difficult to generalize about such a diverse group of women, but the biographical information presents a picture of struggle, sometimes economic, sometimes personal, occasionally both.[13] Vera I. Dmitrieva, for example, was born in 1859, the daughter of a serf who belonged to the princely Naryshkin family. After the emancipation, her family grew increasingly impoverished. Vera's mother had taught her to read, and she prepared herself for high school, but then the family could not afford to send her. Learning of her plight, a local schoolteacher offered to help support the child. Word even reached the writer Nadezhda Khvoshchinskaia, and she sent this ambitious young peasant girl a whole carton of books. Only her grandfather opposed Vera, because, in his words, she refused to do "women's work."

At high school in Tambov province, Vera did well academically, but she often got into trouble with the authorities. From her father she had heard tales of life under serfdom that profoundly shook her faith in the tsar, and when she read *What Is to Be Done?*, it indicated to her, as she put it, "the course of my life." In school, she read Herzen and other radical writers and got to know some genuine revolutionaries, at that time recruiting among students and urging them to go "to the people." After she graduated in 1877, Dmitrieva became a village teacher in order to conduct propaganda among the peasantry in her native Saratov. At the same time, she prepared herself for medical school, and in 1878 she began attending lectures.[14]

Aleksandra Arkhangel'skaia, another student, was born in 1851 in Tula, the daughter of a poor village priest. She remained illiterate until the age of twenty, when she taught herself to read and write. At first, she resolved to train as a midwife; then contact with intellectuals led her to change her plans, and instead she decided to go to medical school. In order to qualify, she needed a certificate that proved she had graduated high school; so at twenty-one she took her place alongside ten-year-olds on a school bench. She finished two years later and entered the St. Petersburg medical courses in 1874.[15]

Iulia Kviatkovskaia (a cousin of Antonina Kwjatkowska, the wife of Mikhail Bakunin) was born in 1859 in Siberia, the fifteenth child of a converted Pole who had risen through the civil service to become governor of his town. The father ran his family in typically patriarchal fashion: None of the children even dared to speak before their father gave permission, not even the eldest son, who held officer's rank. All the children feared him, although with Iulia and her older sister he was occasionally tender and playful. The mother was a kindly, rather passive woman who was forever defending her offspring against their father's despotism. At the urging of a friend of the family, a doctor's wife who had aspired to higher education herself, the mother agreed to send Iulia to high school. The doctor's wife proved influential in other ways, too, as she taught Iulia about different ways of living: that it was healthy for mothers to nurse their own children, that a woman did not have to fuss with her hair all the time.

When Iulia was sixteen, the oldest at home, her father died of alcoholism at forty-two, leaving the family deeply in debt. Adopting men's clothing when she was not at school, Iulia became head of the household. She had already read *What Is to Be Done?* and other works of the

1860s, and because of her family's relative poverty, she vowed to support herself. But there were few opportunities where she lived, and her education had prepared her for little but marriage. For a while she thought of becoming a village schoolteacher; then a brother told her about the medical courses in St. Petersburg. She left high school and began to give lessons in order to earn enough money to go there. When her mother withheld permission to enroll in the courses, Kviatkovskaia managed to get a favorite uncle to stand guardian for her.[16]

Maria Rashkevich, born 1859, was the seventh of eight children in a Jewish family in Odessa. Her father, a wholesaler, died when she was only six, and she grew up relatively unsupervised. She finished high school, then worked for two years giving private lessons and teaching in a Hebrew school. Concurrently, she attended scientific lectures offered by a local professor. When she decided to go to medical school, no one opposed the decision. By contrast, Teofilia Poliak, another Jewish woman, had had to wage such a bitter struggle with her petty bourgeois (*meshchanskaia*) family that it left her, in the words of a friend, "sarcastic, distrustful and pessimistic."[17] Elizaveta Pimenova, born 1855, the daughter of a naval officer, resorted to fictitious marriage in order to circumvent her father, who forbade her to go to medical school.[18] Students such as Maria Mordvinova (born Princess Urusova), who had estates in two provinces, were relatively rare, and even Mordvinova prepared for the courses in secret, and then had to postpone her enrollment on account of her father's opposition.[19]

Because only a highly motivated and unconventional woman would be likely to persevere in such a struggle against family and the traditional female role, a student was, almost by definition, partially radicalized. Many students professed aspirations that when held by women were characterized as nihilist by their society: faith in science and a desire to be independent. They were also altruistic. They wanted to "alleviate the plight of the dispossessed, suffering under the yoke of the struggle against poverty," and to devote themselves entirely to the people.[20] Some women acknowledged having read the radical critics of the early 1860s. Iulia Kviatkovskaia and Vera Dmitrieva found encouragement in their writings. Maria Rashkevich had read Marx as well as the Russian radicals and, like Dmitrieva, had moved in revolutionary circles in Odessa before attending school in St. Petersburg. She studied medicine in order "to be useful to the people through specialized knowledge."[21] Nadezhda Golovina, a young noblewoman from an impoverished family, had worked as a governess in a well-to-do family (about 27 percent of all women medical students were certified as governesses). Her hatred for that work, as well as her reading of radical writers, led her to medicine.[22] Other women had clearly been influenced by the temper of the times.

The government, therefore, had reason to be uneasy about the new student body, and it did everything it could to keep these women in line: Students had to demonstrate their political loyalty. They had to be older than twenty. Each student had to present proof of permission to attend from her parents or husband and proof that she knew a family residing in St. Petersburg that would presumably take responsibility for her. School authorities also attempted to monitor their behavior closely. Within the first week, students received a detailed set of regulations that covered the most petty details of life. They were instructed to behave properly at lectures and were absolutely forbidden to speak up either to approve or to disapprove of their professors. Without the permission of the inspectress of the school, they could not leave the city. They were to wear uniforms at all times and observe strict decorum in their toilette. Should anything "unusual" occur, they were to report it to the inspectress at once.[23]

The inspectress was M. C. Ermolova, a society woman of some standing, whose presence seemed to ensure the respectability of the courses. If Ermolova was in charge, people reasoned, the students' morals could not be so bad, and anxious parents could rest assured that Ermolova would not allow young women to dissect the corpses of naked men. Deeply committed to the well-being of the courses, Ermolova took her responsibilities seriously. For instance, she was never without a supply of hairnets for students who had "forgotten" they had to wear them. Students cheerfully flouted such rules, including the one that forbade them to smoke, so that clashes with the redoubtable Ermolova occurred frequently.[24] Still, their rebelliousness always remained within certain bounds. In 1874, for example, male medical students staged a boycott to protest the behavior of a reactionary professor, and they asked the women students to support them. As student agitation escalated, the women found themselves in a difficult position. "Remember," Ermolova cautioned them, "the fate of the courses depends on you. If you participate in the student movement, the courses will be closed. You'd have to answer for that before *all* women." The women explained their dilemma to the men, most of whom proved sympathetic. Overcoming their desire to participate in the strike, the women stood aside. Women students might disregard regulations concerning behavior, but they carefully avoided clashes over substantive issues. School authorities made no secret of the fact that continuation of the courses depended on the good behavior of the students. They were continually reminded that the whole enterprise was so precarious, its future so doubtful, that "the slightest misstep might compromise the courses and serve to close them."[25]

To further ensure their reliability, women medical students were kept separate from the men medical students, who had the reputation of being the most politically active students in St. Petersburg. Women were assigned their own laboratories and anatomical theater. When the women attended lectures in the school auditorium, a porter preceded them, clearing the corridors through which they had to pass. The women were warned not to visit the student library, because the men sat around "impolitely" in their hats and coats. Instead, they were "advised" to visit the women's library, although its collection of journals and newspapers was not nearly so good. The ostensible reason was to protect the women from insults, but when men and women students did encounter one another, the men proved unfailingly polite. There is only one instance of rudeness on record. One student, dissecting an embryo, left it on a table overnight with a note reading, "embryo of Miss N." to identify it as hers. A number of male students found this simply irresistible, and when Miss N. returned in the morning, she found her note covered with commentary.[26]

Most students led a difficult life. Society was hostile to them. Dmitrieva later remembered how people would call after her: "Hey, vivisectionist!" "Hey, you with the short hair." "Disembowelled many corpses?" Laughter, whistles, and howls would follow her as she walked to school.[27] Many students who were from families unwilling or unable to assist them lived on the edge of destitution. There were no stipends allotted the first class, and only six for the second. People's distrust also made it difficult for students to find tutoring jobs. The few who received money from home contributed most of it to a general fund for needy students. Proceeds from benefit performances and other collections supplemented this. A society to support women students, established in 1876, provided stipends to sixty-eight students drawn from each of the four classes.[28] The following year, impressed by the performance of the first class, a few *zemstva*[29] offered stipends to students who agreed to serve in their medical programs. Nevertheless, applicants continued to outnumber stipends, some of which were inadequate to meet student needs, and some of which failed to arrive on time. When Dmitrieva's *zemstvo* stipend came late one winter, she could afford neither a winter coat nor food, and she became gravely ill with pneumonia. Finally, after fruitlessly complaining to the school authorities, she wrote a letter of protest to a newspaper. This brought immediate action. After she had received her stipend, however, school authorities requested that Dmitrieva retract her accusations in writing. She had put the courses in a dubious light, they told her, "and they barely exist through the mercy of the higher authorities."[30]

Approximately one-fifth of these women students came from St. Petersburg and presumably resided with their families. Most of the rest, especially in the early years, lived in genuine poverty. They usually dwelt in one of the poorer sections of town, renting roach-infested rooms that contained little but a bed, a stool, and a small table. Society women administered the eating houses where most students dined. The food was poor, and at twenty-five kopecks per meal, often it was beyond their means. There was neither time nor money for amusement; so student life assumed a dreary monotony. One student left us an account of her day:

I get up no earlier than 8, no later than 9, even on holidays. In the mornings I drink coffee and arrive at school by nine. As soon as the first lecture is over we race to the porter's lodge, throw on our coats and rush over to another building to get a seat in the first row. Lectures are over by three or four, and we all go off to the eating house...then we go home and start work around five...at seven or eight we have tea and after a short rest start work again. We go to bed no earlier than 12 and sometimes as late as one.[31]

Despite youthful energy and enthusiasm, and a seeming ability to go for days without food, these conditions took their toll. Rates of illness, especially nervous exhaustion, were very high. Of the eighty-nine students entering in 1872, twelve died before graduation, eight of tuberculosis, one of smallpox. Two killed themselves. Four died right before the final examination, and one, the daughter of a rank-and-file soldier who had reached medical school entirely by her own efforts, died during the examination itself. With better funding for subsequent classes, the death rate steadily declined. Even so, by 1880, death had claimed fifteen members of the classes of 1873–7.[32]

The circumstances of student life, especially for those who did not have family in St. Petersburg, tended to isolate women medical students from their society and to strengthen their links with the left. The initial decision to attend school had set them apart from their more conventional sisters. Public hostility and poverty reinforced the isolation. So did study habits. "Life has become very narrow and one-sided, everything outside of medical school forgotten," one young student wrote her sister. She found herself talking only to her "cellmates." "I go out in the street in hope of hearing or seeing something different – but no, on the street, too, everything is the same, the same old cells. The whole Vyborg District is filled with medical students."[33] When Dmitrieva was sick, it was her friends from medical school who took turns looking after her.

Sooner or later, most women medical students made friends in the larger community. Contacts were informal, people were friendly, and students residing in the poorer sections, such as the Vyborg, where the school was situated, came to share apartments, meals, books, and ideas. This community provided women medical students with an important network of support. Many of its members were radicals, and contacts between them and women students seem to have been common from the first. Radicals would ask a favor: to use an apartment for a meeting, or to store illegal publications, for example. Dora Tauber, a Jewish student from Odessa, Adelaida Klein, the daughter of a merchant, and Elizaveta Ob'edova, a noblewoman, all lent their apartments to radicals, and they were by no means atypical.[34]

Involvement in the student community meant events that affected radicals affected women students, too. During the early 1870s, when the populist movement was in its propagandist phase, twenty-eight women medical students participated in one way or another. Then, from late

1875 to the late fall of 1877, things quieted down, as the authorities held most activists in prison and seemed bent on intimidating their supporters. Student activism also declined, to revive again in 1877, when the trials of the Fifty and the 193 set the issues sharply before the educated public.

In the trial of the Fifty, women medical students could recognize women very like themselves. Of the sixteen women defendants, eight had studied medicine in Zurich. Two of these had briefly attended midwife courses connected with the Medical Surgical Academy. They had abandoned lives of comfort and privilege to devote themselves to serving the people. Thus they had been true to the highest ideals of their generation, ideals that most women medical students shared. Among the fifteen spectators who entered the courtroom with counterfeit tickets were two women who had studied at the Women's Medical Courses.[35]

The trial of the 193 involved women medical students still more directly. Two of the defendants at the trial had attended the Women's Medical Courses. Eight more students were implicated in the trial or were called to testify. The police suspected two other students of disseminating the minutes of the trial, which was closed to the public and was reported only in cursory fashion in the press. Three more students assisted political prisoners, and a fourth frequently visited one of the defendants at the trial and sheltered her when she was released from prison.[36]

The trial of Vera Zasulich in 1878 also served to mobilize women students, who followed it closely. The press had reported the Bogoliubov affair, and students shared in the general indignation over this violation of human rights. When Zasulich was first arrested, the authorities thought that she was a student at the Women's Medical Courses, and they prepared to call Ermolova, the headmistress, to testify. To Ermolova's relief, Zasulich, rather than one of her students, had been arrested, but the news disappointed some of the students. "We were sorry that this self-sacrificing girl . . . was not one of us," remembered one student. "What endeared her to us and made her such a heroine was her willingness to sacrifice her young life." They envied her for the courage to act unselfishly according to ideals that they shared: "We thought her the luckiest person in the world, and each of us would have liked to exchange places with her. We felt that the anxiety of the headmistress about the integrity of the courses was very petty in comparison to the great deed that this unknown but precious girl had undertaken." At least one woman medical student participated in the demonstration that celebrated Zasulich's acquittal.[37]

Zasulich's shot introduced the terrorist phase of the movement (see Chapter 9). Few women medical students actually became terrorists, but many seem to have sympathized with the terrorists. Aleksandra Arkhangel'skaia was an interesting example. In the fall of 1878, a dedicated young revolutionary woman tried to recruit her. Arkhangel'skaia, who remained unconvinced by her arguments, and always remained on the sidelines of the revolutionary movement, told the activist: "I'm not sure that the route you have chosen will be the best one for 'the people' later on. I lack the temperament [but] I envy you the fact that you've found your path and will follow it unflinchingly." Dmitrieva remembered how an entire class walked out on a professor who dared insult Aleksandr Soloviev, one of the first to try to assassinate the tsar.[38]

During 1878–9, activism among women students rose markedly. Those women students who came to sympathize with the left found that medical studies paled in importance and seemed selfish and too safe. One of the women who succeeded in combining political organizing and study felt guilty because her commitment to the workers was only partial. "One must give oneself to these people completely and not leave them the remains as I was doing," she told herself. Her revolutionary friends concurred, regarding with a certain disdain those students who remained on the periphery of the movement.[39]

Police records provide a useful measure of the impact of the intensified radical struggle on women medical students. During the 1870s the police were continually on the alert, intercepting mail, infiltrating meetings, ferreting out radicals, and harassing their student sympathizers in an effort to isolate and destroy the revolutionary movement. They detained people for being friendly with a known radical, as well as for genuine crimes such as terrorism. The radical activities of women students were concentrated in two periods: 1873–5 and 1878–9.[40] The "crimes" that brought women to the attention of the police in the early period ranged from "suspicious behavior" to actual propagandizing among workers or peasants. In the later period, the accusations tended to be more serious: involvement with an underground press or association with an attempted assassination, in addition to conducting propaganda.[41]

Women who acquired police records

1873	3
1874	18
1875	7
1876	4
1877	5
1878	17
1879	23
1880	unknown

That a significant minority of women medical students participated in radical activities is certainly understandable. The decision to take part in an illegal movement was probably easier in some respects than their initial struggle against family and conventional female roles. Their personal struggles ordinarily had taken place in relative isolation, whereas radical activities occurred within a sympathetic student community and in the presence of compelling role models. Indeed, living apart from parents in the student community may well have been a key factor in political involvement. We do not know the home provinces for all the women who acquired police records, but we know that fifty-nine of them came from provinces other than St. Petersburg, and one of them was from St. Petersburg. According to a biographical dictionary of the revolutionary movement, eighty-seven women medical students were involved politically to some extent, over 10 percent of the 796 students enrolled in the period 1872–9.[42] A disproportionate number (25 percent) were from noble families, but activists came from all other social categories as well, including one peasant (V. Dmitrieva).

It is likely that the actual numbers involved in political activity were somewhat larger than the figures suggest, and it is likely that some who assisted radicals escaped the attention of the police. Iulia Kviatkovskaia is not listed in the biographical dictionary, but she had two brothers who gave their lives to the movement (Timofei was sentenced to penal servitude in 1877, and Aleksandr was hanged in 1880). Kviatkovskaia shared their ideals and very likely helped them out in ways that were unlikely to get her into trouble. In addition, between 1879 and 1881 she roomed with Elizaveta Olovennikova (also not listed in the dictionary). Olovennikova was a young medical student whose two older sisters were committed revolutionaries and who boasted a rich assortment of ties to the movement. In 1880, the police briefly held Kviatkovskaia, but they neither harassed her nor forced her to answer questions, and she managed to finish school and earn her degree. Arrested in 1881 for radical activity, Elizaveta Olovennikova was not so fortunate. Rosalia Bograd, later the wife of George Plekhanov, a founder of Russian Marxism, succeeded in organizing some urban workers in the late 1870s and also succeeded in eluding the police.[43] Several women medical students distributed illegal literature at the courses. There can be little doubt that a significant proportion of women medical students actively sympathized with the left by the end of the 1870s.

Nevertheless, relatively few women medical students willingly left school, nor did they carry their politics into the classroom. When, for example, student demonstrations erupted in the fall of 1878, women stayed away from them. At the end of November, soldiers, cossacks, and police dispersed an enormous demonstration at the Military School of Medicine in St. Petersburg. Among the several hundred people they detained, not one woman student was to be found. Only in the privacy of their apartments did women meet to discuss the demonstration and voice their support.[44] Between 1872 and 1880, a period of unprecedented student activism, the Women's Medical Courses remained free of disturbances.

Women students exercised caution partly to protect other women who might want to go to school and partly to protect themselves. In 1881, when sixty women students out of a class of ninety did go out on strike in an academic action to force the dismissal of a professor they all disliked, the authorities closed the course for the year.[45] The women were perfectly aware that the fate of the school hinged on their behavior, and many radically inclined students still wanted to earn their degrees. The degree would give them a legitimacy they could obtain in no other way, a legitimacy all the more precious because they had severed other ties and set themselves so much apart from conventional femininity. Vera Figner, who had almost completed her medical studies in Bern when she abandoned them for full-time radical activity, expressed vividly the importance the degree continued to hold for her: "Suddenly I realized that the diploma, that piece of paper of which I'd been so scornful, was in fact precious to me: it enticed me and bound me. It would signify official recognition of my knowledge, evidence that I'd finished what I'd started, achieved the single, absolutely fixed goal I had pursued for so many years with such energy, constancy and self-discipline."[46]

The majority of women medical students, who had spent less time than Figner developing their political ideas and were less committed than she to revolutionary struggle, found it all the more difficult to renounce their initial goals. Thirty-two with police records (more than one-third) completed the program. Others petitioned to resume their studies, but without success.

Graduates of the courses rarely became involved with the police. Professional status appears to have reinforced their conception of medical practice as a legitimate way to act on their ideals. Or, to put it another way, being physicians encouraged them to work within the system. The career patterns for former radicals differed little from the patterns for those who had remained uninvolved or at least had avoided arrest. After graduation, they took up the same kind of work, showed the same social concerns, and experienced the same frustrations. The accomplishments of these graduates were substantial. Their sense of professionalism, of clearing a path for other women, of serving the needy, enabled them to face enormous hardship. These very feelings, however, also served to keep their radicalism in check.

The first test of their abilities occurred in 1877–8. Forty graduates of the courses and twelve fourth-year students (six of the fifty-two had police records) traveled to the front to provide desperately needed medical assistance in the Turkish wars.[47] There they worked under abominable conditions. "Many patients are not even placed in tents, but only under curtains," wrote Varvara Nekrasova from the front. "In order to get to them, you have to bend down and crawl on your knees from one patient to the next. Yesterday I examined thirty people that way – and in addition, you crawl out of there covered with insects."[48]

Their credentials gave them no protection from sexual harassment by military personnel. "The men here have ceased to be people at all," wrote Nekrasova. "They've turned into devils; and they're ready to set up harems and be sultans." She was molested by one general and publicly propositioned by three more, and she wrote that other women staff suffered similar indignities.[49]

Nekrasova, a member of the first graduating class, endured the hardship for the sake of furthering the cause of women: "In the name of advancing our movement forward, I could come to terms with conditions even worse than these – I would not only walk through the mud but wallow in it." Working in complete disregard of her own well-being, she soon caught typhus and died. Another woman reacted to the horrors of war by hanging herself.[50] Some of the women turned to male physicians for support against harassment from military personnel, but they did not join together to make official protests.

Dedicated service at the front earned women physicians praise from every quarter,[51] but it did little to improve their professional status or to gain them the equality they desired after they returned home. The first class of students had performed so well that in 1876 the government changed the title Courses for Learned Obstetricians to Women's Medical Courses and expanded the program to five years, in conformity with the courses in other medical faculties. Nevertheless, many male physicians were suspicious of the graduates. Although their degrees qualified women for regular practice, often they were allowed only into the women's sections of hospitals, and some male physicians would refuse to consult with them. Middle- and upper-class patients sometimes distrusted them, and men would occasionally insult them or make sexual overtures.[52]

Moreover, their certification remained temporary and their legal status undefined, which meant that they had no legal right to positions and no recourse if dismissed from one. In one typical case, a woman attempted to set up a practice and was summoned to the local medical board to present her credentials. She showed them her certificate, which turned out to be useless, because the medical department had not informed the local board that it allowed women physicians to practice. In another instance, a woman sent off her documents to a *zemstvo* to apply for a position and received in response a letter addressed to "Midwife so-and-so." The letter claimed that according to her papers, the applicant was qualified only to practice obstetrics and treat diseases of women and children. Because the *zemstvo* required a physician qualified to treat everyone, the letter rejected her for the position.[53]

Despite the exemplary behavior of women physicians, conservative officials never ceased to be suspicious of them. In 1880, the authorities circulated a confidential memorandum that encouraged provincial governors to consult the Third Section before hiring graduates of the Women's Medical Courses.[54] Generally, women received less money than men for the same services or more onerous services. In 1890, a statistical analysis of the average salaries earned by physicians yielded the following figures:

	Rubles per year
Military physicians (men)	1,390
Civilian physicians (men)	1,007
Zemstvo physicians (men)	1,315
Zemstvo physicians (women)	944
Women physicians as a group	723

Only 4 percent of the women, but 23 percent of the men, earned more than 1,500 rubles per year.[55] The government explicitly acknowledged these wage differentials. In 1894, when the State Council took up the question of reopening the Women's Medical Courses, the fact that "women are usually satisfied with a small remuneration for their labor, and are willing to accept assignments in the most remote places" was one of the most convincing arguments raised in their favor.[56] For these and other reasons, women rarely found the satisfaction they had sought in medical practice. A few could take pride in breaking down barriers against their sex. In 1885, for example, A. F. Zhegina became the first woman to be appointed to the staff of a hospital. She wrote to a friend triumphantly: "If I do nothing else worthwhile in my life, this will provide a bit of comfort in my old age. I have cast at least one more stone amidst the countless stones that have begun to fill the immense chasm that continues to separate one half of humanity from the other."[57] But even Zhegina had originally aspired to devote herself "to the people," and in this aim, like many other women doctors, she proved unsuccessful.

As of 1882, sixty-two women, a slight majority of the women graduates, had gone to work for the *zemstva*. Clinics and hospitals employed fifty-four more. Forty-six had set up private practice, and twelve had become interns or had remained assistants in the military hospitals where they had trained.[58] Because it offered a chance to serve the people and to be in daily contact with them, *zemstvo* work tended to attract the more idealistic women. The peasants ordinarily welcomed them, for they were accustomed to medical care from both landlords' wives and women peasant healers. But such work in rural areas heightened their sense of isolation and often provoked hostility from local society. The desire to serve was frustrated at every turn by lack of proper medications and equipment and by the realization that most of the people's medical problems arose primarily from the conditions of their everyday lives.

A. I. Veretennikova was one of the women who experienced this confrontation between expectations and reality. The daughter of a well-educated family and a cousin of V. I. Lenin, Veretennikova chose medicine in order to devote herself to the people. During her years in school she had pursued her medical studies assiduously, avoiding any sort of political involvement. In difficult moments she fantasized about her future work: "Racing to distant corners of St. Petersburg to give lessons, spending sleepless nights over copying or translation which provided me with barely enough money for the next day, and at the same time visiting clinics and laboratories and studying medicine, in moments of doubt and depression I imagined the brilliant prospects of my future zemstvo work." After graduation, she obtained a post in distant Ufa, among the Bashkirs.[59] There, alien customs and long hours prevented her from having much contact with the people, even though she learned the native language. Supplies were so scarce that she spent half of her salary of 1,500 rubles (when she received it) on medicine. Local officials harassed her at every turn. She found that members of the zemstvo pursued only their own well-being and had no interest in the welfare of the people. Totally exhausted, Veretennikova abandoned the position in 1884 after two years of service. She resumed work two years later in Perm, where she died in 1887, a death her biographer attributed to overwork.[60]

Veretennikova was typical of women physicians in that neither professional status nor work among the people brought her the gratification she had anticipated. Generally speaking, physicians in Russia still lacked the prestige and influence of their Western European counterparts, and practitioners of both sexes had to contend with public indifference and even outright opposition. Women found it more difficult than men because of the widespread prejudice against their sex, which intensified the opposition and sometimes deprived them of even the support of their male colleagues. But still more frustrating was their inability to help the people for whom they were prepared to sacrifice so much. In almost every case their idealism encountered the dismal reality of rural or urban Russia: overwhelming poverty, official hostility and harassment, and, worst of all, helplessness in the face of human misery. None of these factors, however, drove female physicians to radical activity. Commitment to their profession and the absence of a radical milieu kept them on the right side of the law.[61] During the next phase of political upheaval, in the early twentieth century, women doctors who became active, like Anna Shabanova and Maria Pokrovskaia, identified themselves with feminist groups, not radical groups.

In 1881, less than a decade after they had opened, the Women's Medical Courses stopped accepting new students, and in 1887 they ceased to operate. The participation of a minority of women students in illegal activities caused many officials to associate all women students with the women revolutionaries who participated so prominently in the efforts to murder Tsar Alexander II. After his assassination on March 1, 1881, suspicion turned into outright condemnation. No minister would take responsibility for a school that purportedly harbored such dangerous women, and for lack of sponsorship the courses ended, to be reopened only at the end of the century.[62]

During the period of their existence, the courses graduated 691 women physicians. Only a fraction of women medical students acquired police records, and only a tiny minority of these abandoned medical school for full-time political activity, in contrast with the women studying in Zurich. In this sense, official fears about the St. Petersburg students were wildly exaggerated, and the fate of the courses was undeserved. Yet, in another sense, the government was correct: Women medical students tended to be more idealistic and more unconventional than their contemporaries, and toward the end of the 1870s they became increasingly inclined to support the radical sector of their community, even when they were not prepared to devote their lives to revolution. They thus represented an active threat to the sexual status quo and a latent threat to the political order.

In the case of the Women's Medical Courses, the government found itself in a typical dilemma: how to satisfy its needs for trained personnel to provide social services and at the same time maintain control over the idealistic impulses that often led people to seek such training in the first place.

The government was well aware of its dilemma. During the 1870s, one of the primary reasons officials offered to justify advanced courses for women was that such courses would prevent women from becoming revolutionaries.[63] In large part, medical training for women succeeded in this aim, not only in St. Petersburg, but even abroad, where women medical students tended to be far more politically active than at home. Only one of the women who earned their degrees abroad (Aptekman) and only one of the graduates of the St. Petersburg courses (Dmitrieva) came into serious conflict with the police while practicing.

It is therefore particularly ironic that one of the first victims of the repression following Alexander II's assassination was the Women's Medical Courses. More than police persecution, imprisonment, and exile, which left revolutionary women thoroughly undaunted, professional status, with all its limitations, seems to have succeeded in channeling idealistic impulses and in providing one of the most effective of all antidotes to female radicalism.

CHAPTER 9

MORALITY BECOMES ABSOLUTISM

The moral fervor and readiness for self-sacrifice that had prompted hundreds of women to strive for education, then to engage in illegal activities, found fullest expression in the People's Will, a terrorist organization that arose at the end of the 1870s. Composed of a small number of committed revolutionaries, the organization required that they relinquish all other loyalties and renounce all other aspirations, aspirations to personal happiness included, and thus it reinforced the tendency to extremism that almost invariably underlay women's radical activism. The greater a woman's detachment from personal relationships and professional commitments, the more likely it was that her moral fervor would become moral absolutism and her capacity for self-sacrifice would turn into martyrdom.

Their fervent dedication earned women an honored position in the People's Will and a status that was in many respects equal to that of the men. But it also served to perpetuate and intensify revolutionaries' idea of women's special role and thus to reproduce within the movement a sexual division of labor that differed from, but also greatly resembled, the divisions that characterized the very social system revolutionaries aimed to overthrow.

From the very first, women figured prominently in the People's Will. There is no accurate count of the party's membership between its emergence and March 1, 1881, when it succeeded in assassinating Tsar Alexander II. Even the estimates of the number of people in its Executive Committee, its leadership, vary. But all accounts agree that the proportion of women in responsible positions was high, somewhere between one-fourth and one-third of the forty or so people who headed the organization in those years.[1] And women apparently made up a substantial minority of the rank and file as well. In the Executive Committee that took shape at the end of June 1879, eight of the eighteen members were women: Sofia Perovskaia, Vera Figner, Olga Liubatovich, Sofia Ivanova, Tatiana Lebedeva, Anna Sergeeva, Maria Olovennikova-Oshanina, and Anna Iakimova. Although these eight women had traveled a variety of paths to terrorism, they held in common an ethical vision that prompted them to sever their ties to conventional society.

173

For example, Vera Figner, who had managed to resist the temptation to follow the other members of the Fritsche group in going to the people in 1874, was compelled by her conscience to abandon medical school only a year later. Her decision was prompted by Mark Natanson, at that time traveling through Europe trying to establish links among all radicals still at liberty. Natanson stopped off in Bern to urge Figner and Dora Aptekman to cease their studies and return to Russia. Their comrades from the Fritsche group were "perishing," he told them, and "from behind prison walls" they summoned Figner and Aptekman to replace them "in the emptying ranks of propagandist agitators."[2]

Although she was just one semester short of earning her degree, Figner found this appeal almost impossible to resist. She approached the decision in moral terms: Knowing her friends were suffering, how could she refuse to come to their aid, merely for the sake of a diploma, "that piece of paper?" Besides, Figner reasoned, if she truly aimed to serve the people (and not merely indulge her ambition), then she could be just as useful working as a medical aide, for which her studies had already prepared her. Once she viewed the degree that way, there was only one choice Figner could make, and she left Bern soon after Natanson's visit.

Figner's initial experiences in the movement fell far short of her exalted vision. For one thing, she soon discovered that the Fritsche group had not summoned her at all, that in order to recruit her, Natanson had lied. For another, Figner found the movement disunited, the radicals undisciplined and lacking a coherent plan of action, and the workers they recruited "corrupt" and interested only in the money the movement supplied them.[3]

Moreover, she experienced difficulties in adapting her moral fervor to the necessities of struggle. A man who worked with Figner soon after her return complained in a letter that she succumbed too frequently to "childish enthusiasms" and did not take her revolutionary work seriously enough. "Almost daily," he wrote, "I had to nag at her and Shatilova on account of their frivolous attitude toward the cause, and each time, I made them cry, Figner especially." Nevertheless, he concluded, Figner was very sincere and "devoted to the cause to the point of self-sacrifice."[4]

The problem was to temper that devotion with self-discipline. For a while, Figner tried working with the Red Cross, an organization established by Liubov and Aleksandra Kornilova and Larissa Chemodanova, to aid political prisoners. The organization was staffed exclusively by women, who tried to be particularly attentive to the prisoners, because as one woman prisoner recalled, they felt guilty about being free while others were behind bars. Members of the Red Cross collected money, cooked for people who required special nourishment, and provided clothes and books. Their work, in the opinion of another prisoner, was "perfect," and everyone who benefited from it appreciated it deeply.

But women who had joined the movement in order to give themselves to a higher cause found the Red Cross unsatisfactory. Its members were occupied, in fact, with a kind of "women's work": repetitive, nurturing, yielding no measurable product. At the same time, participants risked arrest at any moment. It was no wonder that men busied themselves elsewhere, organizing, writing, working in the countryside. What she was doing fell so far short of Figner's expectations that she actually entertained thoughts of suicide. At that point she found herself a replacement, and in the fall of 1876 she prepared to act directly on her ideals by going to the people.[5]

Before she left, Figner severed still another link with her previous existence by filing for a divorce. Figner, still called Fillipova (her husband's name) in the correspondence of friends, had terminated relations with him in the spring of 1875, when she wrote asking him to stop sending her money. But actually obtaining a divorce was extraordinarily difficult at that time. According to the private correspondence of an acquaintance, Figner received one because Fillipov agreed to testify that he was "incapable of conjugal relations." She resumed the name of Figner, then headed for the countryside.[6]

There, too, nothing went as she had anticipated. Between 1876 and 1879, Figner settled among the people twice. The first time, she lived in the province of Samara, where local officials watched her closely and attributed every act of peasant resistance to her influence. She quickly learned that the conditions of peasant life had left the people more passive than militant and that a handful of propagandists could do little to rouse them. Figner worked desperately hard for three months, trying to treat illnesses she knew full well were economic in origin and therefore beyond repair: incurable stomach ailments caused by insufficient food, syphilis among people of all ages, endless sores and diseases of the skin that resulted from the inconceivably filthy living conditions and the absence of a village bath.

To observe all this was a strain on the nerves of a gently bred noblewoman, however radical. Figner's depression did not lift, and her friends in St. Petersburg grew concerned about her state of mind. "How are your nerves?" inquired Aleksandra Kornilova in a letter, and she cautioned her friend about subjecting herself to such suffering. Figner later wrote that one of the worst parts of this experience in the countryside was her sense of helplessness, of being "lost in a sea of peasants . . . eternally patient and passive." For all her efforts, never did she succeed in "looking into the soul of the people," and never did she utter a word of propaganda. Nevertheless, she would have remained had she not been threatened with arrest.[7]

In the winter of 1877, Figner spent several months in St. Petersburg and then returned to the countryside accompanied by her sister, Evgenia. This time they settled in Saratov, where they worked for ten months,

Vera as a medical aide, Evgenia as a teacher. The one person to join them during that time was Nikolai Morozov, who did so because he was in love with Vera Figner. Figner, her mind on "great ideals," not love, responded unenthusiastically to his declaration, and Morozov left Saratov soon after. The women found themselves cut off from the movement and harassed by local authorities. An investigation launched after a terrorist attempted to assassinate the tsar in April 1879 forced the two women to leave. As many of her comrades had already done, Figner concluded that "the absence of political liberty" prevented propagandists from carrying out their program. She returned to St. Petersburg and offered her services to Land and Liberty.[8]

Figner converted unenthusiastically to terrorism, and only because every other path seemed blocked. She would much have preferred to have remained in the countryside acting directly on her ideals, had circumstances not required her to reject the "moral satisfaction afforded by life among the people" in order to join comrades whose belief in the need for political liberty she increasingly shared.[9] In the summer of 1879, Figner reluctantly joined the People's Will.

Sofia Perovskaia adopted terrorist tactics even less enthusiastically than did Vera Figner, and like her friend, Perovskaia made that decision only after years of fruitlessly trying to act on her ideals in other ways. Soon after her arrest in 1874, Perovskaia's father arranged for her release on bail. (Perovskaia must have found it extremely humiliating to be bailed out by her father, against whom she had struggled so hard for autonomy. But the alternative was years of stagnation in prison. A former comrade wrote that father and daughter had a tearful reconciliation but that their relationship soon deteriorated into hostility.) Fearful of endangering her imprisoned comrades, Perovskaia refrained from any political activity, training instead as a medical aide at a hospital in Simferopol, where her patients reportedly adored her for her gentle and sympathetic care. Perovskaia received certification and was about to set out for her first position when the authorities summoned her to St. Petersburg to appear at the trial of the 193.[10]

Arriving several weeks before the trial began, Perovskaia joined the Red Cross and threw herself into its work. In order to gain access to the men's prison, she became "engaged" to a prisoner, Lev Tikhomirov. Briefly, she even contemplated marrying him so as to mitigate his sentence, for married prisoners usually were sent into exile with their wives, whereas single ones were liable to be kept in prison. "Radicals [radikalki] should really marry, if only for that reason," one woman radical argued, and several women evidently agreed.[11] Perovskaia, however, felt uneasy with an arrangement in which personal relationships were used for political ends. When her mother mistook the engagement for a real one and congratulated her, Sofia flew into a rage. "And even if it were real," she cried, "it's still too intimate to make such a fuss about." The marriage never took place.[12]

When the trial of the 193 got under way, Perovskaia adopted a principled stand, figuring among the "protestors," who refused to mount any defense whatsoever against accusations that to them were so obviously groundless, and before a system they all rejected. She was nevertheless cleared of the charges against her and allowed to go free. Intending to liberate political prisoners, Perovskaia headed south for Kharkov in the company of several comrades.

The group plotted two elaborate escape attempts, renting several apartments, establishing surveillance of the prison, and purchasing the appropriate clothes, weapons, and other equipment. Both attempts failed, and after each failure Perovskaia became furious at the men who had worked with her, blaming them "most unjustly" for what had happened. "How could you fail?" she would mercilessly demand of them.[13]

After that, the others left Kharkov, but Perovskaia remained behind to remove all incriminating evidence. The police arrested her three weeks later as she traveled to her mother's house in the Crimea. Perovskaia managed her own escape quite well. That same evening, while en route to St. Petersburg by train, she offered her guards some tea and waited until they fell asleep. At the next station, Perovskaia opened the door of her compartment, carefully stepped over the guards, jumped off the train, and caught the following train to St. Petersburg.[14]

The price of her liberty was the illegal existence of an underground revolutionary. No longer could she live on her own identity papers, nor could she pursue the work she had trained for. Perovskaia returned to the south once again, hoping to liberate prisoners. Land and Liberty, which previously had assisted with funds and personnel, now deemed other activities more important; so Perovskaia worked almost entirely alone. It was an impossible endeavor, and she eventually had to give it up. Her roommate told us how much it cost Perovskaia to abandon to confinement people with whom she shared so much. For several days, Perovskaia wept silently into her pillow, after her roommate had gone to bed.

By the time Perovskaia returned to St. Petersburg in the winter of 1878–9, these failures had left her more receptive to the idea of political struggle. Still, at the Voronezh conference in June, where radicals tried to iron out their differences, she joined with Figner in attempting to preserve the unity of Land and Liberty. Allowing her feelings to blind her to the realities of the situation, Perovskaia argued that disagreements over tactics arose from misunderstandings, that terror and propaganda were perfectly compatible and could be pursued simultaneously. Several of her comrades characterized her case as one of the best examples of how difficult it was for populists to "tear themselves" from the people in order to engage in political action.[15]

Perovskaia found it so difficult that she continued to work with both Black Repartition and the People's Will until December. That fall she told E. Koval'skaia, then a member of Black Repartition, "You know, if you had anything really serious to do right now, I would go along with you. But your group is not engaged in anything serious." Eager for action, Perovskaia finally cast her lot with the People's Will when she learned that it planned an assassination attempt against the tsar. In the opinion of many who knew her, Perovskaia's decision was based less on tactical considerations than on her desire to retaliate against the government. To her brother she explained: "I'm simply taking my revenge for my good friends who have died on the scaffold and in the fortresses."[16]

Olga Liubatovich, one of the more doctrinaire members of the Fritsche group, had less difficulty accepting terrorism. Exiled to Siberia after the trial of the Fifty, Liubatovich escaped in 1878 and made her way to St. Petersburg, where she quickly reestablished contact with the revolutionary movement. She became the lover of Nikolai Morozov, an early and extreme proponent of terror, and she soon adopted his views. The two subsequently withdrew from the Executive Committee on account of its increasing "Jacobinism," which according to Liubatovich threatened the revolutionary movement with "moral death."[17]

The names of the other women members of the Executive Committee have not yet appeared in this narrative, but they, too, were veterans of the movement. One of them was Maria Olovennikova-Oshanina, born in 1850, the daughter of a noble who, she believed, had become an alcoholic because of his frustrating life as a civil servant. During the 1860s, Oshanina had come under the influence of P. I. Zaichnevskii, the author of Young Russia, who had been exiled to Oshanina's native province of Orel. Zaichnevskii was a Jacobin, who believed that a revolutionary dictatorship, rather than the people, would best be able to solve Russia's problems and transform the society. Oshanina adopted his views. She felt profoundly ambivalent toward the peasantry, which in her own words she both loved and hated for their humility and patience. Oshanina placed her faith in the power of the state. If revolutionaries seized political power, she believed, they would be able to effect the changes they desired and lead the way to socialism. Oshanina had no misgivings whatever about the adoption of terrorist struggle; she was one of its earliest and most ardent proponents.[18]

Sofia Ivanova also had little difficulty in adopting terrorism. Born in 1856 to an army officer who spent practically his whole life on campaigns, Ivanova was one of ten children. She grew up almost unsupervised in a remote part of the Caucasus. From books in the officers' library she learned about a sort of life different from her own "stagnant" life and about new people who had much to teach her. When she turned sixteen, she convinced one of her brothers to take her to Moscow, where she took up sewing, then apprenticed herself as a typesetter at a press run by Ippolit Myshkin. Myshkin soon began printing illegal literature, and as a result, Ivanova was arrested and imprisoned for seven months. In December 1876 she was arrested once again for participating in a demonstration, and because this was her second offense, she was held in prison and tried with the 193, where she figured among the "protestors." Exiled to Siberia, Ivanova managed to escape with the help of her landladies. She returned to St. Petersburg at the end of March 1879, an "illegal," and immediately joined Freedom or Death, a group within Land and Liberty that in the spring of 1879 already espoused terror.[19]

Tatiana Lebedeva had more trouble accepting terrorism as a tactic. Born in 1850, the daughter of a municipal judge, she had lost her mother early. At first a brother's family had taken care of her; then they sent her to the Nikolaevskii Institut, a state-run school for orphans. She got a good education there, but under dreadful conditions. Much later in life, Lebedeva still grew upset when she recalled the physical hunger she had to endure and the epidemics of hysteria that periodically broke out among students. After graduation, she went to the provinces to live with the family of another brother. Her sister-in-law, an ardent proponent of the "ideas of the 1860s," taught peasants to read and organized a club in which women enjoyed equal rights with men. Lebedeva observed these activities but did not participate, and when the family moved back to Moscow she resumed a conventional social life.

In time, however, Lebedeva grew bored. She began to read on her own and to attend pedagogical courses, where she made contact with radicals. Soon she joined a branch of the Chaikovskii circle in Moscow. Because she was financially independent, she rented a place of her own and devoted herself to the activities of her circle. (Her brother, a lawyer and a "man of the sixties," had renounced his share of the inheritance and divided his father's estate equally among his sisters.) Lebedeva was first arrested in 1874 because her apartment housed the radical student library. The police held her for eight months, then released her into her brother's custody. He made her promise to stay away from her radical friends, and after 1875 Lebedeva took no part in the movement, but instead trained as a nurse, passed her examinations, and was about to depart for her first position when she was arrested and incarcerated in 1877, preparatory to the trial of the 193.

Although she was acquitted at the trial, like Perovskaia, Lebedeva never returned to her nursing. Instead, she joined Land and Liberty, ran a library for workers, and did some organizing. In the spring of 1879 she went to Kharkov with Perovskaia to arrange escape attempts. She joined the People's Will after the Voronezh conference, when she severed all ties with her family and went underground.[20]

Anna Iakimova, the daughter of a village priest, was the only woman member of the Executive Committee to come from a relatively humble background. In the early 1870s, Iakimova had been one of Anna

Kuvshinskaia's students in Viatka. She was first arrested in 1875 for spreading seditious propaganda among the peasants. The police held her for a year before shipping her to St. Petersburg to be tried with the 193. Iakimova was acquitted. After her release, she conducted propaganda among peasants and then took up work in a factory. She joined Freedom or Death in the spring of 1879.[21]

We have the least information about Anna Sergeeva. In the memoirs of Sofia Ivanova she appears as "Annushka" the student, who played the role of cook to perfection and who became friendly with the superintendent and all the local shopkeepers. We know neither her social origin nor the date of her birth, because she left the revolutionary movement in the midst of the struggle to assassinate the tsar, and she neither wrote memoirs nor inspired the laudatory biographical sketches that provide much of our information on other women revolutionaries.[22]

Each of these eight women was a tested and experienced revolutionary who had acquired self-discipline and knowledge of conspiratorial practices in the years of struggle. To act directly on their ideals, each of them had set aside education, career, and even family. By the time they joined the People's Will, they had severed virtually all ties to conventional society. There remained only the cause and their comrades.

The regulations of the People's Will reflected this total commitment. They required members to subject their own wills to the will of the majority and to set aside family ties, personal sympathy, friendship, and even love for the sake of their goal. Should it prove necessary, members pledged to give up their very lives. These rules governed the activities of both sexes, but the evidence indicates that the women were more likely than the men to find them morally gratifying as well as tactically unavoidable. Wrote Vera Figner: "Had these rules required less of us, they would have left us unsatisfied. . . . But their severity elevated us . . . and permitted us to feel we embodied an ideal." Anna Korba (born 1849) considered the day she joined the People's Will her happiest. "An enormous joy enveloped me," she remembered. "My heart overflowed with rapture. It seemed to me that the hour was already approaching when I'd give my life for the happiness of 'my people.' I experienced the best day of my life."[23]

Such attitudes shaped other people's perceptions of revolutionary women. "She seemed to us the embodiment of everything elevated, excellent, altruistic and ideal. She was self-sacrificing in matters large and small," reads a typical description, written by another woman. Men found their women comrades equally compelling: "The appearance of one such woman increases a man's courage ten-fold, makes the weak decisive and turns cowards into heroes."[24]

Women's fervent dedication was invaluable to the movement. The Executive Committee never grew very large. In addition to the individuals mentioned earlier, nine more joined between 1880 and 1881, two of them women (Anna Korba and Nadezhda Olovennikova, Maria's younger sister). Other people became rank-and-file members of the organization, and still others, such as women medical students, carried out minor revolutionary errands without actually affiliating with the party. The terrorists unquestionably enjoyed the sympathy and support of a section of the educated public that shared their desire for political liberty, if not their goal of socialist revolution. But although liberal sympathizers might applaud, they remained on the sidelines. In effect, the People's Will consisted of a handful of committed revolutionaries who had pitted themselves against the entire existing order.

Women's extraordinary commitment earned some of them leading roles in the terrorist movement. During two years of terrorist struggle, women members of the People's Will participated in virtually every phase of the party's activity. By and large, their male comrades treated them respectfully and as equals, and the women assumed tasks commensurate with their level of experience, skill, and dedication. The level of women's participation in the Russian terrorist movement contrasts markedly with the activities of their socialist sisters elsewhere in nineteenth-century Europe, who were neither so numerous nor so prominent.[25] In part, the high visibility of Russian women was due to a long-standing commitment on the part of Russian revolutionaries to egalitarian relations; in part it was due to the women's experience and the movement's need to make the utmost use of its scarce human resources. The women's moral stature certainly enhanced their position, too.

Yet women revolutionaries rarely demanded an equal position for its own sake. When they dedicated themselves to the cause, they set aside all "egotistical" concerns, including concern for their own status in the movement. In theory, and for the most part in practice, they had become agents of the organization, committed to carrying out its will. When conflicts arose between equality and the requirements of the struggle, revolutionaries of both sexes readily set equality aside.

This meant that whereas several women assumed positions of immense importance and responsibility, others were assigned tasks on the basis of their gender as well as their skill. One of the most typical examples is housework. As one of the men put it, housework was "woman's work," and the memoirs make it clear that although women enjoyed it no more than men, still women did it. Practical considerations were partly to blame. The demands of conspiracy in a society with strictly defined sex roles made it difficult to delegate housework on any basis but gender, and men took advantage of this to avoid tasks they did not like. Aleksandr Mikhailov, the guardian of party discipline, indirectly revealed his attitude toward the more mundane aspects of revolutionary work when he told Vera Figner that "if the organization told me to wash cups, I'd do that work with the same ardor as the most interesting intellectual work."[26] The fact of the matter is that the organization never told men to wash cups, but quite often told women to do it.

Another example is typesetting. The underground presses of the People's Will carried out the essential service of disseminating the party's ideas, and it was women who did much of the work in them. The life of a typesetter was difficult, not so much because of the risk of arrest but because the need for secrecy was so great that press workers had to keep entirely to themselves and were forbidden even to attend meetings. This made their existence extremely tedious, and many workers simply could not bear it.

Sofia Ivanova had done some typesetting in the past, and she agreed to work for the first underground press. She was registered as its *khoziaika*, a word that in this context translates roughly as housewife. Ivanova's assignment required that she cease to live with her lover, Aleksandr Kviatkovskii, a sacrifice Ivanova made without protest. (Kviatkovskii was married, but apparently did not get on well with his wife.) Kviatkovskii helped to locate the apartment on Sapernyi Lane where Ivanova settled with Nikolai Bukh and Anna Sergeeva at the end of August 1879. Ivanova did not particularly like the isolated life, but she was "eager to be active" and wanted to make herself useful.[27]

Despite her amiable demeanor, Sergeeva liked the work even less. Her lively nature chafed at the restrictions, and she was already involved with Lev Tikhomirov, who visited the press often and who eventually managed to get her a different assignment. Maria Griaznova, born in 1858, a peasant and a seamstress by trade, replaced her. Two other men lived in the apartment illegally and worked in the press.

All five of the residents engaged in setting type, but most of the housework was left to the women. Two of the men, Ivanova recalled, simply would not do it. "Infinitely good natured," the third offered to help however he could. Once, he even proposed to cook, but at this the women drew the line. "We didn't especially trust his culinary skills," Ivanova explained. Ivanova's skills were probably not much better. Tikhomirov, who spent considerable time in the apartment, observed that Ivanova, "like all Russian ladies," knew nothing about housework.[28]

More thoughtful comrades would try to relieve the monotony of the press workers' lives by bringing news of the outside world, as well as manuscripts ready for printing. Sofia Perovskaia proved particularly inventive. To the dismay of A. Mikhailov, who was responsible for maintaining party discipline, Perovskaia would arrange theatre parties for the women who worked in the press. Several times during the winter of 1879–80, Ivanova received theatre tickets, and she arrived at the performances to find Perovskaia and several other friends there. During intermissions they could talk as much as they pleased. Perovskaia regarded these meetings as business, as well as pleasure. Without exchanging ideas, how could they avoid becoming overly specialized? she would inquire. Still, Perovskaia never invited men to these parties, as she always felt more comfortable with women.[29]

Even the routine work of the printing presses involved danger. Late one night in January 1880, the downstairs bell rang, and before the press workers even had time to get out of bed, the police were at their door. Ivanova locked herself in her room, and one by one she fed documents into the fire. Her comrades resisted with firearms, but by the time the police smashed down their door, they had exhausted their ammunition. Before the police reached him, one man used his last bullet to blow his own brains out. Everyone else was arrested.

A second press quickly replaced the first, because publications were the essential element in the party's propaganda. Two women set type for this operation, too: Praskovia Ivanovskaia, born in 1853, the daughter of a village priest, and Liudmila Terenteeva, born in 1862, the daughter of a schoolteacher. Nikolai Kibal'chich, although registered as Ivanovskaia's "husband," did not contribute much to their work, because he was occupied with developing dynamite for the party's assassination attempts.[30]

These women typesetters printed articles that almost invariably had been written by men. It is true that Olga Liubatovich collaborated on two articles with her lover, Nikolai Morozov, who co-edited the party's journal, *The People's Will*, before he and Liubatovich withdrew from the party owing to disagreements over policy. It is also true that Maria Oshanina contributed substantially to an editorial that provided theoretical justification for a seizure of power and that Anna Korba, who wrote several articles and did editorial work, became an editor of *The People's Will* toward the end of February 1881. Still, these women were an insignificant proportion of the twenty or so people who wrote for the paper.[31] Women's participation in the intellectual work of the party contrasts sharply with their high visibility in other revolutionary endeavors. This sexual division of labor appears to have been less a consequence of prejudice than of women's inferior intellectual preparation, which left most of them less able than men to conceptualize and articulate their ideas. When women did possess the intellectual qualifications, as did Oshanina, Korba, and Perovskaia, for example, there is no indication that men discriminated against them or questioned their abilities. Quite the contrary.

For the most part, however, women revolutionaries did not aspire to do intellectual work. With the exception of Oshanina, they had not joined the organization to write articles or shape policy, but because they had come to see terrorism as the only way to attain their goals. Therefore, when women did demand a larger role for themselves in the organization, almost invariably they wanted to participate directly in terrorist activities, particularly assassination attempts against the tsar.

The first attempt required mining the tsar's route as he traveled by train from the Crimea to Moscow in the fall of 1879. In Odessa, Vera

Figner helped Mikhail Frolenko obtain a post as railroad watchman, and with his "wife," Tatiana Lebedeva, Frolenko settled in a cottage by the tracks, where the two, almost strangers, shared a bed so as not to arouse suspicion. Frolenko wrote that Lebedeva, ordinarily very strict concerning her relations with her male comrades, "yielded a little for the sake of the cause," and the two lived peacefully, "like brother and sister." Later, when they grew to know each other better, they fell in love and married. But as Frolenko pointed out, "that was a different matter entirely."[32] The operation was well under way when they had to abandon it because the tsar had chosen an alternate route, and the dynamite was needed elsewhere.

The request for dynamite had come from Moscow, where Lev Gartman and Sofia Perovskaia, posing as the Sukhanovs, had purchased a house on the outskirts of the city, right on the route the tsar would travel. The party also assigned seven others, all male, to the task of digging a tunnel beneath the house, so as to plant a mine under the tracks nearby. They had planned this operation carefully. The Sukhanovs posed as merchants, and they furnished their two-story house accordingly. One wall they covered with enormous cheap portraits of the imperial family; on the wall facing these hung the metropolitan of Moscow and other religious worthies. Each room had its own icon corner, and before each enormous icon Perovskaia set half-burned "marriage" candles. Properly impressed by the couple's piety, the neighbors did not inquire too closely into the odd goings-on next door.

The work on the project proved difficult, even dangerous. The tunnel was lower than a man's height; so the people assigned to digging had to crouch for an entire eight-hour shift, breathing air so foul and stale that occasionally the lamps would blow out and the workers would faint. Mishaps plagued them, too: Rain, snow, and frost would destroy their painstaking progress, and they would lose time making costly repairs. Perovskaia was not assigned to the digging. While the men tunneled, she prepared their meals three times a day, swept and cleaned the rooms, and entertained the visitors who frequently dropped by. This work kept her busy from 5 a.m. until midnight. Nevertheless, when the diggers encountered problems, Perovskaia insisted on doing a share of the work, and she somehow managed to cheer and encourage them all.

On the evening of November 18, 1879, having finally completed the tunnel, they set to work preparing the dynamite. This work was exhausting, because the fumes from the nitroglycerin gave people headaches and made them giddy and nauseous, but Perovskaia managed to stand it longer than the others. The following day it was Perovskaia who gave the signal to Shiriaev to blow up the tsar's train. Shiriaev mistook the tsar's train for a testing train, however, and he exploded the train that followed it. The tsar escaped.[33]

The next attempt occurred the following February. A workman the party had planted in the Winter Palace set off an explosion that destroyed a room, killed eleven people, and wounded fifty-six more. To the dismay of the party, however, the explosion left the tsar himself unharmed. The February attack elicited a swift response. The tsar appointed a commission under General Loris Melikov, who was entrusted with the task of regaining the support of liberal society while crushing the revolutionary movement. Under Melikov's "dictatorship of the heart," repression became more selective and rational. The full force of the police apparatus was unleashed against revolutionaries, but only against revolutionaries, and the government made some concessions to the liberals: less stringent censorship, greater leeway for participation in local affairs. Some people mistook this for a step toward a constitution, but its actual purpose was to separate revolutionaries from their sources of liberal support. Evidence suggests that Melikov's policy succeeded to some extent. On the other hand, it presented the People's Will with new opportunities to organize, and the party hastened to take advantage of them. At the same time, it continued its efforts to assassinate the tsar.

The next attempt occurred in Odessa in April 1880. Anna Iakimova, Sofia Perovskaia, Grigorii Isaev, and Nikolai Sablin joined Vera Figner, who had remained in the south after the attempt of the year before, developing contacts among all levels of society and recruiting for the party. This attempt involved another mining operation under a street the tsar might use. The work had not proceeded very far when Isaev, preparing explosives, blew off three fingers one night. Fortunately, Iakimova, his "wife," kept her presence of mind. Expecting the police to arrive at any moment, she refused to flee. Instead, she bound Isaev's hand, cleaned up the blood and bits of flesh that had spattered the room, and got him to a hospital. Iakimova even managed to be present during the operation to ensure that Isaev would not talk under sedation.[34] The group resumed work, but before they were ready, the tsar passed through town, and they had to abandon the attempt.

These repeated failures affected the morale of some women party members. Vera Figner, for example, grew increasingly dissatisfied with the routine work of organizing intellectuals. Figner was supposed to remain behind in Odessa, maintaining her contacts, after everything had been put in order and all the others had left. But Figner was also eager to leave. She had already asked her departing comrades to request a change of assignment for her and to have the party send someone to whom she could transfer her ties, but growing too impatient to wait any longer, Figner departed for St. Petersburg before her replacement could arrive. This was an extraordinary breach of discipline, and it meant the loss of all Figner's contacts. The Executive Committee reprimanded her severely, but it did not expel her.

There is evidence that Perovskaia was also growing tired of her work, although Perovskaia was not the sort ever to defy party discipline. To one friend she wrote that she was wearying of terrorist struggle. She asked another, a member of Black Repartition, to inform her should things start happening in the countryside. Her brother wrote that around this time Perovskaia became so depressed that she contemplated suicide.[35]

When she started to organize workers, however, Perovskaia began to feel better. Taking advantage of the relative freedom that followed Melikov's "reforms," the party intensified its efforts to reach the working class. With Andrei Zheliabov, a peasant by birth and the party's acknowledged leader, Perovskaia spent her days and evenings among the workers of St. Petersburg. To her friends she would speak joyfully of the progress she and Zheliabov were making, of how the revolution was spreading to new groups: "She spoke as if her child were regaining its health."[36]

That summer, she and Zheliabov became lovers, and in September they began to live together in a conspiratorial apartment. Their affair took just about everyone by surprise. Since her early days in the Chaikovskii circle, Perovskaia had been known as a "rigorist" and even something of a man-hater. Moreover, Zheliabov already had a wife and children, whom he had left in their village when he became a full-time revolutionary. To be sure, Zheliabov himself would not have found his family an obstacle, as he had never let it interfere with his relationships with other women. But what about Perovskaia?

It is undoubtedly no coincidence that when Perovskaia finally fell in love, the man was a peasant. His social origins would have gained her sympathy, even as his masculinity put her on her guard. In the fall of 1879, when Perovskaia still vacillated, Zheliabov fought long and hard to win her for the People's Will. The two came into conflict several times, leading Zheliabov to exclaim in frustration: "You can't do anything with that woman!" Yet he proved as strong-willed as she – the only member of their circle strong-willed enough to be her equal, in the opinion of her friends.[37]

Perovskaia must have loved him very much. There is no other explanation for her abandonment of a personal stance she had held for so long. Only a year earlier she had told her brother Vasilii that as long as the struggle continued, she would never become involved with a man: "That sort of personal happiness would be absolutely impossible for me, because however much I loved a man, every moment of attraction would be poisoned by the awareness that my beloved friends were perishing . . . and that 'the people' still suffered under the yoke of despotism."[38]

There was nothing romantic about their life together. They lived in a tiny, poorly furnished cottage. A cheap cloth covered their table; the samovar handle was broken, the dishes and silverware unmatched. They kept no servant, and Perovskaia did the housework herself. People rarely visited them, but occasionally a woman friend would stop by and help Perovskaia with her chores. Constantly under pressure, the two had little time for relaxation, little time even to be together. Still, when their work went well, or when they both managed to forget it for a moment, it was "a joy to see them, especially her."[39]

Even that bit of happiness proved painfully brief. Both Zheliabov and Perovskaia assumed responsible positions when preparations for another assassination attempt began a few months after they started living together. Agents sent to observe the tsar's movements reported back to Perovskaia. They noted that the tsar traveled by Malaia Sadovaia Street on his weekly trips to the riding academy; so they chose it as the site for the next mining operation. The party purchased a cheese shop, and Anna Iakimova and Iurii Bogdanovich settled above it. From the cellar, people tunneled beneath the street to plant the bombs. Should the tsar fail to pass through the street at the appointed time, two revolutionaries had volunteered to hurl bombs at him. This was a last, desperate effort to achieve the goal of regicide, and the party threw all its resources into it.

Andrei Zheliabov held all the threads of the plot in his hands. Then, on the evening of February 27, just two days before the attack was to occur, the police arrested him. Perovskaia, the only other person fully informed of the details of the plot, was also the only one at liberty with sufficient stature to assume command of the operation. On Sunday, March 1, 1881, the attack would take place as planned. On the evening of February 28, Perovskaia stayed at Figner's apartment and tried to get some rest as Figner and three men assembled the explosives.

On March 1, Perovskaia showed great presence of mind. In fact, the tsar did not go along Malaia Sadovaia Street, where the mine had been planted. But Perovskaia had already activated the backup plan, handing the bombs to the "throwers" and arranging to drop a handkerchief when it came time for them to act. Anticipating the route that the tsar was likely to take, she had the throwers correctly positioned when he rode by at 2:15 p.m. The first bomb fell short, but the second found its target, fatally wounding the tsar and Ignatii Grinevitskii, the man who threw it. The tsar died within an hour, Grinevitskii later that evening.

Afterward, Perovskaia's self-control gave way, and she could only repeat brokenly, "They killed him, they killed him." That night, the conspirators gathered to celebrate their victory; Perovskaia arrived late, pale and in tears. People crowded around to congratulate her, but she would not listen. Instead, she kept insisting that the party devote its remaining resources to rescuing Zheliabov.[40]

When Perovskaia came to her senses and realized that this was impossible, she simply ceased to be concerned for herself. Her comrades encouraged her to escape abroad, but Perovskaia refused. During the nine days before her arrest, she wandered from place to place, always on the move to elude the police. A couple of days before they captured her, she spent the night with Vera Figner. "Verochka, can I sleep at your place?" Perovskaia was careful to inquire. Figner wondered how she could even ask. "I'm asking," Perovskaia replied, "because if they search your place and find me there, they'll hang you." Figner hugged her and showed her the revolver she always kept by her pillow. "With or without you; I'll shoot if they come."[41]

Perovskaia was arrested on March 10, and the trial of the regicides began about two weeks later. During Perovskaia's detention, her mother, who had been summoned from the Crimea, visited daily. The two rarely spoke, but Perovskaia would lie for hours with her head on her mother's lap.

When the trial convened on March 26, there were six defendants: N. Rysakov, A. Zheliabov, N. Kibal'chich, A. Mikhailov, S. Perovskaia, and Gesia Gelfman. Gelfman, a Jew and a member of the petty bourgeoisie, lived in the apartment where the bombs were kept on the eve of the assassination. She belonged to the People's Will, but not to its Executive Committee. Perovskaia did her utmost to protect Gelfman by minimizing her responsibility for the assassination.

It was characteristic of Perovskaia that even after she had ceased to care about herself, she remained concerned for her friends. At the trial she made no effort whatsoever to deny her own part in the assassination. "Having given the signal, I went along Nevskii Prospekt, and across the Kazan bridge, to the opposite side of the Catherine canal, where I stood and watched both explosions," she calmly told the court. But she firmly (and untruthfully) maintained that Gelfman had known nothing about it. The trial lasted only six days. All the defendants were sentenced to death by hanging.

On March 30, Gesia Gelfman requested to see N. N. Kolotkevich, her "husband." After the authorities turned her down, she announced she was pregnant. The execution of Gelfman's sentence was postponed, but the remaining five were hanged on April 3, 1881. A rigorist to the last, in her remaining moments Perovskaia hugged each of her comrades but Rysakov, who had tried to save his own life by giving evidence to the police. Gelfman gave birth in a prison cell on October 12. The child was taken from her and placed in a foundling home, and Gelfman herself died on February 1, 1882.

In the weeks after March 1, the police arrested almost all the remaining members of the Executive Committee. They passed the next two decades in prison or in exile.

The idealistic fervor and willingness to put the welfare of the people ahead of their own that had distinguished the women participants in the movement of the 1870s became most extreme during the terrorist struggle and the long years of incarceration that followed. When they joined the People's Will, women embraced – indeed, seemed to welcome – the chance to obliterate the self. As Vera Figner put it, "I was full of hope and certainty that the cause would make such demands on my mental and moral forces that the personal element would be completely excluded from my life."[42] Women refused to submit to their own "weakness" or special needs, even though, as women, they sometimes experienced debilities that men did not. Olga Liubatovich, although pregnant, nevertheless carried heavy containers of explosive fluid; Perovskaia outlasted the men the night they prepared dynamite; Lebedeva subjected herself to the excruciating headaches nitroglycerin produced, despite her ill-health and her friends' entreaties to stop working. When they requested a change of assignment, almost invariably women wanted a more dangerous one: to be transferred from typesetting or propagandizing to the front lines of terrorist struggle.[43]

Radical women displayed a similar eagerness to assume more than their share of responsibility and punishment. During political trials, women radicals almost never tried to minimize their crimes, and many went so far as to exaggerate them in order to assume responsibility for the acts of others. Sofia Ivanova, who had burned papers while her comrades defended an underground operation, claimed at their trial that she herself had done the shooting. (Two of the male defendants, by contrast, denied they had ever touched a revolver.) "My only desire is to share the fate of my comrades, even if it is capital punishment," Ivanova told the court. Tatiana Lebedeva also exaggerated her crimes at her trial. Lebedeva feared that she would be spared capital punishment. "She did not want to fall behind her comrades, so she did everything she could to help the judges string her up with the others," Mikhail Frolenko, her husband, explained.[44] Despite her efforts, Lebedeva was sentenced to life imprisonment.

Having cut themselves loose from the institutions that might have channeled their idealism into more conventional outlets, many revolutionary women preferred to give their lives to the cause rather than live without it. "To a great extent, we had become indifferent to our own fate," explained Anna Korba. With no concern whatever for their own physical well-being, women prisoners engaged in hunger strikes, arranged escapes, defied their jailors, and in several cases took their own lives when that was the only protest possible against violence done a comrade. When they emerged from twenty or so years of living death, some women, Breshkovskaia, Koval'skaia, Figner, and Ivanovskaia, for example, resumed some form of struggle.

This is not to suggest that revolutionary men were any less committed to their principles, but only that for women the commitment was somehow more absolute and in itself a sort of profession. Records from the Kara prison in Siberia shed interesting light on this. The records provide a variety of data on prisoners – date of birth, social origins, date of arrest, and so forth. According to them, almost every male prisoner had a regular occupation (student, writer, teacher, officer), but only one woman, a medical aide, did. The other twenty women listed either had no entry whatsoever in the occupational category or received a political one, such as "illegal."[45] After they had served their sentences, many radical men took up scientific or other professional work. Few women did, or could.

Instead, they spent their remaining years as revolutionaries, either active or retired. After the Bolshevik Revolution of 1917, most men and women activists of the 1870s kept the memory of their movement alive by recording their own history in books and journals, thus helping to perpetuate into the Soviet period a tradition of women's self-sacrifice that was rooted deep, very deep, in the prerevolutionary past.

CHAPTER 10

THE PERSONAL VERSUS THE POLITICAL

During the 1870s, more than 1,000 Russian women made professional or political commitments: By 1880, close to 800 had attended medical school in Russia, and hundreds more had gone to universities and professional schools in Russia and abroad. More than 400 women had been arrested for radical activities between 1872 and 1879, and several hundred more acquired police records during the two years of intensified political activity that followed.

When women of the intelligentsia entered public life, they assumed roles that were both similar to and different from the roles of men. But whatever roles they played, the women tended to be more fervent than men, more self-sacrificing, and under certain circumstances more likely to go to extremes. Some of these differences can be attributed to cultural expectations of masculinity and femininity that affected the consciousness of even the most self-conscious rebels. A complete explanation, however, must be sought in the family, which shaped the personalities and expectations of individuals of both sexes, but laid far greater claim to the love and loyalty of women. In nineteenth-century Russia, as in Europe and America, women were raised to be family creatures. In addition, socialization, tradition, and law, as well as the absence of alternatives in the larger world, locked women into family life far more closely than men and by defining women primarily as daughters, wives, and mothers, made it far more difficult for them to define themselves as anything else. As a result, ambitious women had to engage in traumatic struggle with one or both parents for the most commonplace male prerogatives, a struggle all the more painful and difficult because it meant divesting themselves of the emotional bonds that not only limited but also enriched their lives.

The need to fight free of family ties shaped women's attitudes toward personal life in ways that ultimately affected their public commitment as well. Having acted according to the moral dimension of the traditional female role, women of the intelligentsia tended to relegate the other aspects to second place, or renounce them altogether. Women were understandably reluctant to relinquish their hard-won freedom for mar-

191

riage and motherhood. "I love the movement," responded the young radical Maria Kolenkina, when asked why men's romantic overtures failed to move her.[1] Other women, like Kornilova, Perovskaia, and the members of the Fritsche group, also tried to postpone or avoid involvement. So did the medical student A. I. Veretennikova. Planning to devote herself entirely to the people, she renounced any thought of marriage and family while at school. A substantial proportion of her fellow medical students shared her decision: Only one-fourth of them married while in school, and it is likely that a significant minority never married at all, an unusual phenomenon in a society where every woman was expected to marry, and just about every woman did.[2] At least one woman physician, Iulia Kviatkovskaia, developed a lifelong relationship with another woman instead.[3]

To say that women of the intelligentsia tried to avoid entanglement in traditional roles, however, is not to suggest that they had no feelings or that they all refused to become emotionally involved. Many of them were passionate and intense women, and some, for all their convictions to the contrary, did fall in love, marry, or have affairs. But even when they did, the necessity of subordinating private satisfaction to public commitment, however difficult, ordinarily remained unquestioned. Wrote Ekaterina Obukhova, a minor revolutionary figure, in the spring of 1878: "There is so much going on in social life right now that I don't understand how personal issues can continue to upset me so much."[4] To avoid interfering with her husband's political commitment, Liubov Kornilova thought of getting divorced when he was released from prison in 1877. "At home, he'll find a son who is totally spoiled, and a wife who is going blind," she wrote Vera Figner, apologizing for raising such an "uninteresting subject." Because she had become "totally decrepit and vile" and could no longer be his comrade in the cause, she feared to burden him, and even considered ending her own life, but could not bring herself to do it.[5] When they joined the revolutionary movement, Vera Figner, Ekaterina Breshkovskaia, Anna Korba, and Elizaveta Koval'skaia, to cite only a few examples, severed ties with husbands who did not share their views. Still other women seemed prepared to suppress their feelings for comrades in order to continue the struggle. Ekaterina Obukhova put it succinctly when she wrote to a friend in 1879 that, for her, the cause always came before any man: "A man who put me above the cause, even in a moment of passion, by admitting it to me would destroy everything that connected us."[6] Olga Liubatovich, "the most fanatical of all the Amazons," who nonetheless succumbed to sexual love, phrased it more dramatically: "Yes, it's a sin for revolutionaries to start a family. Men and women both must stand alone, like soldiers under a hail of bullets. But in your youth, you sometimes forget that revolutionaries' lives are measured not in years, but in days and hours."[7]

Women had an additional reason to avoid sexual relations: They led almost inevitably to pregnancy and so to complex and entangling responsibilities. Women who had vowed to devote themselves to a higher cause could not have found motherhood an appealing prospect. Did they know about contraceptive techniques? We cannot be certain. Women of the intelligentsia, reticent enough about their private lives, were absolutely mute on the subject of sexuality and birth control. However, many of them attended medical school and therefore may have learned some methods of birth control, although the evidence for this is tenuous. One piece of evidence comes from the government, which in 1873 accused the Zurich students of studying "that branch of obstetrics which in all countries is punished by criminal law and despised by honest people" – that is, abortion. Another is provided by Valerian Smirnov, then working in Zurich as an editor of *Forward*. In a letter to his lover, Rosalie Idelson, who was a medical student in Bern, Smirnov recommended the vaginal pessary to cure displacement of the uterus, a cause of "hysteria," "melancholy," and even "neuralgia." A woman, he told her, could learn to insert it for herself. "A woman should be as familiar with her vagina as she is with her nose," Smirnov advised. For several decades, doctors had recommended the pessary, a form of cervical cap, as a means of contraception. So far as we know, Idelson did not become pregnant at this time. Neither did Vera Figner, who was married during her medical-school days.[8]

On the other hand, women medical students, like women of the intelligentsia in general, had not struggled against the family role for the sake of sexual freedom. On the contrary. Like the Fritsche group, who advocated celibacy when they joined the PRSRO, or Perovskaia, who held that sexual maturity began around the age of thirty, these women were disposed to cope with the likelihood of pregnancy by avoiding sexuality rather than by planning for it. When they did become sexually intimate with a man, therefore, they risked becoming pregnant. We know from casual references that nine radical women all conceived in the midst of the struggle. Other women's pregnancies may well have gone unmentioned.[9]

How did women of the intelligentsia feel about motherhood? Here, too, we can catch only occasional glimpses of the complex response motherhood evoked in women who had set their sights on other goals. Elizaveta Pimenova, a medical student in St. Petersburg, found that her children immeasurably complicated her life. Anna Kleiman, who studied medicine in Bern in the late 1870s, faced some painful choices when she became pregnant. If she went by her feelings, she wrote to a friend, then of course she would keep the child, especially as "no other woman, however kind she might be, can look after a child like its mother." Her lover, on the other hand, wanted to give the child to a worker's family to raise. Kleiman found this unacceptable, because although she might be busy, a working-class wife would be busier still. But Kleiman felt that in order to stay in Bern, she would have to give up her child.[10]

We do not know what became of Kleiman's child, but many radical women eventually relinquished theirs for the struggle, even when they found the decision as difficult as Kleiman did. For example, when she set off to work among the people, Ekaterina Breshkovskaia gave her infant son to her sister to raise. Years later, she remembered:

The conflict between my love for the child and my love for the revolution and for the freedom of Russia robbed me of many a night's sleep. I knew that I could not be a mother and still be a revolutionist. Those were not two tasks to which it was possible to give a divided attention. Either the one or the other must absorb one's whole being, one's entire devotion. . . . I was not the only one called upon to make such a sacrifice. Among the women in the struggle for Russian freedom there were many who chose to be fighters for justice rather than mothers of the victims of tyranny.[11]

Olga Schleissner, who left her two children with her parents in Finland after she started organizing for Land and Liberty, was another. She was staying with Vera Figner a year later when she learned that both had died. She never let the loss interfere with her work, but late at night she would crawl into bed, pull the blanket over her head, and abandon herself to silent weeping. Olga Liubatovich found it terribly painful to leave her infant daughter in Geneva when she returned to Russia to rescue her lover: "My heart was numb with grief," she wrote. Despite her care to place the child with a responsible friend, the girl died of meningitis soon after. Another radical woman kept her daughter by her side through two years of terrorist activity, then decided to leave the child with her sister in the summer of 1882. The mother remembered that to part with her was a "painful sacrifice," all the more so as the child soon failed to recognize her mother when she visited. The sister was already raising the daughter of still another woman revolutionary.[12]

In general, very few women left the revolutionary movement for the sake of lovers or children, and it is difficult to find out about the feelings of those who did, because their former comrades were unlikely to re-main in touch with them. For example, we have only the sketchiest information about Anna Sergeeva, a radical who left the movement after becoming the wife of Lev Tikhomirov. From Obukhova we learn about a certain Emily, who got married, became pregnant, and "changed a lot." "She is still sympathetic, of course," Obukhova wrote, "but now her husband and future child come first." What this reordering of priorities meant to Emily, however, Obukhova did not tell us. All the more suggestive, then, are the letters of Larissa Chemodanova, a radical of the early 1870s, who followed her husband, Sergei Sinegub, into Siberian exile. Thirty years later, looking back on her life, Chemodanova found little to satisfy her. She was tired, she wrote to a friend, and it was time for her to get up on the stove and take it easy. But instead, she had to continue working in order to support her children, about whom she complained almost incessantly in her letters. Chemodanova regretted that she was forced to work for her family and not for the good of society.[13]

In general, men handled their personal lives differently than women. It is true that radical men usually respected women's priorities. Everyone on the left condemned flirtation, and even a suggestive look could earn the man a rebuke. In their memoirs, men and women radicals alike comment frequently on the restraint men exercised around women. Nevertheless, although men may have respected the women's priorities, they rarely shared them. Family relationships did not define men's lives as they defined women's. Men were raised to expect a public life as well as a private life and were encouraged to leave home to attend school and establish careers, and so they found the break with family neither so wrenching nor so final. As a result, men found it relatively easy to assume family obligations, for such obligations did not threaten to absorb men completely. Even altruistic and idealistic men went on to marry and establish families of their own, apparently with little of the conflict that their radical sisters experienced.

Evidence indicates that men also regarded sexuality far more casually than women did. As Obukhova carefully weighed the personal against the political, her male friends were delighted to learn she had found a lover. Obukhova had really changed for the better, one wrote another. Since her life had become more "normal," she had grown livelier. "In a word, along with her work she is leading a happy and full personal life," the friend concluded. Valerian Smirnov occasionally attributed the problems of his male friends to sexual abstinence. Of Petr Lavrov, for example, Smirnov wrote: "He's really tired nowadays. . . . A plump woman would really do him some good."[14]

Men were more comfortable than women about seeking personal satisfactions, too. Nikolai Morozov, for example, went to the people in 1878 solely to be near Vera Figner, an act of self-indulgence difficult to imagine in radical women. A year later, when he fell in love with Olga Liubatovich, he again permitted his feelings to overcome him: "From the first hour of our acquaintance, her affect on me was great. . . . Each evening, I ran to Malinovskaia's [where she was staying] in order to see her, to assure myself that she had not been arrested, to exchange with her dreams of the future. I missed her." Nikolai Chaikovskii, whose circle had gained such prominence in the early 1870s and who afterward had experienced an intensely religious phase and spent time in America, became totally absorbed in family concerns at the end of the decade. He refused to abandon his mentally disturbed wife, who was unfaithful to him, and he so wore himself out trying to support his family that his friend and former comrade, Anna Epshtein, wrote to warn him that he would kill himself with work and end by spoiling his children. Another man rather facetiously observed that his propensity for fatherly tenderness might lead him to "extremes."[15] Sergei Kravchinskii, who was responsible for the assassination of Chief of Gendarmes Mezentsev in August 1879, shortly thereafter withdrew from the movement to be with his pregnant wife in Bern and never returned to Russia. Because men were less absorbed by family ties, and therefore found them less binding, many of them experienced far less difficulty than women in establishing personal relationships and maintaining them even in the midst of struggle. As a corollary, even when men committed themselves totally to a cause, they rarely displayed the emotional intensity or the moral absolutism of their women comrades.

Such differences between the sexes did not prevent men and women from collaborating fruitfully, but they did lead to a sort of division of labor that even radicals committed to women's equality had trouble overcoming. This division of labor influenced the kind of work women did for the movement, but more important, it left a profound and enduring stamp on the way radicals of both sexes conceived of women's role, encouraging them to attribute a special mission to women not only during revolutionary struggle but also in the socialist society of the future, when women would again be expected to sacrifice themselves for the good of the collective.

In fact, the Russian radical movement of the 1870s had a rather mixed record in respect to women. On the one hand, women participated in it prominently, and very often on an equal basis with men; on the other, the movement itself virtually ignored both women's issues and the female half of the people.

The special qualities of women revolutionaries provide one explanation for this apparent anomaly, because women's willingness to give themselves absolutely to their cause also shaped their attitudes. Initially, their idealism had led women to join the radical movement and to set aside the woman question, which raised issues that concerned them immediately and personally, for the sake of populism, that is, the cause of others. Through the years of struggle, this ordering of priorities did not change, and it caused women not only to neglect women's issues but also to be strangely insensitive to the plight of their laboring sisters. Judging by memoirs and letters, most populists failed to perceive the patriarchal aspects of peasant life. One exception was Praskovia Ivanovskaia, the daughter of a village priest, a woman of relatively humble origin herself, who observed the special vulnerability of peasant women. In her memoirs she described the sexual advances made by those in power and the double standard that punished only the woman if sexual intercourse between unmarried people led to pregnancy. Another was Ekaterina Breshkovskaia, a noblewoman who was struck by the brutality of peasant men and pleased by the fact that she always got on well with the women. Yet Breshkovskaia condemned peasant women for their "backward" attitudes, observing that peasant men treated her respectfully, whereas peasant women, "as the more conservative element," would always notice the ways she differed from them.[16] Other women propagandists do not mention women at all.

Populist women displayed a similar lack of insight into the position of women factory workers. The women's situation was in many ways worse than that for men: no maternity leave; a literacy rate less than half that for men; salaries from one-half to two-thirds of those for men; far less adequate nourishment.[17] Did this make them harder to organize? Populist women certainly arrived at that conclusion quickly enough. When they went to the factories in the early 1870s, members of the Fritsche group soon despaired of success among working women, whom they found quarrelsome, jealous, and interested only in men. Nadezhda Golovina agreed. Golovina took up factory work in 1874, only to discover that the working conditions and the "character of my female co-workers" made political work impossible. Only Ivanovskaia commented on the universal illiteracy and the driving need that impelled women to tear themselves from family and to turn to factory labor, and even she condemned her female co-workers for being inconsistent and "gypsy-like," for always changing jobs.[18]

Populist ideology was also responsible for the neglect of lower-class women, for it proved no use whatsoever in helping radicals to understand their plight. After the early 1870s, all traces of woman-oriented issues vanished from populist propaganda. Implicit in populism was the assumption that peasants were better, purer, and more moral than revolutionaries themselves. In light of their near worship of the people, how could revolutionaries of the privileged classes impose their own values by criticizing the peasants' personal relationships?

Woman-oriented issues were equally absent from visions of the future. Populists of the 1870s never clearly delineated the society they hoped to achieve, and they disagreed among themselves considerably as to its characteristics, but none of their discussions or disagreements involved the role of women or the status of the family after the revolution. To be sure, the economic and social changes they fought for would benefit women as well as men. Peasants would live better, receive better health care, be better educated. But none of these changes would necessarily alter the profoundly patriarchal peasant way of life: men's contemptuous treatment of women, the frequent beatings, the ubiquitous double standard, the sexual rights of father-in-law over daughter-in-law. If populist women assumed that the revolution would affect any of this, they never said so; consequently, we must conclude either that they failed to see it or that it was not of major concern to them.

As a result, women's participation in the revolutionary movement, which was of such immense value to their cause and so very important to the self-image of the women themselves, yielded no theoretical advances or organizational benefits for the female half of the very people to whom revolutionary women gave their lives, although it certainly yielded a myth.

CONCLUSION: A MIXED LEGACY

On the eve of her execution, Sofia Perovskaia wrote a letter to her mother. Designed to comfort and to reassure, her letter also helps us to understand something of what motivated Perovskaia, and perhaps others like her. All her life, the letter seemed to say, Perovskaia had followed ideals she had learned as a child. She told her mother: "I have always regretted my failure to match your moral integrity." Perovskaia begged her mother not to despair, and to cease tormenting herself. She had no regrets about her fate and would greet it calmly, as she had long anticipated it. "And really, Mamma dear, my fate isn't all that dismal. I have lived according to my convictions; I could not have acted otherwise, and so I await the future with a clear conscience."[1]

Moral integrity. A clear conscience. Absolutes that ring oddly in the ear of the modern reader seemed perfectly natural to many Russians of Perovskaia's time. Religious values still permeated this traditional society. They provided an attractive alternative to the cold and hierarchical relations that characterized the official world, and a standard by which to judge them. Vera Zasulich derived her first moral lessons from the Gospels, and it was her quest for the "crown of thorns" that attracted her to "those who perished," and to revolution. When Vera Figner abandoned medical school for full-time radical activity, she was only following a precept she had learned in her childhood, she wrote. "It was the victory of a principle that had been imprinted long ago on my 13-year-old mind, when I read in the Bible, 'Leave thy father and thy mother, and follow me.' "[2]

Generally speaking, it was Russian women who perpetuated these religious ideals. Most men were too wrapped up in the secular concerns of state and service to pay them much heed, although many continued to find them compelling (as the response to the Fritsche group indicates). The result was a dichotomy between masculine and feminine value systems that the society and culture reproduced and family patterns often reflected, and it led some women to perceive the world in terms of categories that were simultaneously moral and gender-related. They viewed morality, like the capacity for feeling, for suffering, and for self-sacrifice, as essentially feminine, whereas emotional distance, hierarchy, and the arbitrary exercise of power characterized masculinity. New ideas sowed the seeds of discontent because they led women to question the ascendancy of masculinity over femininity, and discontent became rebellion when a significant minority of educated society also started questioning that ascendancy. Elena Gan and Maria Zhukova were among the first to raise the issue, portraying loving and selfless women who, despite their moral superiority, were dominated by emotionally and morally bankrupt men. Neither their heroines nor the authors themselves, however, claimed the right to male prerogatives. Instead, their critique of public life led both Gan and Zhukova to develop a Russian version of the cult of domesticity and to argue that women, within their separate sphere, deserved greater respect and recognition from men, because so long as the political climate remained repressive and opportunities in public life continued to consist primarily of serving the state, to leave the home would mean to become like men and thus to lose women's special qualities. As Praskovia Tatlina, their contemporary, had put it, "men don't recognize their own individuality," because they "slavishly drag out their existence in official circles," whereas women, although treated like slaves, are nevertheless more human because they are more free to feel.[3]

During the reign of Alexander II, the dichotomy between public and private values became transformed into a rationale for women's rebellion against family roles. Beneath the manifest rationalism and scientism of the 1860s lay an ethical vision that was no less powerful for being unarticulated. The philosopher Soloviev captured its essence well in his parody of nihilist views: "Man is descended from the apes; *therefore* we should sacrifice ourselves for our fellow man."[4] It was implicit altruism that made the ideas of the 1860s so appealing to women, for at the same time as progressive opinion challenged the subordination of women to men and family, it also encouraged women to contribute their special energies to the regeneration of society as a whole and to take advantage of new occupations such as midwifery, teaching, and medicine that women could enter without violating their moral self-perception.

In the movement of the 1870s, the ethical vision predominated, and it led hundreds of women to give themselves to the cause. First in their quest for an education, then in illegal activities, and finally in the shift to terrorism, the women of the 1870s attempted to reform and then to transform society according to standards of morality that were religiously based and culturally feminine. Because it promised to ameliorate the lot of the suffering and the oppressed, to end exploitation and to bring about the brotherhood of man, the revolutionary movement appealed to women with the very highest moral expectations. As Figner said of herself and her comrades: "We aspired to a pure life, and to personal sanctity."[5] Such a lofty goal made not only the woman question but also any concern for the self whatever seem trivial.

But to deny oneself did not necessarily mean to dislike oneself. These women, after all, felt they embodied the finest aspects of their cultural heritage. Even if their real connections with the women in their own families had been broken, and the social roles associated with their gender subordinated or rejected, the fact that they acted according to their own ideal of femininity provided an important source of strength and self-affirmation. As Perovskaia wrote her mother: "In every moment of doubt and hesitation, your image has sustained me."[6] Crucial to this was the support of other women, be they mothers or women comrades. Some mothers recognized what their daughters were doing, and it led the mothers to reconcile themselves to their daughters' actions, even when they did not approve. Perovskaia's mother continued to visit her daughter in secret even after she had gone underground and cared for her during Perovskaia's final hours in prison. During the height of the revolutionary movement of the 1870s, Maria Trubnikova, who disapproved of her daughter's involvement, nevertheless allowed her home to be used for meetings of radicals, for storing illegal literature, and even for visits of women such as Sofia Perovskaia, whose terrorist views she herself opposed and whose presence constituted an actual danger.[7] Ekaterina Figner helped her daughter Vera to smuggle funds to emigrés in Geneva, continued to see her after she had gone underground, and faithfully wrote to her in exile. Anna Vasil'evna Armfeld, another noblewoman, openly sympathized with her daughter Natalia's revolutionary goals, took pride in her activity, and assisted her as much as she could. When Natalia was imprisoned in 1878, Anna Vasil'evna obtained the plans of the prison and sought out people to dig a tunnel under her daughter's cell. The work was only half completed when all the prisoners were transferred to Perm. At that point, the mother grew so concerned for her daughter's welfare that she abandoned the capital to follow Natalia into exile.

Friendships between women helped to sustain them, too. Women's networks arose in the 1860s. The triumvirate of Trubnikova, Stasova, and Filosofova was an obvious example, but also significant were the efforts of the Ivanovas, the Zasuliches, and other women to help themselves and each other. Even after the woman question had ceased to be a theoretical concern to the movement of the 1870s, the ties between women remained close and supportive, and in some cases they clearly replicated the relationship between mother and daughter. The members of the Fritsche group, for example, regarded Bardina as a surrogate mother, and she behaved like one. Perovskaia, who was often demanding and difficult in her relationships with male comrades, almost invariably treated the women with tenderness and concern, even arranging outings for them in the very midst of terrorist struggle. Ekaterina Breshkovskaia wrote that the women held in prison before the trial of the 193 were far less likely than the men to become ill, go mad, or die, because the women took far better care of each other.[8] Accounts of prison life indicate that well after the populist movement had come to an end, such concern lingered on, as women prisoners tended each other in sickness and protested, to the point of suicide if necessary, violence done a sister. The memoirs of women radicals provide loving descriptions of their women friends, and their private correspondence indicates how very much they depended on and cared for each other.

It is tempting to idealize women revolutionaries. They were so courageous, so very principled, so utterly self-sacrificing. It is important to keep in mind that their eagerness to sacrifice themselves was sometimes excessive and could damage rather than serve the cause, even as it won them the admiration of their comrades and other contemporaries; in addition, their commitment to terrorism cost many innocent lives without advancing their goals. Moreover, the objectives revolutionary women strove for were neither realistic nor practicable. They unnecessarily idealized the peasantry, and they ignored almost entirely issues that addressed the particular needs of peasant and working women. By contrast with women activists of a later period, some of whom worked for feminist goals within socialist parties in Russia and in the West,[9] Russian women of the 1870s seem to have gained prominence in revolutionary struggles at the price of their awareness of the woman question.

For all that, they were truly remarkable women, strong, determined, and dedicated, willing to give up their lives to make a better world for Russia's suffering masses. Together with the men, they acted as the very conscience of their society. More such women would appear in subsequent decades, but never again would they constitute such a high proportion of activists, and never again would so many assume such prominent positions.

By the next period of serious upheaval, in 1905–6, economic growth and expanded educational opportunities had fostered a sizable feminist movement. Most feminists, however, failed to address the needs of peasants and workers in a meaningful way. To their left, the groups that did so were the Socialist Revolutionaries, the Anarchists, and the Social Democratic parties, Menshevik and Bolshevik. Of these, only the Social Democrats, on the basis of their Marxist principles, theoretically espoused the liberation of women. But only a few extra-ordinary women assumed positions of authority in either party, and fewer still spoke out on issues pertaining to women; when they did, they had to struggle hard to make themselves heard.

Had populist women raised women's issues, would they have fared better? It would, of course, have been utterly out of character, all the more so because all populists believed that the peasants themselves must determine their social system and form of government. Most radical women of the 1870s apparently found it sufficient to have given themselves to their cause and to have acted "not as an inspiration, nor as wives or mothers of men [but] independently, as the equals of men," as Vera Zasulich put it, and to have moved hundreds of women to follow in their footsteps.[10] So in their own fashion they suited themselves.

Nevertheless, although we may not be able to answer the question whether or not they truly served the people, the female half of the people in particular, there is no question that the radical women of the 1870s added a moral dimension to revolutionary politics seldom seen before or since.

NOTES

Introduction to Part I

1 Martin Malia, for example, characterized the intelligentsia as "all men who think independently." In his doctoral dissertation, Anthony Netting described them as "intellectuals despising official society, who have cut loose from it and formed a rival grouping of men." Martin Malia, "What Is the Intelligentsia?" in Richard Pipes, ed., *The Russian Intelligentsia* (New York, 1961), p. 2. Anthony Netting, *Russian Liberalism: The Years of Promise* (Columbia University, unpublished Ph.D. dissertation, 1967), pp. 4–5.

2 Franco Venturi, for example, in his classic *Roots of Revolution* (New York, 1966), discussed in detail the activities and thought of both male and female radicals, but he made no distinction between the motivations of the two. A more recent work by Daniel Brower, *Training the Nihilists* (Ithaca, 1975), rightly identified the radical subculture as a crucial factor in the rebellions of the 1860s and 1870s, and Brower recognized that "only a powerful force could have overcome the emotional and institutional ties binding young women to their designated place in society" (p. 22), but he failed to consider what that force meant for women who rebelled. Adam Ulam, *In the Name of the People* (New York, 1977), simply refused to take radicals seriously at all. In reacting against the adulatory tone of Venturi's work, he employed a sarcastic and patronizing tone, becoming almost nasty in his treatment of the women.

3 There have been some notable exceptions: Richard Wortman, *The Crisis of Russian Populism* (Cambridge, 1967), Daniel Brower, *Training the Nihilists* (Ithaca, 1975), and Michael Confino, "On Intellectuals and Intellectual Traditions in Eighteenth and Nineteenth Century Russia," *Daedalus*, vol. 101, no. 2. Philip Pomper, *Sergei Nechaev* (New Brunswick, 1979) did discuss the "ego strategy of self-sacrifice or self-chosen redemptive suffering for the *narod*" (p. 19) that motivated participants in the movements of the sixties and seventies, but he attempted no analysis of the particular ways that strategy affected women.

4 Richard Stites, *The Women's Movement in Russia: Feminism, Nihilism and Bolshevism, 1860–1930* (Princeton, 1978); Vera Broido, *Apostles into Terrorists* (New York, 1978).

1. Mothers and daughters

1 Dorothy Atkinson, "Society and the Sexes in the Russian Past," in D. Atkinson, A. Dallin, and G. Lapidus, eds., *Women in Russia* (Stanford, 1977), pp. 26–7. Vera Dunham, "The Strong-Woman Motif in Russian Literature," in C.E. Black, ed., *The Transformation of Russian Society* (Cambridge, 1960), pp. 459–83. R. Mathewson, *The Positive Hero in Russian Literature* (New York, 1958).

2 For discussion of the evolution of the woman's role in Europe during this period, see the following: Martha Vicinus, ed., *Suffer and Be Still* (Bloomington, 1973); Patricia

Branca, *Silent Sisterhood* (London, 1977); Bonnie Smith, *Ladies of Leisure* (Princeton, 1981); Renate Bridenthal and Claudia Koonz, eds., *Becoming Visible* (Boston, 1977), especially the essay by Barbara Pope; Edward Shorter, *The Making of the Modern Family* (New York, 1978). For America, see Barbara Welter, "The Cult of True Womanhood," *American Quarterly*, vol. XVIII (Summer 1976); Michael Gordon, ed., *The American Family in Socio-Historical Perspective* (New York, 1973); and Mary Ryan, *Womanhood in America* (New York, 1975).

3 For legislation relating to women, see *Zhenskoe pravo: svod uzakonenii i postavlenii otnoshaiushchikhsia do zhenskogo pola* (St. Petersburg, 1873); later revisions are included in Ia. Orovich [Iakov A. Kantorovich], *Zhenshchina v prave: s prilozheniem vsekh postanovlenii deistvuiushchego zakonodatel'stva, otnoshaiushchikhsia do lits zhenskogo pola* (St. Petersburg, 3rd ed. 1895).

4 The most interesting and most useful treatments are those of Nancy Chodorov, *The Reproduction of Mothering* (Berkeley, 1978), and Dorothy Dinnerstein, *The Mermaid and the Minotaur* (New York, 1977). Nancy Friday, *My Mother, Myself* (New York, 1978) provided a popular but far less thoughtful addition to the literature.

5 Edward Shorter, in *The Making of the Modern Family*, Lloyd de Mause, in his long introduction to *The History of Childhood* (New York, 1974), and Lawrence Stone, in *The Family, Sex and Marriage in England, 1500–1800* (New York, 1977), all welcomed the "progress" in childrearing practices. For an account of lower-class family life and a less negative view of pre-industrial practices, see Louise Tilly and Joan Scott, *Women, Work and the Family* (New York, 1978).

6 See Barbara Alpern Engel, "Mothers and Daughters: Family Patterns and the Female Intelligentsia," in David Ransel, ed., *The Family in Imperial Russia* (Urbana, 1978); this matter will also be treated more fully in Chapter 3 of this book.

7 I. Tiutriumov, "Krestianskaia sem'ia," *Russkaia rech*, vol. I, no. 10 (October 1879), p. 311; Sula Benet, *The Village of Viriatino* (New York, 1970), pp. 97–100, 102.

8 Tiutriumov, pp. 311–12; Benet, pp. 121–2.

9 In the 1840s, by the tsar's order, secondary schools were established for daughters of the clergy to prepare them for their duties as wives. Ruth Dudgeon, *Women and Higher Education in Russia, 1855–1905* (George Washington University, unpublished Ph.D. dissertation, 1975), p. 10. Gregory Freeze, "Caste and Emancipation: The Changing Status of Clerical Families in the Great Reforms," in David Ransel, ed., *The Family in Imperial Russia*.

10 On female occupations, see E. P. Karnovich, *O razvitii zhenskogo truda v Peterburga* (St. Petersburg, 1865).

11 *Domostroi po rukopisam Imperatorskoi Publichnoi Biblioteki* (St. Petersburg, 1867). Quoted by Dorothy Atkinson, "Society and the Sexes in the Russian Past," p. 15. Testimony to its continuing influence can be found throughout Nikolai Dobroliubov's "Temnoe Tsarstvo," in N. A. Dobroliubov, *Sochinenii*, vol. V, translated as "Realm of Darkness," in *Selected Philosophical Essays* (Moscow, 1956), and in the descriptions of merchant life by David McKenzie Wallace, *Russia on the Eve of War and Revolution* (New York, 1961), p. 187, as well as in the plays of Aleksandr Ostrovskii.

12 Ostrovskii's plays provide graphic illustration of this; so does the commentary of Dobroliubov. For one individual's recollections, see Aleksandra Kornilova, "Avtobiografiia," in *Entsiklopedicheskii slovar' "Granat,"* vol. 40, pp. 199–210.

13 The financial status of the nobility has been analyzed by Arcadius Kahan, "The Costs of 'Westernization' in Russia; the Gentry and the Economy in the Eighteenth Century," *Slavic Review*, vol. XXV, no. 1 (March 1966), pp. 40–66. On noble families elsewhere in Europe, see Carolyn Lougee, *Le Paradis des Femmes: Women, Salons and Social Stratification in Seventeenth Century France* (Princeton, 1976); David Hunt, *Parents and Children in History* (New York, 1972); Lawrence Stone, *The Family, Sex and Marriage in England, 1500–1800*; Margaret H. Darrow, "French Noblewomen and

the New Domesticity, 1750–1850," *Feminist Studies*, vol. 5, no. 1 (Spring 1979), pp. 41–65.

14 A. G. Rashin, *Naselenie Rossii za 100 let* (Moscow, 1956), p. 182.

15 *Zhenskoe pravo*, pp. 110–11.

16 George Fedotov, *The Russian Religious Mind*, 2 vols. (Cambridge, 1966), vol. II, pp. 77–9. I am deeply grateful to Gregory Freeze for directing me to important sources in this area and for sharing with me his impressive knowledge of the subject.

17 Marc Raeff, *Origins of the Intelligentsia, the Eighteenth Century Nobility* (New York, 1966), p. 122. Memoirs of women often report mothers who ran estates for themselves. See, for example, E. Vodovozova, *Na zare zhizni*, 2 vols. (Moscow, 1964), vol. I, especially pp. 122–3; Ekaterina Zhukovskaia, *Zapiski* (Leningrad, 1930); A-va [A. N. Kazina], "Zhenskaia zhizn'," *Otechestvennye zapiski* (March 1875), (April 1875), (May 1875).

18 E. Vodovozova, *Na zare zhizni*, vol. I, p. 126.

19 My own model is based primarily on Nancy Chodorow's excellent article, "Family Structure and Feminine Personality," in Michelle Rosaldo and Louise Lamphere, eds., *Women, Culture and Society* (Stanford, 1974).

20 A-va [A. N. Kazina] "Zhenskaia zhizn'," *Otechestvennye zapiski*, (March 1875), p. 221.

21 Ekaterina Iunge, *Vospominaniia* (Moscow, 1933), p. 213.

22 See, for example, Jessica Tovrov, "Mother-Child Relationships among the Russian Nobility," in D. Ransel, ed., *The Family in Imperial Russia*, and Karolina Pavlova, *A Double Life* (Ann Arbor, 1978). On mothers changing their minds, see Vodovozova, *Na zare zhizni*, vol. II, p. 175.

23 Avdotia Panaeva, *Semeistvo Tal'nykovykh* (Leningrad, 1928).

24 Vera Figner, *Zapechatlennyi trud*, 2 vols. (Moscow, 1964), vol. I, p. 58.

25 See Raeff, *Origins*.

26 E. Likhacheva, *Materialy dlia istorii zhenskogo obrazovaniia v Rossii* (St. Petersburg, 1899–1901), pp. 250–1; J. L. Black, *Citizens for the Fatherland* (Boulder, 1979), chapter 7.

27 Anna Evdokimovna Labzina, *Vospominaniia: 1785–1828* (St. Petersburg, 1914; reprinted by Oriental Research Partners, Newtonville, Mass., 1974), p. 2.

28 Labzina, p. 21.

29 Labzina, pp. 42, 58, 72–3.

30 There are many examples of such self-indulgent behavior in Sergei Aksakov's *A Family Chronicle* (New York, 1961).

31 See, for example, the accusations of Prince Mikhail Shcherbatov in *On the Corruption of Morals in Russia* (London, 1969), pp. 227–35; also, A. Levshin, "Zhenskie nravy i vospitanie proshlogo veka," *Kolos'ia* (January 1887), p. 160, and Serafim Shashkov, *Sobranie sochinenii*, 2 vols. (St. Petersburg, 1898), vol. I, pp. 813–16. Additional evidence, although far less negative, for the Westernization of upper-class women is to be found all through the memoirs of F. F. Vigel' (1786–1856), *Zapiski* (Moscow, 1928; reprinted by Oriental Research Partners, Newtonville, Mass., 1974).

32 Black, *Citizens for the Fatherland*, pp. 142–50 and chapter 7. Vigel provided numerous examples of aristocratic men who honored and respected their well-educated wives. Likhacheva estimated that there were seventy women writers during Catherine's reign: *Materialy*, pp. 264–9. See also N. N. Golitsyn, *Bibliograficheskii slovar' russkikh pisatel'nits* (St. Petersburg, 1889).

33 Praskovia Tatlina, "Vospominaniia Praskov'i Nikolaevny Tatlinoi," *Russkii arkhiv* (1899), pp. 190–6, 199–200.

34 Tatlina, p. 201.

35 Marc Raeff, *The Decembrists* (Englewood Cliffs, 1966), pp. 75, 94, 111, 113, 115.

36 For an unsatisfactory examination (but excellent bibliography) of the Decembrist wives, see A. Mazour, *Women in Exile: The Wives of the Decembrists* (Tallahassee, 1975); also Glyn Barrett, *The Rebel on the Bridge* (Athens, Ohio, 1975).

37 Richard Stites, *The Women's Liberation Movement in Russia: Feminism, Nihilism and Bolshevism, 1860–1930* (Princeton, 1978), p. 116.

38 Alexander Herzen, *My Past and Thoughts* (an abridgement of the lengthier *Byloe i dumy*) (New York, 1974), p. 42.
39 Vera Figner, "Zheny Dekabristov," *Katorga i ssylka* no. 21 (1925), p. 237.

2. Rising expectations and shattered dreams

1 For an analysis of this phenomenon, see Marc Raeff, *Origins of the Russian Intelligentsia* (New York, 1966).
2 See, for example, the discussion of the evolution of Herzen's ideas in Martin Malia, *Alexander Herzen and the Birth of Russian Socialism* (New York, 1965). Also see Isaiah Berlin, "A Marvellous Decade, 1838–1848: The Birth of the Russian Intelligentsia," *Encounter*, vol. IV (June 1955), pp. 27–39, and Edward Brown, *Stankevich and His Moscow Circle* (Stanford, 1966). For an examination of the impact of romantic ideas earlier in the nineteenth century, see Marc Raeff, "Russian Youth on the Eve of Romanticism: Andre I. Turgenev and Ilis Circle," in Alexander and Janet Rabinowitch, eds., *Revolution and Politics in Russia* (Bloomington, 1972).
3 These abortive affairs are discussed elsewhere: Malia, *Alexander Herzen*; Brown, *Stankevich*; E. H. Carr, *Michael Bakunin* (New York, 1937); P. Miliukov, "Liubov idealistov tridtsatykh godov," in *Iz istorii russkoi intelligentsii* (St. Petersburg, 1903).
4 This was initially the view even of the liberal critic Vissarion Belinskii. In 1840 he wrote that "the unavoidable result of these profound and excellent ideas is the dissolution of the holy bonds of matrimony, parenthood and family – in short, the total transformation of the state first into a beastly and outrageous orgy, and then into a phantom, fashioned out of words written on air." Quoted by Richard Stites, *The Women's Liberation Movement in Russia: Feminism, Nihilism and Bolshevism, 1860–1930* (Princeton, 1978), p. 21.
5 Jonathan Beecher and Richard Bienvenu, eds., *The Utopian Vision of Charles Fourier* (Boston, 1971), pp. 195–6.
6 Malia, *Alexander Herzen*, pp. 274–5; Stites, *Women's Liberation Movement*, p. 21.
7 Nicholas Riasonovsky, *Nicholas I and Official Nationality in Russia* (Berkeley, 1969), pp. 91, 94.
8 E. O. Likhacheva, *Materialy dlia istorii zhenskogo obrazovaniia v Rossii*, 4 vols. (St. Petersburg, 1899–1901), vol. II, pp. 135, 173–6.
9 Likhacheva, vol. III, p. 9.
10 A-va [A. N. Kazina] described institute life in the late 1840s and early 1850s in "Zhenskaia zhizn'," *Otechestvennye zapiski*, no. 4 (1875), p. 402. She wrote: "Ties with family, with everyone at home are broken; it is hard to imagine how one could keep on loving people whom one does not see for years on end, and if one does see them, then only very rarely, and under such peculiar circumstances that intimate conversation is impossible, let alone the demonstration of feeling" (A-va, p. 297). In 1844, a committee appointed to consider the question of girls' education once again addressed the problem of separating girls from their families. While granting that family education was the best preparation for family life, the committee nevertheless concluded that because most noble families remained both too poor and too ignorant to invest in the education of their daughters, state-sponsored education remained necessary. Likhacheva, *Materialy*, vol. III, pp. 41–2.
11 Likhacheva, *Materialy*, vol. I, pp. 167–8.
12 E. Vodovozova, *Na zare zhizni*, 2 vols. (Moscow, 1964), vol. I, p. 470.
13 *Zapiski staroi Smolianki* (St. Petersburg, 1898), p. 149.
14 Vodovozova, *Na zare zhizni*, vol. I, pp. 86–7.
15 Quoted by S. Ia. Shtraikh [Streich], *Sestry Korvin-Krukovskie* (Moscow, 1934), pp. 9–10.
16 Likhacheva, *Materialy*, vol. II, p. 241; vol. III, pp. 215–16, 265.

17 Tatiana Passek, *Iz dal'nykh let'*, 2 vols. (Moscow, 1963), vol. I, p. 324.

18 Passek, vol. I, p. 358.

19 Avdotia Panaeva, *Vospominaniia* (Moscow, 1972). Marina Ledkovsky, "Avdotya Panaeva: Her Salon and Her Life," *Russian Literature Triquarterly*, no. 9 (Spring 1974). Karolina Pavlova, *A Double Life* (Ann Arbor, 1978). Carr, *Michael Bakunin*. A. A. Kornilov, *Molodye gody Mikhaila Bakunina* (Moscow, 1915). Ogareva's diary is quoted by M. Gershenzon, "Materialy po istorii russkoi literatury i kultury. Russkaia zhenshchina 30-kh godov," *Russkaia mysl'*, vol. XI (December 1911), p. 55.

20 See, for example, V. Belinskii's review of Gan's works in *Otechestvennye zapiski*, vol. XXI (1845), pp. 1–24. Of Zhukova, Belinskii wrote that "the main virtue of Zhukova's stories, and a worthy one it is, consists of her ability to tell a story with full, lively and passionate feminine feeling." V. Belinskii, *Polnoe sobranie sochinenii* (Moscow, 1954), vol. IV, p. 113.

21 E. N. [E. Nekrasova], "Elena Andreevna Gan, 1814–1842, biograficheskie ocherki," *Russkaia starina*, vol. 51 (1886), pp. 337–8. As is the case with all the biographical material concerning Gan, there is some disagreement as to how rebellious the Princess Dolgorukova really was. N. A. Fadeeva, Gan's younger sister, wrote that Elena Pavlovna, their mother, was far too dutiful and moral and too attached to her grandparents to oppose their will. N. A. Fadeeva, "Elena Pavlovna Fadeeva," *Russkaia starina*, vol. 52 (1886), pp. 749–51.

22 There is no full-length biography of Gan, but there exist a number of biographical sketches, some of them containing her letters in whole or in part. The sketches occasionally disagree on details of her life, at times quite sharply. The best is E. N. [E. Nekrasova], "Elena Andreevna Gan." For a more critical approach there is A. V. Starcheskii, "Roman odnoi zabytoi romanistki," *Istoricheskii vestnik*, no. 8–9 (1886), and a rebuttal to it, written by Gan's sister, her daughter, and a friend, in *Istoricheskii vestnik*, no. 11 (1886), pp. 456–64. Gan's daughter, the writer V. P. Zhelikhovskaia, also published a short biography of her mother, which includes excerpts from a number of letters: "Elena Andreevna Gan v 1835–1842," *Russkaia starina*, vol. 53 (1887), pp. 733–66. Also see M. Gershenzon, "Materialy po istorii russkoi literatury i kultury."

23 Z. R-va [Gan], "Ideal," *Biblioteka dlia chteniia*, no. 21 (1837), p. 131. Her daughter remembered these dinners well. The officers, she wrote, would fill the little room with smoke, so that her mother always left right after dinner to take refuge in the nursery with the children. Zhelikhovskaia, p. 740.

24 Z. R-va, "Ideal," p. 131. In a letter of October 1838 she described with distaste their bivouac in the Caucasus: "I live in a smelly, damp, cold hut; from my windows I can see a village church to the East, to the West a cemetery on a hill, covered with crosses that are about to fall down; to the South a large stable, to the West another building belonging to the battery, further off the steppe, sand and swamp." Gershenzon, "Materialy," p. 62. Not all women so disliked following the troops with their husbands. See, for example, Varvara Bakunina, "Persidskii pokhod v 1796 godu," *Russkaia starina*, vol. 53 (1887), pp. 343–74.

25 Z. R-va, "Sud sveta," *Biblioteka dlia chteniia*, no. 38 (1840), p. 19.

26 "Ideal," p. 128.

27 "Ideal," pp. 118–44.

28 Z. R-va, "Medalion," *Biblioteka dlia chteniia*, no. 34 (1839); "Teofania Abbadzhio," *Biblioteka dlia chteniia*, no. 44 (1841); "Sud sveta," "Naprasnyi dar," *Otechestvennye zapiski*, vol. XXI (1842); "Liubon'ka," *Otechestvennye zapiski*, vol. XXV (1842).

29 Quoted by Zhelikhovskaia, pp. 744–5.

30 Quoted by Gershenzon, "Materialy," p. 59.

31 Quoted by Gershenzon, "Materialy," p. 65.

32 Quoted by Starcheskii, "Roman odnoi zabytoi romanistki," p. 521.

33 "Ideal," p. 144.

34 "Naprasnyi dar," pp. 38–9.
35 Quoted by Gershenzon, "Materialy," pp. 59–66.
36 Starcheskii, "Roman odnoi," pp. 513, 526. Until the very eve of her death she contin-
    ued to work in order to provide for her children. See Nekrasova, p. 572.
37 Even when she was with her mother, Zhelikhovskaia remembered, it was her nurse
    who held her. It took her a long time to realize that the money her mother earned by
    writing was being spent on her education. Zhelikhovskaia, pp. 2–3.
38 Quoted by Starcheskii, "Roman odnoi," p. 512.
39 Quoted by Nekrasova, p. 563. In the same letter to her sister, in which she excused
    herself for hiring governesses, she also explained that she could not teach religion to
    her children because of her own doubts about her faith. See also Zhelikhovskaia,
    pp. 760–1.
40 "As far as the number of my literary children are concerned, that's something else.
    They aren't so costly and fate, that blind tyrant, doesn't interfere." Starcheskii, "Roman
    odnoi," p. 512.
41 Given the attitude toward women writers at the time, this is hardly surprising. The
    very same issue of Biblioteka dlia chteniia that published a story by a woman writer also
    contained a short story about women writers – a vicious attack on their alleged vanity
    and self-centeredness. "It's all right for a woman to be a writer," the author conceded,
    "so long as she does it for economic reasons: to support herself or her family, but not if
    she does it for fame or to advance herself. Such women should never marry, they are a
    curse to their husband and family." "Zhenshchina-pisatel'nitsa," Biblioteka dlia chteniia,
    no. 23 (1837).
42 The only biographical source for Zhukova is M. S. Konopleva, "Maria Zhukova,"
    Golos Minuvshago, no. 7 (1913).
43 "Provintsialka," Biblioteka dlia chteniia, no. 24 (1837), pp. 299, 340; quoted by Konopleva,
    p. 29.
44 "Samopozhertvovanie," in Povesti M. Zhukovoi (St. Petersburg, 1841), p. 25.
45 "Moi kurskie znakomtsi," in Povesti, pp. 209, 218, 221–2.
46 On Sand, see Curtis Cate, George Sand: A Biography (Boston, 1975).
47 V. Belinskii in Otechestvennye zapiski, vol. XXI, pp. 8–9.
48 Richard Wortman, The Development of a Russian Legal Consciousness (Chicago, 1976).
49 Praskovia Tatlina, "Vospominaniia Praskov'i Nikolaevny Tatlinoi," Russkii arkhiv (1899),
    p. 220.
50 S. Shashkov, Sobranie sochinenii, 2 vols. (St. Petersburg, 1898), vol. I, p. 650; M. Portugalov,
    Zhenshchina v russkoi khudozhestvennoi literature XIX veka, 1823–1876 (St. Petersburg,
    1917), p. 8.
51 "Zhorzh Zand," Otechestvennye zapiski, no. 6 (June 1877), p. 441.
52 Her story is told by Malia in Alexander Herzen, by E. H. Carr in The Romantic Exiles
    (Boston, 1961), by Miliukov, Iz istorii russkoi intelligentsii, and at greater length by P.
    Guber, Kruzhenie serd'tsa (Leningrad, 1919). Some of Natalie Herzen's letters have
    been published in M. Gershenzon, Russkie propili, vol. I, and Russkaia starina, no. 1–3
    (1892), pp. 771–92.
53 Quoted by Carr, p. 17.
54 A. Herzen, My Past and Thoughts (New York, 1974), p. 131.
55 Quoted by Miliukov, Iz istorii, pp. 130–1; Guber, Kruzhenie serd'tsa, p. 56.
56 Quoted by Miliukov, Iz istorii, p. 132.
57 Quoted by Malia, Alexander Herzen, p. 173.
58 A little over a week after her elopement, Natalie wrote: "Here is the harmony, the
    prayer, the heaven, the life of angels about which I have dreamed, for which I lived
    expectantly these twenty years," Russkaia starina, p. 788. In September 1838 she wrote:
    "Imagine! Sashenka and I have been parted only one hour in the last two weeks. Oh,
    how happy I am!" Gershenzon, Russkie propili, p. 791.

59   Natalie Herzen, *Russkai starina*, p. 789.
60   Miliukov, *Iz istorii*, p. 152.
61   Miliukov, *Iz istorii*, p. 152.
62   Malia, *Alexander Herzen*, p. 264.
63   Natalie Herzen, *Russkai starina*, p. 238; quoted by Guber, *Kruzhenie serd'tsa*, p. 165.
64   Natalie Herzen, *Russkaia starina*, p. 255.
65   Natalie Herzen, *Russkaia starina*, p. 254.
66   Quoted by Carr, *The Romantic Exiles*, p. 41; Natalie Herzen, *Russkaia starina*, pp. 258–9.
67   Quoted by Carr, *The Romantic Exiles*, p. 75. Carr described the struggle between Herzen and Herwegh, and their respective allies, in fine and often painful detail.

3. Searching for a politics of personal life

1   See, for example, Terence Emmons, *The Russian Landed Gentry and the Peasant Emancipation of 1861* (London, 1968), and Elena Shtakenshneider, *Dnevnik i zapiski (1854–1886)* (Moscow, 1934; reprinted by Oriental Research Partners, Newtonville, Mass., 1980).
2   Evidence of this ferment can be found in the work of E. Vodovozova, *Na zare zhizni*, 2 vols. (Moscow, 1964), vol. II, pp. 33–45, as well as the work of Shtakenshneider, especially the entries for 1855–66.
3   Reginald Zelnik, "The Sunday School Movement in Russia, 1859–1862," *Journal of Modern History*, vol XXXVII (June 1965), pp. 151–70.
4   Cynthia Whittaker, "The Women's Movement during the Reign of Alexander II: A Case Study in Russian Liberalism," *Journal of Modern History*, supplement to vol. 48, no. 2 (June 1976), p. 38. E. O. Likhacheva, *Materialy dlia istorii zhenskogo obrazovaniia v Rossii*, 4 vols. (St. Petersburg, 1899–1901), vol. III, p. 96. Richard Stites, *The Women's Liberation Movement in Russia: Feminism, Nihilism and Bolshevism, 1860–1930* (Princeton, 1978).
5   These figures are cited in *Zhenskoe obrazovanie* (1878), p. 92.
6   N. Dobroliubov, "Temnoe tsarstvo," *Sochinenii*, vol. V; translated as "Realm of Darkness," in *Selected Philosophical Essays* (Moscow, 1956).
7   Dobroliubov, *Sochinenii*, vol. V, pp. 247, 364.
8   See, for example, articles on that subject in *Rassvet*, a journal for genteel young ladies, which was approved by the government for use in secondary schools. Other representative pieces include N. I. Pirogov, "Voprosy zhizni," *Morskii sbornik* (1856); S. Andreeva, "Drugaia pora," *Otechestvennye zapiski*, vol. 134 (1861); "Zhaloba zhenshchiny," *Sovremennik* (May 1857), p. 58. Memoirs by women influenced by these ideas are often critical of their own mothers. E. Vodovozova, *Na zare zhizni*, vol. I, part I. A-va [A. N. Kazina], "Zhenskaia zhizn'," *Otechestvennye zapiski* (March 1875), pp. 203–59.
9   Evgenia Konradi, in *Zhenskii vestnik*, no. 1, pp. 42–3. See also Nadezhda Suslova-Erisman's book review of Maria Manassein, "O vospitanii detei v pervye gody zhizni," in *Arkhiv*, vol. 6, no. 4 (December 1870), pp. 21–31. See Vodovozova, vol. II, pp. 85–8. Also see the pedagogical articles of A-va [A. N. Kazina] in *Otechestvennye zapiski*, vol. 217 (December 1874), pp. 193–229; vol. 220 (June 1875), pp. 337–66; vol. 227, (August 1876), pp. 383–410; vol. 229 (December 1876), pp. 281–322.
10   N. V. Shelgunov, L. P. Shelgunova, and M. L. Mikhailov, *Vospominaniia v dvukh tomakh* (Moscow, 1967), vol. I, p. 137. There was also an enormous increase in the number of journals devoted to children and childcare. Titles such as *Kindergarten, The Children's Journal, Children's Reading*, the *Russian Pedagogical News*, and *Education* are merely representative examples.
11   N. I. Pirogov, "Voprosy zhizni," is quoted in *Sbornik pamiati Anny Pavlovny Filosofovoi*, 2 vols. (Petrograd, 1915), vol. I, p. 10. John Shelton Curtiss, "Russian Sisters of Mercy in the Crimea, 1854–1855," *Slavic Review*, vol. XXV, no. 1 (March 1966), pp. 84–100. Similar in tone to Pirogov's work is F. T-l', "O nian'kakh," *Zhurnal dlia vospitaniia*, vol. III (1858), pp. 443–63: "Nobody would deny that besides her duties towards her

children, every woman has still other unavoidable obligations towards her husband,
herself and the society to which she belongs."

12 Maria Vernadskaia, *Sobranie sochinenii* (St. Petersburg, 1862), pp. 99–103, 113–15, 136.

13 M. M. Mikhailov, "Zhenshchiny, ikh vospitanie, i znachenie v sem'e i obshchestve,"
Sovremennik (April, May, August, 1860). On the triangle, see Tatiana Bogdanovich,
Liubov liudei shestidesiatykh godov (Leningrad, 1929). For more details, see Richard
Stites, "M. L. Mikhailov and the Emergence of the Woman Question," *Canadian Slavic
Studies* (Summer 1969), pp. 178–99.

14 For the debates, see Vodovozova, *Na zare zhizni*, vol. II, and Shtakenshneider, *Dnevnik
i zapiski*.

15 See F. T-l', "O nian'kakh," and Vodovozova, *Na zare zhizni*, vol. II, pp. 119–35, for
examples of the connections between family and social concerns. For the contrasting
European and American experiences, see the following: Lawrence Stone, *The Family,
Sex and Marriage in England, 1500–1800* (New York, 1977); Edward Shorter, *The Making
of the Modern Family* (New York, 1978); Eli Zaretsky, *Capitalism, the Family and Personal
Life* (New York, 1976); Barbara Welter, "The Cult of True Womanhood," *American
Quarterly*, vol. XVIII (Summer 1976), pp. 151–74; Nancy Cott, *The Bonds of Womanhood*
(New Haven, 1977).

16 Quoted by V. I. Semevskii, "N. D. Khvoshchinskaia-Zaionchkovskaia," *Russkaia mysl'*,
no. 10 (1890), pp. 73–4. For an examination of these antifamily ideas as they were
developed by revolutionaries of the late nineteenth and early twentieth centuries, see
Richard Stites, *The Women's Liberation Movement in Russia*, chaps. VI, VIII, and XI.

17 Likhacheva, *Materialy*, vol. III, p. 468.

18 E. A. Slovtsova-Kamskaia, "Zhenshchina v sem'e i obshchestve," *Istoricheskii vestnik*
(August 1881), pp. 766, 779–80.

19 S. Ashevskii, "Russkoe studenchestvo v epokhu shestidesiatykh godov," *Sovremennyi
mir* (August 1907), pp. 20–1. See also L. F. Panteleev, *Vospominaniia* (Moscow, 1958),
pp. 213–15; and Whittaker, "The Women's Movement," pp. 39–40.

20 E. F. Iunge, *Vospominaniia* (Moscow, 1933), p. 216.

21 Likhacheva, *Materialy*, vol. III, pp. 472–4; Whittaker, "The Women's Movement," pp.
40–2.

22 Whittaker, "The Women's Movement."

23 Quoted by Daniel Brower, *Training the Nihilists* (Ithaca, 1975), p. 213.

24 Natalia Ivanina *née* Shpilovskaia, "Otchet o voskresnoi zhenskoi shkole," *Russkii in-
valid*, no. 197 (September 14, 1860), pp. 737–8.

25 Biographical information on Trubnikova was provided by her daughter and her sister.
Olga Bulanova-Trubnikova, *Tri pokolenii* (Moscow, 1928), pp. 136–7. Vera Cherkesova,
"Maria Vasilevna Trubnikova," *Zhenskoe delo*, vol. XII (December 1899), pp. 15–37.

26 *Sbornik pamiati Anny Pavlovny*, vol. I, p. 120. See also V. Stasov, *Nadezhda Vasilevna
Stasova, vospominaniia i ocherki* (St. Petersburg, 1899).

27 *Sbornik pamiati Anny Pavlovny*, vol. I, p. 73.

28 The two-volume collection, *Sbornik pamiaty Anny Pavlovny*, is devoted to Filosofova
and the movement she helped to lead. For a good general account of the activities of
all three women, see Richard Stites, *The Women's Liberation Movement in Russia*, chap.
III.

29 Bulanova-Trubnikova, *Tri pokolenii*, pp. 80–1.

30 The charter was provided by Bulanova-Trubnikova, *Tri pokolenii*, p. 89.

31 Quoted in *Sbornik pamiati Anny Pavlovny*, vol. I, p. 128.

32 Accounts of efforts to establish the Society for Inexpensive Lodgings can be found in
E. Shtakenshneider, *Dnevnik i zapiski*, pp. 349–57; Stasov, *Nadezhda Stasova*, pp. 214–15;
Sbornik pamiati Anny Pavlovny, vol. I, pp. 125–36. What remained was a far more
modest undertaking that had originated two years before: a translating cooperative,
headed by Trubnikova, Stasova, and Filosofova and employing around twenty-three
women. As the firm "Stasova and Trubnikova" publications, the collective lasted until

1869. It was responsible for translating and publishing important children's books, including the works of Hans Christian Andersen. For a list of their publications, see N. N. Golitsyn, *Bibliograficheskii slovar' russkikh pisatel'nits* (St. Petersburg, 1889), entry for Trubnikova.

33 Bulanova-Trubnikova, *Tri pokolenii*, p. 104; Likhacheva, *Materialy*, vol. III, pp. 497–9; Shtakenshneider, *Dnevnik i zapiski*, pp. 408–9, 420–1. On Solodovnikova, see B. Koz'min, *Revoliutsionnoe podpol'e v epokhu belogo terrora* (Moscow, 1929), pp. 18–24.

34 An excellent account of the "liberal" struggle for women's higher education has been provided by Whittaker, "The Women's Movement." For a more detailed version, see Ruth Dudgeon, *Women and Higher Education in Russia 1855–1905* (George Washington University, unpublished Ph.D. dissertation, 1975).

35 Konradi's letter was reproduced in B. Sapir, ed., *Lavrov – Years of Emigration*, 2 vols. (Dordrecht, 1974), vol. I, p. 315.

36 E. Konradi, *Zhenskii vestnik*, pp. 40–2.

4. Daughters against parents

1 Sofia Kovalevskaia, *Sonya Kovalevsky: Her Recollections of Childhood* (New York, 1895), p. 93.

2 See the essays by Dmitry Pisarev, N. N. Strakhov, Appollon Grigorev, and Alexander Herzen in I. Turgenev, *Fathers and Sons*, R. E. Matlaw, ed. (New York, 1966).

3 Sergei Stepniak-Kravchinskii, *Underground Russia* (New York, 1883), p. 4.

4 See Daniel Brower, "Fathers, Sons and Grandfathers," *Journal of Social History* (Summer 1969), p. 343.

5 I want to thank Professor Roberta Manning for generously allowing me to use her manuscript on the Russian nobility, on which I have based this discussion.

6 A look at volume I, part 2, of the biographical dictionary, *Deiateli Russkogo revoliutsionnogo dvizhenii; bio-bibliograficheskii slovar'* (Moscow, 1927), reveals dozens of women who acquired police records for such vague crimes as "political unreliability" or "professing the doctrine of nihilism."

7 E. I. Bervi, "Iz moikh vospominaniia," *Golos Minuvshago* (May 1915), pp. 122–4.

8 Materials on the Korvin-Krukovskii family include the following: Ia. A. Shtraikh, *Sestry Korvin-Krukovskie* (Moscow, 1934); I. S. Knizhnik-Vetrov, *Russkie Deiatel'nitsy pervogo Internatsionala i Parizhskoi Kommuny* (Moscow, 1964); S. V. Kovalevskaia, *Vospominaniia i pis'ma* (Moscow, 1951), translated into English under the title *Sonya Kovalevsky: Her Recollections of Childhood*.

9 This is the expression that her sister, Sofia, used to describe the impact of the emancipation in her novel *Vera Vorontsoff* (Boston, 1895).

10 Shtraikh, *Sestry*, p. 12; Sofia Kovalevskaia, *Vospominaniia i pis'ma*, pp. 70–2.

11 Shtraikh, pp. 16–17.

12 Knizhnik-Vetrov, *Russkie*, pp. 45, 139, 162–3, 188–9.

13 For accounts of several other Russian women who played equally prominent roles in the Commune, see Knizhnik-Vetrov.

14 A-va [A. N. Kazina], "Zhenskaia zhizn'," *Otechestvennye zapiski*, no. 3 (March 1875), p. 172; Bervi, "Iz moikh," p. 125.

15 Ekaterina Zhukovskaia, *Zapiski* (Leningrad, 1930), pp. 20–1; Shtraikh, *Sestry*, p. 17.

16 Maria K. Tsebrikova, "Vospominaniia," *Zvezda*, no. 6 (1935), p. 191.

17 See V. I. Semevskii, "N. D. Khvoshchinskaia-Zaionchkovskaia," *Russkaia starina*, no. 1–3 (1891).

18 N. D. Khvoshchinskaia, *Povesti i rasskazy* (Moscow, 1963), pp. 185–6.

19 See Aleksandr Smirnov, *Pervaia Russkaia zhenshchina-vrach* (Moscow, 1960); *Pervyi Zhenskii Kalendar' na 1901 g.*, P. N. Arian, ed. (St. Petersburg, 1901).

20 N. S. "Rasskaz v pis'makh," *Sovremennik*, vol. CII, no. 7–8 (1864), pp. 141–68.

21 Actually, Khvoshchinskaia displayed some ambivalence, too. She wrote: "It is possible to throw over one's stupid and cruel family, to renounce one's attachments and to take up work – but that would be to live by halves, and that in itself is abnormal; it creates its own griefs and discomforts." Quoted by Semevskii, "N. D. Khvoshchinskaia-Zaionchkovskaia," *Russkaia starina*, p. 67.

22 I. M. Krasnoperov, *Zapiski raznochintsa* (Moscow, 1929).

23 Kovalevskaia, *Vospominaniia i pis'ma*, p. 100.

24 Parental power over daughters, the law read, is absolute. Marriage limits it, but does not do away with it. What that meant for unmarried daughters over the age of majority, the law did not specify. See the collection *Zhenskoe pravo* (St. Petersburg, 1873) or Ia. Kantorovich, *Zakony o zhenshchinakh* (St. Petersburg, 1899).

25 E. P. Karnovich, *O razvitii zhenskogo truda v Peterburge* (St. Petersburg, 1865), especially pp. 16, 69–70.

26 E. Kozlinina, *Za polveka* (Moscow, 1913), p. 313. Wrote Olga Bulanova-Trubnikova, with slight exaggeration: "The only work for women was as governess, class mistress, actress or seamstress, but in all these areas the supply exceeded the demand." *Tri pokolenii*, p. 88.

27 The salaries were given by Karnovich, pp. 50–7. A governess, he wrote, generally earned less than 200 rubles per year, but this included room and board (pp. 99–100). For rents, see Reginald Zelnik, *Labor and Society in Tsarist Russia* (Stanford, 1971), chap. 7. He wrote that in 1857 there were no more than sixty-six buildings in the entire city where housing could be found for less than ten rubles per year (see p. 241). Also see James H. Bater, *St. Petersburg: Industrialization and Change* (Montreal, 1977), chap. 7.

28 Quoted in *Sbornik pamiaty Anny Pavlovny Filosofovoi*, 2 vols. (Petrograd, 1915) vol. II, pp. 102–3.

29 E. A. Shtakenshneider, *Dnevnik i zapiski* (Moscow, 1934), p. 325.

30 For the commune, see Kornei Chukovskii, *Liudi i knigi shestidesiatykh godov* (Leningrad, 1934). Ekaterina Zhukovskaia, *Zapiski*, provided a rather biased and polemical, but nonetheless interesting, account. Also see E. Vodovozova, *Na zare zhizni*, 2 vols. (Moscow, 1964), vol. II, pp. 484–91.

31 See Zhukovskaia, *Zapiski*, especially pp. 22–3, 33–5.

32 See Zhukovskaia, *Zapiski*, pp. 154–6; the *Bio-bibliograficheskii slovar'*, vol. I; Z. Bazileva, "K istorii pervykh artelei raznochintsev," *Voprosy istorii sel'skogo khoziaistva krest'ianstva i revoliutsionnogo dvizhenii v Rossii* (Moscow, 1961), p. 208.

33 Zhukovskaia, *Zapiski*, p. 167; Chukovskii, *Liudi i knigi*, p. 231.

34 Vodovozova, *Na zare zhizni*, vol. II, p. 490.

35 Vodovozova, vol. II, p. 199.

36 Vodovozova, vol. II, p. 201.

37 Vera Zasulich, "Nechaevskoe delo," *Gruppa "Osvobozhdenie Truda"* (Moscow, 1924), vol. II, p. 25; Vodovozova, vol. II, pp. 200–1. Because the court refused to recognize the seamstresses as "the personification of labor," it ordered the machinery to be returned to its owner.

38 E. Garshina, "Nekotorye ob'iasneniia po povodu voprosa o zhenskom trude," *Sanktpeterburgskie Vedomosti*, no. 102. Also see "Pochemy inogda plokho udaiutsia zhenskie arteli," *Sovremennik*, no. 4 (1865).

39 P. Gaideburov, "Zametki na stat'iu G-zhi Garshinoi," *Sanktpeterburgskie Vedomosti*, no. 113.

40 Iulii Zhukovskii, "Zatrudneniia zhenskogo dela," *Sovremennik*, vol. 101, no. 3 (December 1863).

41 Quoted by N. S. Strakhov, *Iz istorii literaturnogo nigilizma* (St. Petersburg, 1890), p. 398.

42 Zasulich, "Nechaevskoe delo," pp. 18–19.

43 Vodovozova, *Na zare zhizni*, vol. II, pp. 118–19.

44 *Sbornik pamiati Anny Pavlovny*, vol. II, p. 79.

45 Tatiana Bogdanovich, *Liubov liudei shestidesiatykh godov* (Leningrad, 1929), pp. 95, 110, 144.

46 S. G. Svatikov, "N. D. Nozhin," *Golos Minuvshago* (October 1914), pp. 30–1; Baron A. I. Del'vig, *Moi vospominaniia* (Moscow, 1913), vol. III, pp. 344–7; N. K. Mikhailovskii, "V peremezhku," *Polnoe sobranie sochinenii* (St. Petersburg, 1909), vol. IV, p. 271.

47 E. Vilenskaia, *Revoliutsionnoe podpol'e v Rossii (60-e gody XIX v)* (Moscow, 1965), and *Khudiadov* (Moscow, 1969).

48 M. M. Klevenskii, "Materialy ob I. A. Khudiakove," *Katorga i Ssylka*, no. 45–46 (1928), pp. 222–3.

49 I. A. Khudiakov, "Iz vospominanii shestidesiatnika," *Istoricheskii vestnik*, no. 11 (1906), p. 405.

50 Klevenskii, "Materialy," pp. 222–3; Khudiakov, "Iz vospominanii," p. 405.

51 Khudiakov, pp. 405–6.

52 See Vilenskaia, *Revoliutsionnoe podpol'e*, Khudiakov, and German A. Lopatin, *Avtobiografiia, pokazaniia, stat'i* (Petersburg, 1922), p. 140.

53 Kovalevskaia, *Vospominaniia i pis'ma*. Beatrice Stillman, "Sofya Kovalevskaya: Growing up in the 'Sixties," *Russian Literature Triquarterly*, no. 9 (Spring 1974).

54 Stillman, pp. 284, 286.

55 Kovalevskaia, *Sonya Kovalevsky*, p. 175; Stillman, pp. 284–5.

56 Both Kozlinina, *Za polveka*, and Vilenskaia, *Revoliutsionnoe*, gave some details on women's communes during the early 1860s.

57 Quoted by Richard Stites, *The Women's Liberation Movement in Russia: Feminism, Nihilism and Bolshevism, 1860–1930* (Princeton, 1978), p. 50.

58 Charles Moser, *Anti-Nihilism in the Russian Novel of the 1860s* (The Hague, 1964), has provided a handy synopsis of several of these works.

59 Quoted by V. A. Badanov and P. N. Andreev, "Obshchestvennaia deiatel'nost N. P. Suslovoi," *Sovetskoe zdravookhranenie*, and by D. Brower, *Training the Nihilists* (Ithaca, 1975), p. 222.

60 Nozhina was placed under surveillance in 1865 for "a dangerous frame of mind" (*obraz mysli*) and for belonging to a "nihilist tendency." So were many other men and women.

5. The nigilistka *as radical: an unequal partnership*

1 M. L. Alekseev and B. P. Koz'min, eds., *Politicheskie protsessy 60-kh godov* (Moscow, 1923), p. 267. The Zhukovskii quote was cited by V. Bazanov, *Iz literaturnoi polemiki 60-kh godov* (Petrozavodsk, 1941), p. 113.

2 E. S. Vilenskaia, *Revoliutsionnoe podpol'e v Rossii (60-e gody XIX v.)* (Moscow, 1965), p. 391.

3 E. Ia. Polivanova, "Teni proshlogo," *Istoricheskii vestnik*, vol. 117 (1909), p. 774.

4 E. S. Vilenskaia, "Proizvoditel'nye assotsiatsii v seredine 60-kh godov, XIX v.," *Istoricheskie zapiski*, vol. 68 (1961), pp. 63–4. This work is the major source for the information on the Ivanovas' cooperative.

5 Vilenskaia, p. 63; B. Koz'min, *Revoliutsionnoe dvizhenie 1860-kh godov* (Moscow, 1932), pp. 144–5.

6 Ekaterina Breshkovskaia, "Iz vospominanii," *Golos Minuvshago*, no. 10–12 (1918), p. 221; L. Deich, "Chernyi Peredel'," *Istoriko-Revoliutsionnyi Sbornik*, vol. II (Leningrad, 1924), p. 292.

7 M. M. Klevenskii, *Ishutinskii kruzhok i pokushenie Karakozova* (Moscow, 1938), p. 47; E. Vilenskaia, *Khudiakov* (Moscow, 1969), pp. 117–22.

8 Vilenskaia, *Revoliutsionnoe podpol'e*, p. 278.

9 R. V. Fillipov, *Revoliutsionnaia narodnicheskaia organizatsiia* (n.p., 1964), p. 164. This is the only source that refers to her statement on women.

10 Quoted by Vilenskaia, *Revoliutsionnoe podpol'e*, p. 277.

11 E. Ia. Polivanova, "Teni proshlogo." The memoir used for this episode is of cloudy origin. Neither the name of Polivanova nor that of Radetskaia can be found in the

literature of the sixties. On the other hand, almost all the other names mentioned in the account are easily authenticated, and the memoir itself is written in a very straightforward fashion, without polemics, despite its somewhat sensational material. It is the fairness of the account, the lack of anger and recrimination, and the candor of its author, together with her obvious sympathy for the revolutionary movement, that argue for its authenticity.

12   A. Uspenskaia, "Vospominaniia shestidesiatnitsy," *Byloe*, no. 18 (1922), p. 20.

13   Uspenskaia, pp. 20–21.

14   B. Engel and C. Rosenthal, eds., *Five Sisters: Women Against the Tsar* (New York, 1975), p. 65; Vera Zasulich, *Vospominaniia* (Moscow, 1931), p. 11. By contrast with the picture of abandonment that Zasulich presented in her memoirs, her sister Aleksandra wrote that Vera kept in contact with her mother and sisters by visiting them every summer. Uspenskaia, "Vospominaniia," p. 20.

15   Engel and Rosenthal, p. 69; Zasulich, p. 15.

16   Uspenskaia, "Vospominaniia," p. 23.

17   Uspenskaia, p. 26.

18   Uspenskaia, pp. 31, 33.

19   B. Koz'min, *Revoliutsionnoe podpol'e v epokhu belogo terrora* (Moscow, 1929), p. 128; Vilenskaia, *Revoliutsionnoe podpol'e*, p. 327.

20   The authorship of this document remains highly controversial. A number of historians, among them E. H. Carr and Franco Venturi, have considered Bakunin to be the primary author. I am inclined to agree with M. Confino, who argued convincingly that it was composed by a group of revolutionaries, including Nechaev, L. Nikiforov (who married Ekaterina Zasulich), and Peter Tkachev. See M. Confino, ed., *Daughter of a Revolutionary* (La Salle, 1973), pp. 32–5, 221–35. In any case, Nechaev's behavior conformed perfectly to the precepts outlined in the catechism.

21   B. Bazilevskii, ed. [Vasilii Ia. Iakovlev], *Gosudarstvennye prestupleniia v Rossii v XIX veka* (Stuttgart, 1903), vol. 1, p. 336. Confino, pp. 228–9.

22   Zasulich, *Vospominaniia*, p. 60; Engel and Rosenthal, *Five Sisters*, pp. 73–4; Philip Pomper, *Sergei Nechaev* (New Brunswick, 1979), pp. 108–10, 118–19. For remarkably similar treatment of Natalie Herzen, the daughter of Aleksandr and Natalie Herzen, see the correspondence reproduced by Confino, *Daughter*, pp. 157–84, especially page 182, where Nechaev once again declares his love to obtain something he wants.

23   Material about the female defendants is based on *Deiateli revoliutsionnogo dvizheniia: bio-bibliograficheskii slovar'*, and Bazilevskii, *Gosudarstvennye prestupleniia*, vol. I.

24   Uspenskaia, "Vospominaniia," p. 21.

25   B. Koz'min, *Nechaev i nechaevtsy* (Moscow, 1931), p. 32.

26   The three were Anna Dementeeva, Vera Zasulich, and Varvara Aleksandrovskaia. See Bazilevskii, *Gosudarstvennye prestupleniia*, pp. 350–1, 369, 387–9, and Koz'min, *Nechaev i nechaevtsy*, pp. 137–9. As an informer, Aleksandrovskaia proved absolutely useless.

27   For Tkachev's life and ideas, see Deborah Hardy, *Petr Tkachev, The Critic as Jacobin* (Seattle, 1977).

28   Bazilevskii, *Gosudarstvennye prestupleniia*, pp. 307–15.

29   Boris Koz'min, "Okolo nechaevskogo dela," *Katorga i Ssylka*, no. 6 (1923), pp. 57–9.

30   Dementeeva eventually completed medical school in France and set up a practice there in 1888. In 1903 she obtained permission to return to Russia, where she worked as a physician until her death in 1922. I. Dzhabadari, who met Tkachev in Zurich in the early 1870s, has left us a rather pathetic picture of her. "During our talk a young, rather plump and coquettish lady walked back and forth in the room, frequently stopping before a large mirror, primping, straightening her hair, fixing her dress. This annoyed me very much. It attracted our attention and interrupted our conversation. She was Tkachev's wife...and according to my friends, who knew her well, she had no serious meaning in the revolutionary movement." I. S. Dzhabadari, "Protsess 50-ti," *Byloe* (September 1907), p. 184.

31 Actually, Russian women who traveled abroad in the late 1860s found many more opportunities for action than those who remained in Russia. Anna Korvin-Krukovskaia, Elizaveta Dmitrieva, and E. Barteneeva all played active roles in the Paris Commune of 1871. Dmitrieva, in particular, was an important organizer of working women. I. S. Knizhnik-Vetrov, *Russkie deiatel'nitsy Pervogo Internatsionala i Parizhskoi kommuny* (Moscow, 1964).

32 "Revoliutsionnoe i studencheskoe dvizhenie 1869 g. v otsenki Tret'ego otdeleniia," *Katorga i Ssylka*, no. 10 (1924), pp. 110, 116, 118–9.

33 Arthur Lehning, ed., *Michael Bakunin, Selected Writings* (London, 1973), p. 83.

34 *Literaturnoe nasledstvo*, vol. 41–42, pp. 141, 147–9.

Introduction to Part III

1 A. F. Koni, *Vospominaniia o dele Very Zasulich* (Moscow, 1933), pp. 138–9.

6. From feminism to radicalism

1 Biographical works on Perovskaia include the following: V. L. Perovskii, *Vospominaniia o sestre* (Moscow, 1927); *Sofia Perovskaia* (Petersburg, 1921); E. A. Pavliuchenko, *Sofia Perovskaia* (Moscow, 1962); "K biografiiam A. I. Zheliabova i S. L. Perovskoi," *Byloe* (August 1906); Vera Figner, *Zapechatlennyi trud* (Moscow, 1964), vol. I, pp. 274–5. See also Perovskaia's farewell letter to her mother, which was reprinted by S. M. Stepniak-Kravchinskii, *Sochineniia* (Moscow, 1958).

2 Aleksandra Kornilova-Moroz, "Perovskaia i osnovanie kruzhka Chaikovtsev," *Katorga i Ssylka*, no. 22 (1926).

3 Aleksandra Kornilova-Moroz, "Avtobiografiia," in *Entsiklopedicheskii slovar' "Granat"* (Moscow), vol. 40, pp. 203–7; Kornilova-Moroz, "Perovskaia i osnovanie," pp. 9–10.

4 Elizaveta Koval'skaia, "Avtobiografiia," in *Entsiklopedicheskii slovar' "Granat"* (Moscow), vol. 40, p. 141; E. Koval'skaia, "Moi vstrechi s S. L. Perovskoi," *Byloe*, no. 16 (1921), p. 43; Barbara Engel and Clifford Rosenthal, eds., *Five Sisters: Women against the Tsar* (New York, 1975), p. 216.

5 Kornilova-Moroz, "Perovskaia," pp. 12–13.

6 Kornilova-Moroz, "Perovskaia," p. 18.

7 Perovskii, *Vospominaniia*, p. 51.

8 Kornilova-Moroz, "Perovskaia," p. 19.

9 Koval'skaia, "Moi vstrechi," p. 43; Engel and Rosenthal, *Five Sisters*, pp. 213–14.

10 S. V. Kovalevskaia, *Vospominaniia i pis'ma* (Moscow, 1961), p. 141.

11 E. Koval'skaia, "Moi vstrechi s Lazarem Goldenbergom," *Katorga i Ssylka*, no. 3 (1924), p. 89.

12 Anna Kuvshinskaia, who later joined the Chaikovskii circle, had taught in a parochial school for girls in Viatka. Before they fired her for "sowing the seeds of nihilism," Kuvshinskaia managed to influence a number of her pupils. One of them later wrote: "I'm indebted to our teacher, Anna Kuvshinskaia, for giving me intellectual direction and a political perspective." Kuvshinskaia taught her students to read critically, obtained books for them, and had them read aloud to each other while they did needlework. Larissa Chemodanova, one of her students, also joined the Chaikovskii circle. A. Iakimova, "Avtobiografiia," in *Entsiklopedicheskii slovar' "Granat"* (Moscow), vol. 40, pp. 623–4.

13 E. Koval'skaia, "Iz moikh vospominanii," *Katorga i Ssylka*, no. 21 (1926), pp. 30–1.

14 Kornilova-Moroz, "Avtobiografiia," p. 208.

15 Kornilova-Moroz, "Perovskaia," p. 16.

16 Koval'skaia, "Moi vstrechi s S. L. Perovskoi," p. 44.

17 Kornilova-Moroz, "Perovskaia," p. 19.

18 *Revoliutsionnoe Narodnichestvo*, 2 vols. (Moscow, 1965), vol. I, p. 235.

19 Kornilova-Moroz, "Perovskaia," p. 18. In an account by a participant in the Chaikovskii circle, written around 1880, the proposal was described as follows: "Here Aleksandrov for the first time attempted to propagate his original views on free love. But here, too, he failed. However young the members of the women's circle were, they nevertheless quickly realized that Aleksandrov wanted to lead them into some kind of swamp." *Revoliutsionnoe Narodnichestvo*, vol. I, p. 217.

20 Koval'skaia, "Iz moikh vospominanii," p. 33.

21 Koval'skaia, "Moi vstrechi s S. L. Perovskoi," p. 45; Engel and Rosenthal, *Five Sisters*, p. 217.

22 As one male comrade put it, radical circles could absorb entirely a person's feelings, sympathies, passions, and thoughts. In such circles, "the feeling of friendship becomes a living embodiment not only of tenderness but also of the highest intellectual principles. Friendship achieves such depth and force that it far exceeds even the closest blood relations." Stepniak-Kravchinskii, *Sochineniia*, p. 456.

23 Kornilova-Moroz, "Avtobiografiia," p. 207.

24 I. E. Deniker, "Vospominanii," *Katorga i Ssylka*, no. 11 (1924), p. 27.

25 *Protsess 193-kh* (Moscow, 1906), p. 6; L. Tikhomirov, *Zagovorshchiki i politsii* (Moscow, 1930), p. 105.

26 For one of the more detailed accounts of a fictitious marriage that turned into a charming love story, see Sergei Sinegub, *Zapiski Chaikovtsa* (Moscow, 1929), pp. 18–82. Also see Nikolai Charushin, *O dalekom proshlom* (Moscow, 1926). For a sarcastic commentary, see [L. Tikhomirov], *V podpol'e* (St. Petersburg, 1907).

27 Kornilova-Moroz, "Avtobiografiia," p. 213.

28 *Revoliutsionnoe Narodnichestvo*, vol. I, p. 220.

29 Skvortsova left because of pressures from her family; we do not know why the men left.

30 "Neizdannye pis'ma S. L. Perovskoi," *Krasnyi Arkiv*, vol. III (1923), p. 245. These letters are among the only documents that Perovskaia has left us.

31 Ibid., pp. 246–9.

32 "Sofia Perovskaia v Stavropole," *Katorga i Ssylka*, no. 14 (1925), p. 249.

33 Peter Kropotkin, *Memoirs of a Revolutionist* (New York, 1970), p. 304.

34 P. L. Lavrov, *Narodniki-Propagandisty 1873-1878 godov* (Leningrad, 1925), p. 69.

35 V. Bogucharskii [Vasilii Iakovlev], *Aktivnoe narodnichestvo 70-kh godov* (Moscow, 1912), p. 153.

36 N. Asheshov, *Sofia Perovskaia* (Petersburg, 1921), p. 19.

37 "Starik," "Dvizhenie semidesiatykh godov po Bol'shomy protsessu," *Byloe*, no. 12 (1906), p. 70.

7. Heroines and martyrs

1 Vera Figner, "Studencheskie gody," *Golos Minuvshago*, no. 2 (February 1923), p. 181.

2 Vera Figner, *Zapechatlennyi trud*, 2 vols. (Moscow, 1964), vol. I, pp. 57–8.

3 Vera Figner, *Polnoe sobranie sochineniia*, 6 vols. (Moscow, 1929), vol. V, p. 26.

4 Figner, *Zapechatlennyi trud*, vol. I, p. 59.

5 Figner, *Polnoe sobranie sochineniia*, vol. V, p. 20.

6 Figner, *Zapechatlennyi trud*, vol. I, p. 60.

7 Ibid., p. 100.

8 Ibid., p. 100.

9 Figner, *Polnoe sobranie sochineniia*, vol. V, p. 30.

10 Kuliabko-Koreskii, who knew both Figner and her husband in Zurich, wrote that it was not Filippov's love of science that drew him abroad. "Terribly in love with his beautiful wife, he could not oppose her stubborn striving to go abroad and study medicine, and not wishing to part with her, he retired and followed her to Zurich." N. G. Kuliabko-Koreskii, *Iz davnikh let'* (Moscow, 1931), p. 40.

11 Figner, *Polnoe sobranie sochineniia*, vol. V, p. 39.

12 Figner, *Zapechatlennyi trud*, vol. I, p. 114.

13 J. M. Meijer, *Knowledge and Revolution* (Assen, The Netherlands, 1955), p. 60.

14 International Institute of Social History, Amsterdam, Smirnov Archive (hereafter called IISH, Smirnov Archive).

15 Barbara Engel and Clifford Rosenthal, eds., *Five Sisters: Women against the Tsar* (New York, 1975), p. 13.

16 A. A. Ul'ianovskii, *Zhenshchiny v protsesse 50-ti* (St. Petersburg, 1906), p. 28.

17 According to its regulations, the founders intended the circle to foster women's intellectual development and help them obtain education by means of debates and lectures. Any woman who spoke Russian and was willing to take an active part could be a member. IISH, Smirnov Archive; Engel and Rosenthal, *Five Sisters*, p. 28; Figner, *Polnoe sobranie sochineniia*, vol. V, p. 47.

18 Figner, *Polnoe sobranie sochineniia*, vol. V, pp. 27, 47.

19 Five of those present, Beta Kaminskaia, Sofia Bardina, E. Zavadskaia, A. Khorzhevskaia, and S. Grebnitskaia, were later to die by their own hands.

20 IISH, Smirnov Archive; Engel and Rosenthal, *Five Sisters*, p. 9.

21 On the Fritsche, see Amy Knight, "The Fritsche: A Study of Female Radicals in the Russian Populist Movement," *Canadian Slavic Studies*, vol. 9, no. 1 (Spring 1975), pp. 1–18.

22 Engel and Rosenthal, *Five Sisters*, p. 145; S. M. Stepniak-Kravchinskii, "Olga Liubatovich," in *Sochineniia* (Moscow, 1958), vol. I, p. 588.

23 S. M. Stepniak-Kravchinskii, *Biographie de Sophie Bardina* (Geneva, 1900), pp. 9–10.

24 D. I-va [Dora Aptekman], "Iz zapisok zemskogo vracha," *Russkaia Mysl'*, vol. XII (1884), pp. 48–9.

25 Evgenia Subbotina, *Na revoliutsionnom puti* (Moscow, 1928), pp. 6, 10, 12.

26 Figner, *Polnoe sobranie sochineniia*, vol. VI, p. 72; V. A. Badanov and G. A. Vladimirova, "Russkaia koloniia v Tsurikhe," *Sovetskoe zdravookhranenie*, no. 10 (1969), p. 73.

27 I. S. Dzhabadari, "Protsess 50-ti," *Byloe*, no. 9 (1907), p. 182.

28 IISH, Smirnov Archive; Ul'ianovskii, *Zhenshchiny*, pp. 10, 54.

29 Figner, *Polnoe sobranie sochineniia*, vol. VI, p. 64.

30 Stepniak-Kravchinskii, *Bardina*, pp. 8–9.

31 Vera Figner, "Studencheskie gody," *Golos Minuvshago* (October 1922), p. 168; Boris Sapir, ed., *Lavrov – Years of Emigration*, 2 vols. (Dordrecht, 1974), vol. 2, p. 46.

32 IISH, Smirnov Archive.

33 Engel and Rosenthal, *Five Sisters*, pp. 6, 12.

34 Ibid., pp. 13–15.

35 "Iz avtobiografii Very Figner," *Byloe* (August 1917), pp. 113, 163.

36 Dzhabadari, "Protsess 50-ti," p. 183; "Iz avtobiografii Very Figner," p. 162; Ul'ianovskii, *Zhenshchiny*, p. 31.

37 IISH, Smirnov Archive; "Iz pokazanii V. N. Figner," *Byloe*, no. 7–8 (1906), p. 4; Figner, *Polnoe sobranie sochineniia*, vol. V, p. 94.

38 Marx did have his Russian female adherents, even at this time. Among them, Elizaveta Dmitrieva and Olga Levashova worked quite closely with him in the late 1860s and early 1870s and were active in the Paris Commune. See I. S. Knizhnik-Vetrov, *Russkie deiatel'nitsy pervogo Internatsionala i Parizhskoi Kommuny* (Moscow, 1964).

39 L. Barrive, *Osvoboditel'noe dvizhenie v tsarstvovanie Aleksandra II* (Moscow, 1909), p. 127.

40 See Arthur Lehning, ed., *Michael Bakunin. Selected Writings* (London, 1973), especially p. 83. From the program of the Slavic section of the International, 1872.

41 Vera Figner, "Studencheskie gody," *Golos Minuvshago* (January 1923), pp. 35–6.

42 Vera Figner, "Studencheskie gody," *Golos Minuvshago* (February 1923), pp. 131–2; Ul'ianovskii, *Zhenshchiny*, p. 55; Figner, "Studencheskie gody" (January 1923), p. 38.

43 Figner, *Polnoe sobranie sochineniia*, vol. V, pp. 98–9.

44 Figner, "Studencheskie gody" (January 1923), pp. 38–9.

45 Engel and Rosenthal, *Five Sisters*, pp. 19–20; Figner, "Studencheskie gody" (January 1923), pp. 35–6; Vera Figner, "Posle universiteta," *Golos Minuvshago*, no. 3 (March 1923), p. 98.
46 Engel and Rosenthal, *Five Sisters*, p. 29.
47 Letter of V. Smirnov, a friend and ally of Petr Lavrov, to Buturlin, December 4, 1872. Hoover Institute, Nikolaevskii Archive; S. M. Dionesov, "Russkie Tsiurikhskie studentki-medichki v revoliutsionnom dvizhenii 70-kh godov XIX stoletii," *Sovetskoe zdravookhranenie*, no. 11 (1973), p. 72.
48 Meijer, *Knowledge*, pp. 141–2.
49 Smirnov to Buturlin, June 8, 1973, Nikolaevskii Archive; "Iz avtobiografii Figner," p. 163.
50 Meijer, *Knowledge*, pp. 208–12.
51 Engel and Rosenthal, *Five Sisters*, p. 26.
52 Information on the careers of women with police records can be found in *Deiateli revoliutsionnogo dvizhenii v Rossii. Bio-bibliograficheskii slovar'*, 3 vols. (Moscow, 1927), vol. II.
53 M. P. Dragomanov, *Detoubiistvo, sovershaemoe russkim pravitel'stvom* (Geneva, 1877), pp. 4–5.
54 I. S. Dzhabadari, "Protsess 50-ti," *Byloe*, no. 9 (1907), pp. 180–6.
55 Figner, "Studencheskie gody" (October 1922), pp. 180–1.
56 Engel and Rosenthal, *Five Sisters*, p. 27.
57 Nikolai Morozov, *Povesti moei zhizni*, 3 vols. (Leningrad, 1947), vol. I, p. 434.
58 See Amy Knight, "The Fritsche." Also see R. Stites, "All Russian Social Revolutionary Organization," in *The Modern Encyclopedia of Russian and Soviet History*, vol. 1, pp. 170–2.
59 Dzhabadari, "Protsess 50-ti" *Byloe*, no. 10 (1907), pp. 169–70. Vera Figner wrote: "It must be mentioned that the men opposed the women entering factories. They felt that the work was beyond the women's strength, and that they did not look like factory workers." Vera Figner, "Protsess 50-ti," *Katorga i Ssylka*, no. 33 (1928), p. 13.
60 Dzhabadari, "Protsess 50-ti" no. 10 (1907), p. 170.
61 Ul'ianovskii, *Zhenshchiny*, pp. 62–3; L. Deich, *Rol' Evreev v russkom revoliutsionnom dvizhenii* (Moscow, 1926), vol. 1, p. 91.
62 Ibid., pp. 31, 35.
63 Engel and Rosenthal, *Five Sisters*, pp. 29–31; Dzhabadari, "Protsess 50-ti" no. 10 (1907), p. 171.
64 Letter of E. Obukhova, dated March 6/23, 1877. Hoover Institute, Nikolaevskii Archive. Figner, *Polnoe sobranie sochineniia*, vol. V, p. 95. Olga Liubatovich was probably responsible for this demand. Dzhabadari suggested that it was she who wrote the charter in Zurich, and Kravchinskii described her as the most nihilistic of women, "rejecting marriage and love as unsuitable for a revolutionary." Dzhabadari, "Protsess 50-ti" no. 10 (1907), pp. 172–3; Stepniak-Kravchinskii, *Sochineniia*, p. 588.
65 Dzhabadari, "Protsess 50-ti" no. 10 (1907), pp. 173–6. Their program can be found in the work of B. Itenberg, *Revoliutsionnoe narodnichestvo*, vol. I, pp. 118–23.
66 Subbotina, *Na revoliutsionnom puti*, pp. 17–18.
67 "Pamiati V. I. Aleksandrovoi-Natanson," *Gruppa "Osvobozhdenie Truda,"* vol. II, p. 326.
68 Engel and Rosenthal, *Five Sisters*, p. 30; A. Kiperman, "Narodnicheskaia propaganda sredi ivanovovoznesenskikh rabochikh v 1875 gg.," *Istoriia SSSR*, no. 3 (1961), pp. 139–42.
69 *Gosudarstvennoe prestuplenie*, vol. II, p. 170.
70 *Obshchina*, no. 8–9, p. 9.
71 Ul'ianovskii, *Zhenshchiny*, pp. 56–9; Figner, *Polnoe sobranie sochineniia*, vol. V, p. 191.
72 N. B. Panukhina, " 'Protsess 50-ti' kak akt revoliutsionnoi bor'by," *Istoriia SSSR*, no. 5 (1971), pp. 49, 54; S. M. Stepniak-Kravchinskii, *Izbrannye*, p. 397.
73 Figner, *Polnoe sobranie sochineniia*, vol. V, p. 197.

74 Quoted by Ul'ianovskii, *Zhenshchiny*, p. 38.
75 B. Bazilevskii, ed. [Vasilii Ia. Iakovlev], *Gosudarstvennye prestupleniia v Rossi v XIX veka* (Stuttgart, 1903), vol. II, pp. 404–5; Knight, "The Fritsche," p. 16; Obukhova, March 6/23, 1877, Hoover Institute.
76 Ul'ianovskii, *Zhenshchiny*, p. 51; Figner, *Polnoe sobranie sochineniia*, vol. V, p. 99.
77 E. Salova, "Avtobiografiia," in *Entsiklopedicheskii slovar' "Granat,"* vol. 40, p. 398.
78 Figner, *Zapechatlennyi trud*, vol. I, p. 208.

8. Finding a legitimate outlet

1 V. Smirnov to Rosalie Idelson, June 24, 1876. Hoover Institute, Nikolaevskii Archive.
2 *Vrach*, no. 34 (1880), p. 556.
3 Apart from the sciences, the Lublian courses in Moscow offered Russian language, Russian history, world history, geography, and languages. The first year, sixty-five of the students (about one-third) concentrated in physics and forty-six in mathematics; the following year those numbers had nearly doubled. E. S. Nekrasova, "Zhenskie vrachebnye kursy v Peterburge," *Vestnik Evropy* (December 1882), p. 282; Sophie Satina, *Education of Women in Pre-Revolutionary Russia* (New York, 1966) (reproduction of typewritten copy); Ruth Dudgeon, *Women and Higher Education in Russia, 1855–1905* (George Washington University, unpublished doctoral dissertation, 1975), chap. II.
4 Cynthia Whittaker, "The Women's Liberation Movement during the Reign of Alexander II: A Case Study in Russian Liberalism," *Journal of Modern History*, vol. 48 (June 1976), p. 41.
5 E. Likhacheva, *Materialy dlia istorii zhenskogo obrazovaniia v Rossii* (St. Petersburg, 1899–1901), vol. IV, p. 542.
6 See Chapter 7 of this volume.
7 This statement was made in a speech to the council of the University of Saint Vladimir in Kiev in 1870, calling for better training for midwives. Quoted by S. M. Dionesov, "Stranitsy iz istorii zhenskogo vrachebnogo obrazovaniia v Rossii v XIX veke," *Sovetskoe Zdravookhranenie*, vol. 29 (1970), p. 64. Moscow province figures cited by Nancy Frieden, "Child Care: Medical Reform in a Traditionalist Culture," in D. Ransel, ed., *The Family in Imperial Russia* (Urbana, 1979), p. 237.
8 In a statement to the Council of Ministers, dated December 15, 1870; the chief of police had advised against allowing a woman to serve in any official capacity. Such work, the chief of police warned, "would tear her away from hearth and home and stifle desire to become a good wife and mother. Such a woman would become independent, and would instinctively be contemptuous of everything that had once been her principal vocation." Likhacheva, *Materialy*, vol. IV, pp. 544–5.
9 Likhacheva, *Materialy*, vol. IV, p. 543.
10 Vera Figner, "K biografii V. N. Figner," *Byloe*, no. 5–6 (1906), p. 4.
11 Nekrasova, "Zhenskie vrachebnye kursy," p. 814.
12 *Vrach*, no. 34 (1880), p. 556.
13 Students of the first class left few accounts of their backgrounds, but it is safe to assume that their experiences differed little from those of the women who followed them.
14 V. I. Dmitrieva, *Tak bylo* (Moscow, 1930).
15 A. A. Shibkov, *Pervyi zhenshchiny-mediki Rossii* (Moscow, 1961); S. A. Iakobson, *Zemskii vrach A. G. Arkhangel'skaia* (Moscow, 1958).
16 Iulia A. Kviatkovskaia, *Vospominaniia vrachei Iulii A. Kviatkovskoi i Marii P. Rashkevich* (Paris, 1937).
17 R. M. Plekhanova, "Nasha zhizn' do emigratsii," *Gruppa "Osvobozhednie Truda,"* no. 6, p. 76.
18 E. Pimenova, *Dni minuvshie* (Leningrad, 1929), p. 97.
19 Obituary in *Russkaia mysl'*, no. 2 (1883), pp. 178–9; N. Pozniakov, *Vrach M. P. Mordvinova* (St. Petersburg, 1883), p. 3.

20 Pozniakov, p. 4; A. I. Veretennikova, "Zapiski zemskogo vracha," *Novyi Mir*, no. 3 (1956), p. 206.
21 Kviatkovskaia, *Vospominaniia*, pp. 154, 158–9, 224–5.
22 Nadezhda Golovina-Iurgenson, "Avtobiografiia," *Entsiklopedicheskii slovar' "Granat*," vol. 40, p. 73.
23 Nekrasova, "Zhenskie vrachebnye kursy," p. 828; Likhacheva, *Materialy*, vol. IV, pp. 552–5.
24 A. Shabanova, "Iz pervykh let' zhenskogo meditsinskogo obrazovaniia," in E. Letkova, ed., *K svetu* (St. Petersburg, 1904), p. 294; Nekrasova, "Zhenskie vrachebnye kursy," p. 828.
25 Pimenova, *Dni minuvshie*, pp. 104–5; Sh., "Zhenskie vrachebnye kursy," *Vestnik Evropy*, vol. 1 (1886), p. 350.
26 Nekrasova, "Zhenskie vrachebnye kursy," pp. 827–8.
27 Dmitrieva, *Tak bylo*, p. 167.
28 The program of the Society to Help Women Students was printed in *Otechestvennye zapiski*, vol. 226 (1876), pp. 218–20.
29 The *zemstvo* was an organ of self-government in rural areas. Some of its more important responsibilities were for education and medical care.
30 Dmitrieva, *Tak bylo*, pp. 167–71; E. S-va, "Zhenskie Vrachebnye Kursy v SPb," *Zhenskoe obrazovanie* (1877), p. 113.
31 Nekrasova, "Zhenskie vrachebnye kursy," pp. 834–6.
32 *Vrach*, no. 35 (1880), p. 580; Nekrasova, "Zhenskie vrachebnye kursy," p. 841.
33 E. Nekrasova, *Iz proshlogo zhenskikh kursov* (Moscow, 1886), p. 91.
34 The examples are all drawn from *Deiateli revoliutsionnogo dvizhenii v Rossii. Bio-bibliograficheskii slovar'*, 3 vols. (Moscow, 1927–9), vol. II. A careful reading of this invaluable reference work yields dozens of such cases.
35 Both had dropped out, but one soon resumed her studies and earned her degree in 1882.
36 This was Anna Formakovskaia, the daughter of a village priest, and a school friend of the defendant, Anna Iakimova. The two maintained their friendship even after Iakimova had gone underground. Formakovskaia died of tuberculosis before finishing school. Anna Iakimova, "Bol'shoi protsess ili protsess 193kh," *Katorga i Ssylka*, no. 37 (1927), pp. 28–9.
37 R. M. Plekhanova, "Stranitsa iz vospominanii o V. I. Zasulich," *Gruppa "Osvobozhdenie Truda*," no. 3 (1925), pp. 82–3.
38 A. Pribyleva-Korba, "*Narodnaia Volia.*" *Vospominaniia o 1870–1880kh gg.* (Moscow, 1926), p. 31; Dmitrieva, *Tak bylo*, p. 174.
39 R. M. Plekhanova, "Perifereinyi kruzhok 'Zemli i Voli,' " *Gruppa "Osvobozhdenie Truda*," no. 4 (1925), p. 102. We know that several other women combined organizing efforts with medical studies. Among them were Maria Bondyreva, Elizaveta Rebrova (both of whom had already drawn the attention of the police), and Vera Kazas.
40 The biographical dictionary covering the later period is unfortunately incomplete, but published sections suggest that political activity remained high through 1880 and 1881.
41 The figures of involvement with the police are somewhat misleading, in part because some of the entries do not give the precise date of arrest, in part because some of the people listed became involved with the police several times. In such cases, I have listed the date of first involvement, even when subsequent activities were more serious.
42 My own count is eighty-seven. Pavluchkova estimated eighty, p. 64. Dionesov, using documents from the Third Section, wrote that forty-six women medical students were called to testify at political trials between 1873 and 1878. Dionesov, "Stranitsy," p. 66.
43 Plekhanova, "Perifereinyi kruzhok," p. 102.
44 Kviatkovskaia, *Vospominaniia*, pp. 160–1.
45 Dmitrieva, *Tak bylo*, pp. 196–7.

46 Barbara Engel and Clifford Rosenthal, eds., *Five Sisters: Women against the Tsar* (New York, 1975), p. 33; Vera Figner, *Polnoe Sobranie Sochinenii v shesti tomakh* (Moscow, 1929), vol. V, pp. 142–3.

47 Shibkov, *Pervyi*, pp. 81–2.

48 Z. Okun'kova-Gol'denger, ed., *Delo: Sbornik literaturno-nauchnyi* (Moscow, 1899), p. 64.

49 Her letters were reprinted in *Otechestvennye zapiski*, no. 5 (1878), pp. 124–8.

50 V. S. Nekrasova, "Studentka na voine," *Russkaia Mysl'* (June-July 1898), p. 116. Rosalia Bograd, who also went to the front, confirmed Nekrasova's account. Everywhere she looked, she saw medical personnel treated poorly, the sick cared for inadequately, and military authorities engaged in theft and corruption. Her wartime experiences served to reinforce her radicalism. Plekhanova, "Perifereinyi kruzhok," p. 93.

51 In recognition of their service in the Turkish War, in 1878 the tsar officially granted the female graduate the right to be known as a "woman physician" (*Zhenshchina vrach*).

52 Shabanova, "Iz pervykh," pp. 297, 304; Kviatkovskaia, *Vospominaniia*, p. 81.

53 Okun'kova-Gol'denger, *Delo*, p. 30; *Zhenskoe obrazovanie*, no. 2 (February 1881), pp. 129–30.

54 Dionesov, "Stranitsy," p. 66.

55 Quoted in *Spravochnaia kniga dlia vrachei* (St. Petersburg, 1890), vol. I, pp. 119–20.

56 *Gosudarstvennyi sovet. Otchet po deloproizvodstvo Gos. Sovet za sessiiu 1894–5*, p. 359.

57 Quoted by E. Shchepkina, "Pamiati dvukh zhenshchin-vrachei," *Obrazovanie*, no. 5–6 (1896), p. 103.

58 P. O. Sushchinskii, *Zhenshchina vrach v Rossii* (St. Petersburg, 1883), p. 17.

59 In this, she was preceded by V. Kashevarova-Rudneva, the first woman physician in Russia, who had been granted permission to study medicine so that she might treat Bashkirian women.

60 Veretennikova, "Zapiski," pp. 206–7; Shchepkina, "Pamiati," pp. 92–102.

61 See the memoirs of Kviatkovskaia, Rashkevich, and Pimenova. Also see M. E. Pokrovskaia, *Kak Ia byla gorodskim vrachem dlia bednykh* (St. Petersburg, 1903); S. A. Iakobson, *Zemskii vrach A. G. Arkhangel'skaia*.

62 Likhacheva, *Materialy*, pp. 536–64.

63 Whittaker, "The Women's Liberation Movement," pp. 54, 59.

9. Morality becomes absolutism

1 For various estimates, see Anna Pribyleva-Korba, "Narodnaia Volia," *Vospominaniia o 1870–1880kh gg.* (Moscow, 1926), p. 51; Nikolai Asheshov, *Sofia Perovskaia* (Petersburg, 1921), p. 91; *Narodovol'tsy. Sbornik III* (Moscow, 1931), p. 11; and Franco Venturi, *Roots of Revolution* (New York, 1966).

2 Vera Figner, "Studencheskie gody," *Golos Minuvshago* (February 1923), pp. 137–8.

3 Figner, "Mark Andreevich Natanson," *Katorga i Ssylka*, no. 56 (1929), p. 143; *Zapechatlennyi trud*, vol. I, p. 134.

4 Hoover Institute, Nikolaevskii Archive, file no. 183, box 1, folder 3. The letter is dated October 18, 1876. Its author, D. Aivazov, was a minor radical figure who emigrated abroad in the mid-1870s and remained there.

5 Sofia Ivanova, "Vospominaniia o S. L. Perovskoi," *Byloe*, no. 3 (1906), p. 85; Catherine Breshkovsky, *Hidden Springs of the Russian Revolution* (London, 1931), p. 111.

6 Figner, *Zapechatlennyi trud*, vol. I, p. 155; V. I. Smirnov to R. Idelson, Dec. 10, 1877, Hoover Institute, Nikolaevskii Archive.

7 "Pis'ma uchastnikov protsessa 193-kh," *Krasnyi arkhiv*, no. 5 (1924), p. 137; Vera Figner, *Zapechatlennyi trud*, vol. I, p. 155.

8 Nikolai Morozov, *Povesti moei zhizni*, 3 vols. (Leningrad, 1947), vol. II, pp. 314–19; A. I. Ivanchin-Pisarev, *Khozhdenie v narod* (Moscow, 1929), pp. 78–9; Figner, *Zapechatlennyi trud*, vol. I, p. 171.

9 Figner, *Zapechatlennyi trud*, vol. I, p. 275.

10 "K biografiiam A. I. Zheliabova i S. L. Perovskoi," *Byloe*, no. 8 (1906), p. 121; S. M. Stepniak-Kravchinskii, *Izbrannoe* (Moscow, 1958), pp. 454–5.

11 E. Obukhova, letter dated November, 1877. Hoover Institute, Nikolaevskii Archive, file no. 183.

12 V. Perovskii, *Vospominaniia o sestre* (Moscow, 1927), p. 85.

13 S. Stepniak-Kravchinskii, *Podpol'naia Rossiia* (Moscow, 1958), pp. 95–6; S. N. Valk, ed., *Arkhiv "Zemli i Voli" i "Narodnoi Voli"* (Moscow, 1932), p. 43; E. Bogucharskii, ed., *Revoliutsionnaia zhurnalistika semidesiatykh godov* (Paris, 1905), pp. 338–44; "K biografiiam A. I. Zheliabova i S. L. Perovskoi," p. 122.

14 I. Tiutchev, *Revoliutsionnoe dvizhenie 1870–1880 gg.* (Moscow, 1925), p. 66; Stepniak-Kravchinskii, *Podpol'naia Rossiia*, p. 448.

15 Olga Liubatovich, "Dalekoe i nedavee," *Byloe*, no. 5 (1906), p. 222; Figner, *Zapechatlennyi trud*, vol. I, p. 192; *Bor'tsy za svobodu* (Moscow, 1917), pp. 8–9.

16 Ekaterina Koval'skaia, "Moi vstrechi s S. L. Perovskoi," *Byloe*, no. 16 (1921), pp. 47–8; V. L. Perovskii, "Moi vospominanii," *Katorga i Ssylka*, no. 17 (1925), p. 72. See also *Sofia L'vovna Perovskaia* (London, 1882), pp. 20–1, and "K biografiiam Zheliabova i Perovskoi," p. 126.

17 B. Engel and C. Rosenthal, eds., *Five Sisters: Women Against the Tsar* (New York, 1975), p. 177.

18 On Oshanina, see N. S. Rusanov, *Iz moikh vospominanii* (Berlin, 1923), pp. 126–8; G. F. Cherniavskaia-Bokhanovskaia, *Maria Nikolaevna Olovennikova* (Moscow, 1930); A. Pribyleva-Korba, *Vospominaniia*, p. 111.

19 Sofia Ivanova, "Avtobiografiia," in *Entsiklopedicheskii slovar' "Granat,"* vol. 40; "Vospominaniia o S. L. Perovskoi," and *Pervaia tipografiia "Narodnoi voli"* (Moscow, 1928).

20 E. Dubenskaia i O. Bulanova, *Tatiana Ivanovna Lebedeva* (Moscow, 1930); M. Frolenko, "Tatiana Ivanovna Lebedeva-Frolenko," *Katorga i Ssylka*, no. 2 (1924); A. Pribyleva-Korba, *Vospominaniia*, pp. 98–9.

21 Anna Iakimova, "Avtobiografiia," in *Entsiklopedicheskii slovar' "Granat,"* vol. 40; "Bol'shoi protsess ili protsess 193-kh," *Katorga i Ssylka*, no. 37 (1924); V. A. Novitzkii, *Iz vospominanii zhandarme* (1929), p. 238.

22 S. Ivanova, *Pervaia tipografiia "Narodnoi Voli."*

23 Figner, *Zapechatlennyi trud*, vol. I, p. 208; Pribyleva-Korba, *Vospominaniia*, p. 45.

24 M. El'tsina-Zak, "Iz vstrech s pervomartovtsami," *Katorga i Ssylka*, no. 12 (1924), pp. 126–8.

25 See M. Boxer and J. Quataert, eds., *Socialist Women* (New York, 1978), for case studies of women's role in Western European socialist movements.

26 Figner, *Zapechatlennyi trud*, vol. I, p. 229.

27 Ivanova, *Pervaia tipografiia*, p. 9.

28 Ivanova, *Pervaia tipografiia*, pp. 11, 14; N. Bukh, "Pervaia tipografiia 'Narodnoi Voli'," *Katorga i Ssylka*, no. 57–8 (1929), pp. 72–3; [Lev Tikhomirov], *V podpol'e* (St. Petersburg, 1907), p. 140.

29 Ivanova, "Vospominaniia o S. L. Perovskoi," p. 87.

30 Praskovia Ivanovskaia, "Pervye tipografii 'Narodnoi Voli'," *Katorga i Ssylka*, no. 24 (1926); "L. D. Terenteeva," *Katorga i Ssylka*, no. 76 (1931).

31 See D. Kuz'min [E. E. Kolosov], *Narodovol'cheskaia zhurnalistika* (Moscow, 1930), pp. 175–203.

32 Figner, "Avtobiografiia," in *Entsiklopedicheskii slovar' "Granat,"* vol. 40, p. 469; "Iz pokazanii V. N. Figner," *Byloe*, no. 7–8 (1906); *Zapechatlennyi trud*, vol. I. pp. 214–15; Frolenko, "Tatiana Ivanovna Lebedeva-Frolenko," p. 226.

33 "Hartmann's Revelations," *New York Herald*, July 30, 1881.

34 N. M. Druzhinin, *Chlen ispolnitel'nogo komiteta partii "Narodnaia volia" Anna Vasilevna Iakimova* (Moscow, 1926), pp. 34–5.

35 Asheshov, *Sofia Perovskaia*, pp. 71–2, 88–9; Perovskii, "Vospominanii," p. 72.

36 Ivanovskaia, "Pervye tipografii," p. 50.

37 Figner, *Bor'tsy za svobodu*, pp. 4–5; Asheshov, *Sofia Perovskaia*, p. 76; D. Footman, *Red Prelude* (London, 1968).

38 Perovskii, "Vospominaniia," p. 72.

39 *Delo 1-go Marta 1881 g.* (St. Petersburg, 1906), pp. 17, 22–3; Galina Cherniavskaia-Bokhanovskaia, "Avtobiografiia," *Katorga i Ssylka*, no. 43, p. 27; Footman, *Red Prelude*, p. 147.

40 E. Sidorenko, "Iz vospominaniia o 1-m Marta 1881 goda," *Katorga i Ssylka*, no. 5 (1923), pp. 50–3; "Avtobiografiia," in *Entsiklopedicheskii slovar' "Granat,"* vol. 40, p. 418.

41 Figner, "Sofia Perovskaia," *Byloe*, no. 4–5 (1918), p. 10.

42 Figner, *Zapechatlennyi trud*, vol. I., p. 134.

43 See, for example, Praskovia Ivanovskaia, "Idillia," *Russkie zapiski*, no. 8 (1916), translated in *Five Sisters*, pp. 104–5.

44 N. Bukh, "Pervyi protsess narodovol'tsev," *Katorga i Ssylka*, no. 8 (1931), pp. 126–7, 137; Frolenko, "Tatiana Ivanovna Lebedeva-Frolenko," p. 229.

45 Hoover Institute, Nikolaevskii Archive.

10. The personal versus the political

1 Alice Blackwell, ed., *The Little Grandmother of the Russian Revolution* (Boston, 1919), p. 28.

2 Of the degree of student spinsterhood, the journal *Vrach* had this to say: "Spinsterhood, as we know, is one of the most powerful causes of the development of various neuroses and psychoses, and a mass of other infirmities, which could prove a major obstacle to successful medical practice," no. 34 (1880), p. 557. The figures on the proportion of married women physicians are derived by the very rough method of counting hyphenated names listed in the *Rossisskii meditsinskii spisok* for 1904, pp. 416–31. One source suggests a marriage rate of approximately one-third for a later generation of women physicians. See E. Ia. Belitskaia, "Poliklinicheskaia pomoshch v dorevoliutsionnom Peterburge i uchastie v nei zhenshchin-vrachei," *Sovetskoe zdravookhranenie*, no. 10.

3 E. Shchepkina, "Pamiati dvukh zhenshchin-vrachei," *Obrazovanie*, no. 5–6 (1896), pp. 92–101.

4 Hoover Institute, Nikolaevskii Archive, file no. 183.

5 "Pis'ma uchastnikov protsessa 193-kh," *Krasnyi arkhiv*, no. 5 (1924), pp. 134–5.

6 Nikolaevskii Archive, file no. 183.

7 S. M. Stepniak-Kravchinskii, "Olga Liubatovich," in *Sochineniia* (Moscow, 1958), vol. I, p. 588; Olga Liubatovich, "Dalekoe i nedavnee," *Byloe*, no. 6 (1906), p. 131.

8 The government decree was translated by J. Meijer, *Knowledge and Revolution* (Assen, 1955). Nikolaevskii Archive, file no. 32, letter dated December 10, 1875. On the pessary, see Norman Himes, *Medical History of Contraception* (New York, 1970).

9 The nine women were Aleksandra Obodovskaia, Liubov Serdiukova, Olga Schleissner, Sofia Ivanova, Ekaterina Obukhova, Anna Iakimova, Gesia Gelfman, Olga Liubatovich, and Galina Cherniavskaia.

10 E. Pimenova, *Dni minuvshie* (Leningrad, 1929), p. 104; International Institute of Social History, Amsterdam, Smirnov Archive.

11 Blackwell, *Little Grandmother*, pp. 39–40.

12 Vera Figner, "Mark Andreevich Natanson," *Katorga i Ssylka*, no. 56 (1929), p. 147. Liubatovich, "Dalekoe i nedavnee," pp. 129–31; Sergei Kravchinskii, "Olga Liubatovich," in *Sochinenii* (Moscow, 1958), pp. 597–8; Galina Cherniavskaia-Bokhanovskaia, "Avtobiografiia," *Katorga i Ssylka*, no. 43, pp. 27–31.

13 Nikolaevskii Archive, file no. 183, letter dated June 23, 1877; Hoover Institute, Volkhovskii Collection, box number 4.

14 A. Elsnits to Zemphira Ralli, undated letter. Nikolaevskii Archive, file no. 183, box 2; Smirnov to Idelson, November 21, 1875.

15 A. I. Ivanchin-Pisarev, *Khozhdenie v narod* (Moscow, 1929), pp. 78–9; Nikolai Morozov, *Povesti moei zhizni*, 3 vols. (Leningrad, 1947), vol. II, pp. 314–19; Hoover Institute, Chaikovskii Archive; Nikolaevskii Archive, file no. 183, letter of V. Gol'shtein dated September 22, 1874.

16 Ekaterina Breshkovskaia, "Vospominaniia propagandistky," *Byloe*, no. 5 (1906), pp. 320–1; Blackwell, *Little Grandmother*, pp. 41–75.

17 In 1897, 21.3 percent of working women were literate, as compared with 56.5 percent of working men. See Rose Glickman, "The Russian Factory Woman, 1880–1914," in D. Atkinson, A. Dallin, and G. Lapidus, eds., *Women in Russia* (Stanford, 1977).

18 Nadezhda Golovina, "Avtobiografiia," in *Entsiklopedicheskii slovar' "Granat,"* vol. 40, p. 74; Praskovia Ivanovskaia, "Avtobiografiia," in *Entsiklopedicheskii slovar' "Granat,"* vol. 40, p. 156.

Conclusion: a mixed legacy

1 The letter is reprinted in S. Stepniak-Kravchinskii, *Izbrannoe*, pp. 470–1.

2 Vera Zasulich, *Vospominaniia* (Moscow, 1931), pp. 15–16; Vera Figner, *Polnoe sobranie sochinenii*, vol. 5, p. 144.

3 Praskovia Tatlina, "Vospominaniia Praskov'i Nikolaevny Tatlinoi," *Russkii arkhiv* (1899), pp. 199–200.

4 Quoted by Dmitrij Tschizewskij, *Russian Intellectual History* (Ann Arbor, 1978), p. 217.

5 Vera Figner, *Zapechatlennyi trud*, vol. I, p. 275.

6 Stepniak-Kravchinskii, *Izbrannoe*, p. 470.

7 Olga Bulanova-Trubnikova, *Tri pokolenii* (Moscow, 1928), pp. 146ff.

8 V. A. Anzimirov, *Kramol'niki* (Moscow, 1907), p. 96; Catherine Breshkovsky, *Hidden Springs of the Russian Revolution* (London, 1931), p. 112.

9 See M. Boxer and J. Quataert, eds., *Socialist Women* (New York, 1978), and Richard Stites, *The Women's Liberation Movement in Russia: Feminism, Nihilism and Bolshevism, 1860–1930* (Princeton, 1978), chaps. VII, VIII, and IX.

10 Zasulich, *Vospominaniia*, p. 31.

BIBLIOGRAPHIC ESSAY

There is a wealth of primary sources available to the reader who would like to pursue this topic further. In English, Karolina Pavlova, *A Double Life* (Ann Arbor, 1978), has provided a fictional account of an aristocratic young woman's existence during the prereform period. *Sonya Kovalevsky: Her Recollections of Childhood* (New York, 1895) recorded the unhappy early years of the woman who went on to become one of Europe's first female mathematicians. Elizaveta Vodovozova, in *A Russian Childhood* (London, 1961), an abridgement of the lengthier *Na zare zhizni* (Moscow, 1964), has provided another account of childhood and adolescence, as well as a vivid description of the social ferment of the early 1860s. For the 1870s, Vera Figner's *Memoirs of a Revolutionist* remains one of the best sources available, although this translation of the two-volume *Zapechatlennyi trud* (Moscow, 1964) omits much useful material. The work edited by Barbara Engel and Clifford Rosenthal, *Five Sisters: Women against the Tsar* (New York, 1975), contains the memoirs of Vera Figner, Vera Zasulich, Olga Liubatovich, Praskovia Ivanovskaia, and Elizaveta Koval'skaia. See also Catherine Breshkovsky, *Hidden Springs of the Russian Revolution* (Oxford, 1931). Sergei Stepniak-Kravchinskii, in *Underground Russia* (London, 1883), has provided colorful pen-portraits of many radical women of the 1870s.

The sources available to readers with a knowledge of Russian are far greater, particularly if they are interested in the women of the 1860s and 1870s. In the Nikolaevskii Archive of the Hoover Institute and the Smirnov collection of the Institute for Social History in Amsterdam, I found rich documentary evidence concerning the personal lives of female students and political activists. Documents, letters, and personal reminiscences of the people who participated in the movements of the 1860s and 1870s have been published in the journals *Byloe, Katorga i Ssylka, Golos Minuvshago,* and *Krasnyi Arkhiv.* Tatiana Bogdanovich, ed., *Liubov liudei shestidesiatykh godov* (Leningrad, 1929), and N. V. Shelgunov, L. P. Shelgunova, and M. L. Mikhailov, *Vospominaniia,* 2 vols. (Moscow, 1967), have documented early efforts to restructure relationships between the sexes. *Sbornik pamiaty Anny Pavlovny Filosofovoi,* 2 vols. (Petrograd, 1915), is a compendium of primary and secondary material covering the first decades of the women's movement in Russia. Useful documentary collections containing materials on revolutionary women include the following: S. N. Valk, ed., *Arkhiv "Zemli i Voli" i "Narodnoi Voli"* (Moscow, 1932); B. Itenberg, ed., *Revoliutsionnoe narodnichestvo,* 2 vols. (Moscow, 1965); B. Bazilevskii, ed., *Gosudarstvennye prestupleniia v Rossii v XIX veka* (Paris, 1905), vols. II and III; *Protsess 193-kh* (Moscow, 1906); *Delo 1-go Marta 1881 g.* (St. Petersburg, 1906).

Published memoirs have also provided primary sources for this volume. Many appeared in the journals cited earlier. Of those published in book form, I found the work of Tatiana Passek, *Iz dal'nykh let',* 2 vols. (Moscow, 1963), one of the few memoirs we have of a woman of the first generation of the intelligentsia, to be a rich resource for the details of women's lives in the second third of the nineteenth century. Elena A. Shtakenshneider, *Dnevnik i zapiski* (Moscow, 1934; reprinted by Oriental Research Partners, Newtonville,

Mass., 1980), Elizaveta Vodovozova, *Na zare zhizni*, 2 vols. (Moscow, 1964), and Ekaterina Zhukovskaia, *Zapiski* (Leningrad, 1930), have provided useful firsthand accounts not only of women's lives but also of the social ferment of the 1860s and the ways it affected female participants. For the 1870s, Vera Figner's *Polnoe sobranie sochineniia v shesti tomakh* (Moscow, 1929) is the most comprehensive account. Also see *Entsiklopedicheskii slovar' "Granat"* (Moscow), vol. 40, which contains brief autobiographies of many prominent activists of the 1870s, and *Deiateli revoliutsionnogo dvizhenii v Rossii. Bio-bibliograficheskii slovar'* (Moscow, 1929), which provides information on the origins, backgrounds, and political activities, as well as bibliographic references, for virtually everyone who acquired a police record during the reign of Alexander II.

The most useful secondary source in English is the work of Richard Stites, *The Women's Liberation Movement in Russia: Feminism, Nihilism and Bolshevism, 1860–1930* (Princeton, 1978). Stites has provided a wealth of information and bibliographic references for the major figures of the period I have studied. In Russian, the best work is that of Elena Likhacheva, *Materialy dlia istorii zhenskogo obrazovanii v Rossii* (St. Petersburg, 1899–1901). This four-volume study ranges far beyond its topic of women's education to explore the circumstances of women's lives and the birth and development of the Russian women's movement. For the first generation of women of the intelligentsia, who have left us relatively few primary sources, I found most helpful the work of Mikhail Gershenzon, "Materialy po istorii russkoi literatury i kultury. Russkaia zhenshchina 30-kh godov," *Russkaia mysl'*, vol. XI (December 1911), E. H. Carr, *The Romantic Exiles* (Boston, 1961), and P. Miliukov, "Liubov idealistov tridsatykh godov," in *Iz istorii russkoi intelligentsii* (St. Petersburg, 1903). Background information on the status and role of women in nineteenth-century Russia can be found in two studies: D. Ransel, ed., *The Family in Imperial Russia* (Urbana, 1978); Dorothy Atkinson, Alexander Dallin, and Gail Lapidus, eds., *Women in Russia* (Stanford, 1977).

INDEX

abortion, 193
adultery, 28, 36–7, 41–2; *see also* sexual relations
Alarchin courses, 60, 98, 105, 110, 112, 113, 115, 127, 157
Aleksandrov, Vasilii, 113, 116, 118, 120, 122
Aleksandrova, Varvara, 133, 144, 145, 149, 150, 151, 154
Aleksandrovskaia, Varvara, 98–9
Alekseeva, Ekaterina, 89
Alekseeva, Maria, 89
Alexander II, 45, 47, 49, 50, 172, 173, 200
anarchism, 145, 202
Anserova, Ekaterina, 135
Aptekman, Dora, 133, 134, 144, 146, 147, 172, 174
Aptekman, Osip, 112, 134
Arkhangel'skaia, Aleksandra, 160, 165–6
Armfeld, Anna, 201
Armfeld, Natalia, 201

Bakunin, Mikhail, 10, 22, 101, 140–1, 144
Bakunin, Varvara, 10
Bardina, Sofia, 128, 131–3, 136, 137, 138, 139, 140, 141, 144, 145, 149, 150, 151, 152, 153, 154, 201
Beliaeva, Elizaveta, 98, 115
Belinskii, Vissarion, 22–3, 35–6
Bervi, E., 65
Bervi-Flerovskii, F., 65; *The Position of the Working Class in Russia*, 116
Bestuzhev courses, 61
Black Repartition, 107, 178, 186
Blavatskaia, Elena, 35
Boborykina, Iulia, 98
Bogdanovich, Iurii, 187
Bogoliubov, A., 107, 165
Bograd, Rosalia (Plekhanova), 167
Bolsheviks, 202
Breshkovskaia, Ekaterina, 189, 192, 194, 196–7, 202
Bukh, Nikolai, 182

"Catechism of a Revolutionary," 97
Catherine the Great, 16, 23
celibacy, 141, 149–50; *see also* sexual relations
Chaikovskii circle, 113, 120, 122, 124–5, 179
Chaikovskii, Nikolai, 113, 121, 122, 195–6
Chemodanov, Vasilii, 121
Chemodanova, Larissa, 120–1, 122, 124, 174, 194–5
Chernyshevskaia, Olga, 80–1
Chernyshevskii, Nikolai, 72–3, 74, 80–1, 93, 96; *What Is to Be Done?*, 72–4, 77, 79, 80, 112, 123, 160
Chikoidze, Mikhail, 145, 151
childbearing, 10
childrearing, 11–12, 14, 17, 23, 26, 39, 41; radical views of, 51–2, 53, 87, 93, 140
communes, 74, 75, 76, 77, 79, 84, 89, 92, 96, 117–18
contraception, 113, 193
cooperatives, producers, *see* workshops, collective
Courses for Learned Obstetricians, 61, 105, 125, 143, 158, 161–3, 169
Crimean War, 45, 53

Dashkova, E., 16
Decembrist Movement, 18, 20
Decembrist wives, 17–19
Dementeeva, Anna, 99–100

division of labor, sexual, 181–2, 183, 184, 196; *see also* women's work
divorce, 18, 53, 175, 192
Dmitrieva, Vera, 159–60, 161, 163, 164, 166, 167, 172
Dobroliubov, Nikolai, 51; "Realm of Darkness," 51
domesticity, ideology of, 6, 24, 27, 32, 200
Domostroi, 9
Dzhabadari, Ivan, 136, 140, 145, 146, 147, 148, 149, 150, 151

education, women's, 14, 16, 23 5, 27, 52 3; advanced, 60, 61; and discontent, 24, 105, 109–10; 167; Institute, 23–5, 129, 179; secondary, 50–1, 53
Engelhardt, Anna, 59
Epshtein, Anna, 196
Ermolova, M., 162, 165
Evreinova, Anna, 71

Fadeeva, Elena, 28
family, 7, 9, 23, 27, 45–6, 53–4, 70, 72, 191, 199; challenges to, 21, 45–6, 51, 63, 66, 113, 114, 200; and men's radicalism, 195–6; radical circles as surrogate for, 107, 120, 124–5, 136; and women's radicalism, 107–8, 191, 194–5, 199–200
"Fatherly Advice to my Daughter," 24
feminism, 22, 34, 61, 74, 84, 110, 115, 171, 202
Figner, Ekaterina, 10, 128–9, 130, 135, 142, 201
Figner, Evgenia, 175–6
Figner, Lidia, 130, 131, 133, 144, 145, 149, 151, 154
Figner, Nikolai, 128, 129, 130
Figner, Vera, 10, 13, 19, 133, 135, 136, 145, 154, 158, 173, 183–4, 187, 192, 193, 194, 195; early life, 128–31; as a radical activist, 174–6, 180, 185, 188–9, 199, 200–1; student years, 131, 132, 138–9, 140, 141, 142, 144, 146–7, 168
Filippov, Aleksei, 130, 138–9, 175
Filosofov, Vladimir, 58
Filosofova, Anna, 56, 58, 59–61, 201
Fourier, Charles, 22, 73, 75
"Freedom or Death," 179, 180
Fritsche group, 128, 133, 135–6, 137, 139–42, 143–4, 145, 146, 147, 149, 150, 154, 174, 192, 197, 199, 201
Frolenko, Mikhail, 184, 189

Gan, Elena, 28–33, 35–6, 200; "The Futile Gift," 31; "Ideal," 29, 30, 31; "Liubon'ka," 31; "Medalion," 30–1; "Society's Judgment," 31; "Teofaniia Abbadzhio," 31
Gan, Petr, 29, 30
Garshina, E., 78–9, 91
Gartman, Lev, 184
Gelfman, Gesia, 188
Golovina, Nadezhda, 161, 197
Gonetskaia, Aleksandra, 26
Gospels, the, 94, 141, 199
governesses, 12, 25, 51, 71, 72, 88, 94, 161
Griaznova, Maria, 182
Grinevitskii, Ignatii, 187

"Hell" (*Ad*), 88, 90–1
Herwegh, Georg, 41–2
Herzen, Aleksandr, 19, 22–3, 27, 28–42, 56
Herzen, Natalie, 37–42

228